Collins

Collins

German

Phrasebook
and Dictionary

German Phrasebook and Dictionary

Other languages in the
Collins Phrasebook and Dictionary series:
French, Greek, Italian, Japanese, Mandarin,
Polish, Portuguese, Spanish, Turkish.

HarperCollins Publishers
Westerhill Road, Bishopbriggs,
Glasgow G64 2QT

www.collinslanguage.com

First published 2004
This edition published 2008

Reprint 10 9 8 7 6 5 4 3 2 1 0

© HarperCollins Publishers 2004, 2008

ISBN 978-0-00-726455-1

Typeset by Davidson Pre-Press Graphics Ltd,
Glasgow

Printed in Malaysia by Imago

Contents

3

Your *Collins German Phrasebook and Dictionary* is a handy, quick-reference guide that will help make the most of your stay abroad. Its clear layout will save valuable time when you need that crucial word or phrase. Download free all the essential words and phrases you need to get by from www.collinslanguage.com/talk60. These hour long audio files are ideal for practising listening comprehension and pronunciation. The main sections in this book are:

Everyday Germany - photoguide
Packed full of photos, this section allows you to see all the practical visual information that will help with using cash machines, driving on motorways, reading signs, etc.

Phrases
Practical topics are arranged thematically with an opening section, Key talk containing vital phrases that should stand you in good stead in most situations. Phrases are short, useful and each one has a pronunciation guide so that there is no problem saying them.

Eating out
This section contains phrases for ordering food and drink (and special requirements) plus a photoguide showing different places to eat, menus and practical information to help choose the best options. The menu reader allows you to work out what to choose.

Grammar
There is a short Grammar section explaining how the language works.

Dictionary
And finally, the practical 5000-word English-German and German-English Dictionary means that you won't be stuck for words.

So, just flick through the pages to find the information you need and listen to the free audio download to improve your pronunciation.

Useful websites

Accommodation

www.bed-and-breakfast.de

www.deutsche-pensionen.de (guest houses, holiday homes and apartments)

www.djh.de (youth hostels)

www.europeanhostels.com (hostels)

www.hrs.com (hotel reservation service)

www.landtourismus.de (farm holidays)

Culture & Activities

www.deutsches-museum.de (museum of technology and science in Munich)

www.gastroscout.com (restaurant guide for Germany, Austria and Switzerland)

www.germany-christmas-market.org.uk (about German Christmas markets)

www.germanwine.de

www.oktoberfest.de

www.smb.spk-berlin.de (site of the 16 national museums in Berlin)

Currency Converters

www.x-rates.com

Driving

www.drivingabroad.co.uk

www.tank.rast.de (German motorway service stations, with route planner)

Foreign Office Advice

www.fco.gov.uk/travel

www.dfat.gov.au (Australia)

www.voyage.gc.ca (Canada)

Health advice

www.dh.gov.uk/travellers

www.thetraveldoctor.com

www.smartraveller.gov.au (Australia)

www.phac-aspc.gc.ca (Canada)

Internet Cafés

www.cybercafes.com

Passport Office

www.ukpa.gov.uk

www.passports.gov.au (Australia)

www.pptc.gc.ca (Canada)

Pets

www.defra.gov.uk/animalh/quarantine

Sightseeing

www.bayern.by (guide to Bavaria)

www.berlin-tourist-information.com

www.germany-info.org

www.germany tourism.co.uk (tourist board)

www.hamburg-tourism.de

www.k-d.com (Rhine cruises)

www.koeln.de (Cologne)

www.leipzig-online.de (Leipzig)

www.muenchen.de (Munich)

www.unesco-welterbe.de (Unesco world heritage sites in Germany)

Austrian National Tourist Office: www.austria-tourism.at

Switzerland Tourism: www.myswitzerland.com

Transport

www.bahn.de (German railway)

www.dfds.co.uk (ferry)

www.eurostar.com (Channel Tunnel)

www.germanwings.com (German budget airline)

www.poferries.com (ferry)

www.raileurope.com (Info on Train travel and passes available)

www.superfast.com (ferry)

www.lufthansa.co.uk (German airline)

Weather

www.bbc.co.uk/weather

We've tried to make the pronunciation under the phrases as clear as possible. Words are split up to make them easy to read but don't pause too long between syllables. German is not hard to pronounce and once you get used to unfamiliar letters or letter combinations, you will find yourself reading straight from the German.

Notice the differences in the way the language is written. The most obvious is that all nouns begin with capital letters. There is also a letter which doesn't exist in English – **ß** – which is like **ss**.

Most letters are pronounced in the same way as their English equivalents. However, when they appear at the end of a word **b** is pronounced like **p**, **d** like **t**, and **g** like **k**; and **v** is pronounced like **f**. **S** is pronounced like **sh** in **shock** before **p** and **t** when they are at the beginning of a word, and when it is combined with **ch**.

The umlaut ¨ often appears over German vowels and makes a difference to the pronunciation. Two sounds, **ö** and **ü**, are rather different from anything in English. We show **ö** as **ur'** because the nearest sound to it is in English words like 'hurt', but don't roll the r! The sound of **ü** can be made if you purse your lips and try to say **ee**. We give this sound as **oo** in the pronunciation.

A final **e** is always pronounced, and sounds like **a** in sof**a** or **e** in Porsch**e**. So German **bitte** sounds like English 'bitter' (but without the r).

The syllable to be stressed is the one in **bold type**. Here are a few other rules to be aware of:

German	sounds like	example	pronunciation
au	ow	**Auto**	**ow**to
äu	oy	**Säule**	**zoy**-le
ch	kh	**ich**	ikh
ei	'eye'	**ein**	ine
		zwei	tsvy
ie	ee	**sie**	zee
eu	oy	**neun**	noyn

Everyday photoguide

Everyday Germany

Open Some small shops tend to close over lunchtime, but generally shops are open from morning till early evening Mon-Fri. Saturday opening times may vary slightly. There is no Sunday shopping in Germany.

Deutsche means German. Germany is **Deutschland**.

No Admittance The word for 'forbidden' or 'prohibited' is **verboten**.

Pay Here
Kasse means 'till/checkout'.

No Exit
Kein means 'no'.

Entrance
(for vehicle)

Exit
(for vehicle)

Opening Hours

Fahrt comes from **fahren** 'to drive', so **Einfahrt** and **Ausfahrt** are used on road signs. **Gang** comes from **gehen** 'to walk', so you see **Eingang** and **Ausgang** on signs for pedestrians.

Banks in Germany can be identified by the word **Bank** or **Sparkasse**. **Reise Bank** is a bureau de change, also called **Wechselstube**.

Prices are written with a comma. This is 3 euro and 70 cents per kilo. Germany is metric – weights are in kilos.

Euro The euro replaced the former **deutschmark**.

Öffnungszeiten

Opening Times Bank opening hours are generally from 9am–4pm Mon–Fri. Some may open for a few hours on Saturday. All banks are closed on Sundays.

The euro is the currency of Germany. It breaks down into 100 euro cents. Notes: 5, 10, 20, 50, 100, 200, 500. Coins: 1 and 2 euros, 50, 20, 10, 5, 2 and 1 cents. Some European countries have their own words for cents but Germans use the same word and

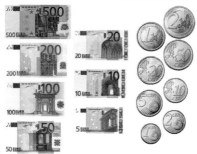

pronunciation as English. **Euro** is pronounced **oy**-roh. Euro notes are the same throughout Europe. Coins carry a different design from each member country on the back.

Cash machines operate the same as at home.
Abbruch = cancel
Korrektur = error
Bestätigung = proceed

Automat gibt Rückgeld
Change Given

Geldautomat Cash Machine (ATM)

HIRSCH APOTHEKE

Pharmacy
Pharmacists can give treatment advice. Supermarkets don't sell medicines.

Quittung Receipt

Bitte wählen Sie
Kennzahl eingeben   Taste drücken

Please Select

zahlbar mit

Pay With

NOTDIENST DER APOTHEKEN

MO	COSMOS-APOTHEKE Dotheimer Str. 14-18 Tel. 303470	PARACELSUS-APOTHEKE Schatthalden 37a Tel. 502755
DI	DAIMLER-APOTHEKE Schweihoffstr 20 Tel. 92804	WELLRITZ-APOTHEKE Schweihoffstr 8-10 Tel. 409587

There is usually one pharmacy open for emergencies (**Notdienst**).

← **Krankenhaus**

Hospital You have to ring a local number for an ambulance (displayed in phone boxes), but if you need one urgently, you can ring 110 or the fire brigade on 112.

◀ NOTAUFNAHME

The A&E department is called the **Notaufnahme**.

HOTEL

— GARNI —

☎ 06326 / 708 - 0

A **Hotel garni** is a small hotel offering bed and breakfast.

PENSION

A **Pension** is like a guesthouse.

Haus Sonnblick
Gasthof Laschitz

Gasthof Löffler
Komfortzimmer

A **Gasthof** is usually a pub or winebar that has rooms.

Empfang

Reception

Germans are very recycling-conscious and you must use the correct bin for rubbish.

brown = biodegradable, blue = paper, black = general waste, yellow = packaging carrying the recycling symbol.

DER GRÜNE PUNKT

ZIMMER

Rooms/Vacancies

zu vermieten

To Rent

Ferien unter'm Rohrdach

Ferienhaus   Zimmer

frei   belegt

Accommodation

Ferienhaus
frei

Ferienhaus is a self-catering holiday house. **Frei** shows that there is availability.

Zimmer
belegt

The word **belegt** means that it is full up (no vacancies).

Postboxes are yellow. Most post offices are open from 8am to 6pm Monday to Friday and 8am to 2pm Saturday.

verboten

Prohibited

Außer Betrieb

Out Of Order

TOILETTEN RESTROOMS

WC

Toilets There aren't many public toilets in Germany and wherever you go you will be expected to pay, or at least leave a tip for the attendant. Look for them in shopping centres, some larger department stores or in bigger cities try railway stations or public buildings. You can also follow the city signpost system.

NICHTRAUCHER-ZONE!
Bitte nehmen Sie Rücksicht auf die Nichtraucher. Danke für Ihr Verständnis.

No Smoking Zone
Smoking is not allowed on public transport or in public buildings except in designated areas.

Trinkwasser

Drinking Water
The word for water is **Wasser** (**vas**-er).

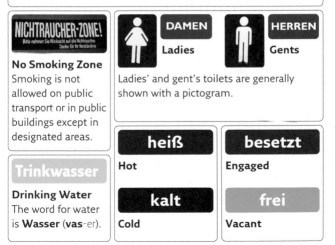

DAMEN Ladies

HERREN Gents

Ladies' and gent's toilets are generally shown with a pictogram.

heiß

Hot

besetzt

Engaged

kalt

Cold

frei

Vacant

Timetables

Tage		Days
Montag	**mon**-tahk	Monday
Dienstag	**deens**-tahk	Tuesday
Mittwoch	**mit**-vokh	Wednesday
Donnerstag	**donn**ers-tahk	Thursday
Freitag	**fry**-tahk	Friday
Samstag	**zams**-tahk	Saturday
Sonntag	**zon**-tahk	Sunday

Fahrplan
Timetable

HEUTE
Today

MORGEN
Tomorrow

NOTDIENST
DER APOTHEKEN

MO — COSMOS-APOTHEKE / PARACELSUS-APOTHEKE
DI — DAIMLER-APOTHEKE / WELLRITZ-APOTHEKE
MI — APOTHEKE AM SÜDBAHNHOF / APOTHEKE IM RAD
DO — KUR-APOTHEKE / APOTHEKE AM SEDANPLATZ
FR — MARIEN-APOTHEKE / VATER-FREIBERG APOTHEKE
SA — BAHNHOF-APOTHEKE / SESSELS-APOTHEKE
SO — APOTHEKE AM MARKT / CAROLUS-APOTHEKE

Abbreviations for days of the week on a duty pharmacy signboard.

Monate		Months
Januar	**yan**-ooar	January
Februar	**feb**-rooar	February
März	mehrts	March
April	ap-**reel**	April
Mai	mye	May
Juni	**yoo**-nee	June
Juli	**yoo**-lee	July
August	ow-**goost**	August
September	sep-**tem**ber	September
Oktober	ok-**to**ber	October
November	no-**vem**ber	November
Dezember	dayt-**sem**ber	December

Wochenmarkt
Di, Fr, Sa 7 - 14 Uhr

Weekly Market
Tuesday, Friday, Saturday from 7am-2pm.

12

Tickets

KARTEN HIER ERHÄLTLICH!

Buy Tickets Here! Karten is the general word for 'tickets'.

Fahrkarten

Tickets (for public transport)

Busfahrkarten

Bus Tickets

Validate Here

ReiseZentrum

Travel Centre You can buy tickets and get information here.

You have to validate any ticket you buy for public transport in a validating machine. These are found at the entrance of buses, train platforms and metro stations. Simply insert your ticket in the slot for punching.

Ankunft

Arrivals abb. to **an**

Abfahrt

Departures

13

---

2. Wählen Sie bitte Ihre Fahrkarte

Einzelfahrt	Tageskarte	Sammelkarte	Zuschlag
zum sofortigen Fahrtantritt	gültig ab Kauf bis Betriebsschluß	vor Fahrtantritt entwerten	(pro Person) zusätzlich zur Fahrkarte
Taste drücken	Taste drücken	Taste drücken	Taste drücken

Choose Your Ticket Type

Zuschlag supplement

Einzelfahrt single ticket **Tageskarte** day ticket **Sammelkarte** multiple tickets (must validate for each journey)

Tickets

Getting around

Behringstraße

Emil von Behring
1854 - 1917
Arzt und Bakteriolog.
Nobelpreisträger

Street signs are usually blue and white. They often have additional info about the person or event the street was named after.

Pedestrian City Signs

St. Stephan
Chagall-Fenster
Altstadt
Dom
Gutenbergmuseum
Rheinschiffe

Schloß Lustheim
1.2.3

The numbers under the sign tell you the house numbers you can find.

Altstadt — Old Part Of Town

Dom — Cathedral

Innenstadt — Town Centre

Neustadt/Weinstr. 8 km
NW-Mußbach 5 km

Distances are in kilometres. Yellow roadsigns are for out of town destinations.

● **Standort**
You Are Here

Bahnhof
Railway Station

RECHTS
Right

LINKS
Left

north **Nord**

West west

Ost east

Süd south

Most German cities operate an integrated transport system so all kinds of transport are part of one network and any of them will take your ticket. Buy your ticket in advance and validate it in the machine on board the bus or tram. With **U-Bahn** and **S-Bahn** you validate your ticket on entering the station or platform. You can find ticket machines at some bus stops. The word for stop is **Haltestelle** (hence the **H**).

Hauptbahnhof
Main Station

← zu den Zügen
To The Trains

Richtung
Direction

| 10 54 | Departure | **Abfahrt** | Départ | DB |

Zeit	Zuglauf		Ziel	Gleis	Hinweis
10 56	S1		FRANKFURT HÖCHST	20	
10 57	ICE	KS-Wilhelmshöhe Göttingen-Hannover	HAMBURG-ALTONA	7	
11 02	RB	Ffm Süd-Ffm Ost	HANAU	5	
11 03	IR	3ed Nauheim-Gießen	Wetzlar-Siegen-W.-Hagen	DÜSSELDORF	15	
11 05	ICE	← Flughafen	Mannheim	STUTTGART	6	←

Departure Board Zeit = Time, **Zuglauf** = Via, **Ziel** = Destination, **Gleis** = Platform, **Hinweis** = Info

Metro U-Bahn is the metro system. Lines are colour coded and numbered.

S-Bahn is the suburban train system.

Driving

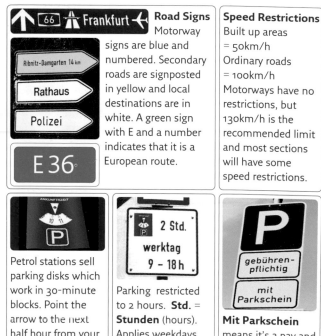

Road Signs
Motorway signs are blue and numbered. Secondary roads are signposted in yellow and local destinations are in white. A green sign with E and a number indicates that it is a European route.

Speed Restrictions
Built up areas = 50km/h
Ordinary roads = 100km/h
Motorways have no restrictions, but 130km/h is the recommended limit and most sections will have some speed restrictions.

Petrol stations sell parking disks which work in 30-minute blocks. Point the arrow to the next half hour from your start time.

Parking restricted to 2 hours. **Std.** = **Stunden** (hours). Applies weekdays from 9am–6pm.

Mit Parkschein means it's a pay and display zone.

This sign means you give way to the priority road (yellow diamond). Drivers on the priority road must indicate when turning. Drivers on the top secondary road must yield to drivers on the bottom, as they are on their right.

Austrian motorway toll sticker valid for 10 days, 2 months or a year. Austrian and Swiss motorways, unlike German, aren't free. In Switzerland stickers are valid for a year.

If you break down on the motorway, put on your warning lights and place your warning triangle about 100m behind the car. An arrow on the distance indicator will show you which way the nearest phone is (never more than 1 km away). The police will arrange for a recovery vehicle to come to you.

Water   Air

Spaces Watch out, **Frei** means spaces, not free parking!

Autobahn

Motorway Signs are in blue.

66 is the number of the motorway.

Ausfahrt

Exit This sign indicates the exit number. (21)

Benzin
Unleaded Petrol

Super
Premium

Diesel
Diesel

Shopping

 **Netto** is a supermarket chain, **Fleischer** is a butcher's and **Bäcker** is a baker's. Shops are usually open morning till early evening, Monday to Saturday but times vary. There is no Sunday opening (except in tourist areas). Petrol stations selling snacks, bread, drinks, etc, are open on Sundays. Baker's can also open on Sunday mornings.

 **Please leave your bags in the car** At some of the supermarkets you aren't allowed to take any bags (except handbags) in with you. If you need plastic carriers, you have to pay for them.

 **Pay Here**

 **Reductions**

 UG Basement **Untergeschoss**

EG Ground Floor **Erdgeschoss**

 **1.OG** First Floor **1. Obergeschoss**

 In most supermarkets you have to use a coin (usually 1 euro) or a special plastic coin to release the trolley.

 Wochenmarkt Di,Fr,Sa 7 - 14 Uhr

Weekly Market Tue, Fri, Sat 7am–2pm. These times vary from town to town, but most of them have a market on Saturday.

Bread You can find many varieties of bread in Germany.
Schwarzbrot = very dark bread
Vollkornbrot = wholemeal bread
Weißbrot = white bread

Kilojoule (kJ)	111	— kjoules
Kilokalorien (kcal)	26	— calories
Eiweiß	0,7g	— protein
Kohlenhydrate	5,6g	— carbohydrates
Fett	0,1g	— fat

Nutrition Label

Bio

Organic Health food shops selling organic products are called **Bioladen** or **Reformhaus**.

Vollfettmilch | Full Fat Milk

Halbfettmilch | Semi-Skimmed Milk

Magermilch | Skimmed Milk

Glutenfreies Produkt
Gluten-Free

OBST / GEMÜSE
Karin Ohler

Fruit/Vegetables

Artischocken
frisch und zart
kg nur 7,20

nur means 'only';
ab means 'from' and
Stück means 'each'.

Auch für Mikrowelle
Suitable To Microwave

Keeping in touch

Postbox
Collection times are marked. A red dot indicates that there is a Sunday collection. It should also list the nearest postbox (**nächster Briefkasten**) with collection times.

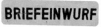

Letterbox

Post Office Logo

Most payphones take phonecards not coins.

 **Airmail**

There are internet cafés in most cities, and many public libraries provide internet access. The most common service provider is T-Online. Websites end in **.de** for **Deutschland**.

International Dialling Codes

UK oo 44	Australia oo 61
USA/Canada oo 1	Germany oo 49
Austria oo 43	Switzerland oo 41

Germans use 'at' as in English.

Phone numbers are given in single digits.			
21	882	03	48
zwei, eins	acht, acht, zwei	null, drei	vier, acht

www.
is pronounced **veh veh veh poonkt**

Key talk

Key talk

• Among friends you will hear **hallo!** or **hi!** and **tschüss!** (bye) but avoid these unless you know the person well.
• In southern Germany and Austria you often hear the greeting **Grüß Gott** for 'hello'.
• In Switzerland you will hear **Grüezi** for 'hello', **Ade** for 'goodbye'.

yes	ja	ya
no	nein	nine
that's fine	das ist gut so	das ist goot zoh
please	bitte	**bi**-te
thank you	danke	**dang**-ke
a pleasure!	bitte!	**bi**-te!
hello	guten Tag	**goo**ten tahk
goodbye	auf Wiedersehen	owf **vee**der-zayn
good night	gute Nacht	**goo**te nakht
excuse me	Entschuldigung	ent**shool**-digoong
sorry	Verzeihung	fer-**tsy**-oong
pardon?	wie bitte?	vee **bi**-te?

21

• Here is an easy way to ask for something ... just add **bitte**

a...	einen... ('der' words)	**ine**-en...
a coffee	einen Kaffee	**ine**-en ka**fay**
2 coffees	zwei Kaffee	tsvy ka**fay**
a...	eine... ('die' words)	**ine**-e...
a bottle	eine Flasche	**ine**-e **fla**-she
2 bottles	zwei Flaschen	tsvy **fla**-shen

a...	ein... ('das' words)	ine...
a Pils	ein Pils	ine pils
2 Pils	zwei Pils	tsvy pils
a coffee and two Pils, please	einen Kaffee und zwei Pils, bitte	**ine**-en ka**fay** oont tsvy pils, **bi**-te

• To catch someone's attention use **Entschuldigung!** You can use the same word for 'sorry' when bumping into someone, etc.
• **Bitte** means 'please' but **bitte schön** or **bitte sehr** is also used for 'here you are' when passing something to somebody.

I'd like.../ we'd like...	ich möchte.../wir möchten...
	ikh **mur'kh**-te.../veer **mur'kh**-ten...
I'd like an ice cream	ich möchte ein Eis
	ikh **mur'kh**-te ine ice
we'd like to visit Potsdam	wir möchten Potsdam besuche
	veer **mur'kh**-ten **pots**-dam be**zoo**khen
do you have...?	haben Sie...?
	hah-ben zee...?
do you have any milk?	haben Sie Milch?
	hah-ben zee milkh?
do you have stamps?	haben Sie Briefmarken?
	hah-ben zee **breef**-marken?
do you have a map?	haben Sie eine Landkarte?
	hah-ben zee **ine**-e **lant**-kar-te?
how much is it?	was kostet das?
	vas **kos**tet das?
how much does ... cost?	was kostet...?
	vas **kos**tet...?
how much is the cheese?	was kostet der Käse?
	vas **kos**tet der **kay**-ze?
how much is the room?	was kostet das Zimmer?
	vas **kos**tet das **tsim**mer?
how much is a kilo?	was kostet ein Kilo?
	vas **kos**tet ine **kee**lo?
how much is it each?	was kostet es pro Stück?
	vas **kos**tet es pro shtook?

Key talk

• Germans tend to be more formal than the British or Americans and there is also some truth in the cliché that Germans are compulsive law abiders. Jay walking is not very common and littering is subject to very high fines in some cities.

• Germany is very recycling conscious. There are different coloured bins for different types of rubbish.

where is...?/ where are...?	wo ist...?/wo sind...?
	voh ist...?/voh zint...?
where is the station?	wo ist der Bahnhof?
	voh ist der **bahn**-hof?
where are the toilets?	wo sind die Toiletten?
	voh zint dee twa-**let**-ten?
is/are there...?	gibt es...?
	gipt es...?
is there a restaurant?	gibt es ein Restaurant?
	gipt es ine restoh-**rong**?
where's there a chemist?	wo gibt es eine Apotheke?
	voh gipt es i**ne**-e apoh-**tay**-ke?
are there reductions?	gibt es Ermäßigung?
	gipt es er-**may**-sigoong?
is there a golf course?	gibt es einen Golfplatz?
	gipt es i**ne**-en **golf**-plats?
there is/are no...	es gibt kein (das)/keinen (der)/keine (die and plural)...
	es gipt **ki**ne/**kine**-en/**kine**-e...
there is no hot water	es gibt kein heißes Wasser
	es gipt kine **hy**-ses **vas**ser
there are no towels	es gibt keine Handtücher
	es gipt **kine**-e **hant**-tookher
I need...	ich brauche...
	ikh **brow**-khe...
I need help	ich brauche Hilfe
	ikh **brow**-khe **hil**-fe
I need a receipt	ich brauche eine Quittung
	ikh **brow**-khe i**ne**-e **kvi**-toong

• Politeness and respect are very important to Germans. You always shake hands on meeting (especially for the first time). Normally the older person proffers their hand first.
• Except among friends and young people, the transition from the formal **Sie** to the informal **du** has to be mutually agreed and is often sealed with a toast.

can I...	kann ich...
	kan ikh...
can I phone?	kann ich telefonieren?
	kan ikh taylay-fo-**neer**en?
can I book a ticket?	kann ich ein Ticket buchen?
	kan ikh ine **ti**cket **boo**-khen?
where can I...?	wo kann ich...?
	voh kan ikh...?
where can I buy tickets?	wo kann ich Karten kaufen?
	voh kan ikh **kar**-ten **kow**fen?
where can I hire a bike?	wo kann ich ein Fahrrad leihen?
	voh kan ikh ine **fah**-rat **lye**-en?
when?	wann?
	van?
when is breakfast/ lunch?	wann gibt es Frühstück/Mittagessen?
	van gipt es **froo**-shtook/**mi**tahk-essen?
when does it open?	wann ist geöffnet?
	van ist ge-**ur'f**net?
when does it close?	wann wird geschlossen?
	van virt ge**shlo**ssen?
yesterday	gestern
	gestern
today	heute
	hoy-te
tomorrow	morgen
	morgen
this morning	heute Morgen
	hoy-te **mor**gen
this afternoon	heute Nachmittag
	hoy-te **nakh**-mitahk

tonight	heute Abend
	hoy-te **ah**bent
is it open/closed?	ist es geöffnet/geschlossen?
	ist es ge-**ur'f**net/ge**schlo**ssen?

• Abbreviations for Mr and Mrs are **Hr.** for **Herr** and **Fr.** for **Frau**.
Fräulein (Miss) is considered old-fashioned or even discriminatory
nowadays. A woman of any age should be addressed as **Frau**.
• **Vorname** means 'first name', **Nachname** means 'surname'.
Always use a person's title (Dr, Prof, etc), if you know it.

how are you?	wie geht es Ihnen?
	vee gayt es **ee**-nen?
fine, thanks. And you?	danke, gut. Und Ihnen?
	dang-ke, goot. oont **ee**-nen?
what is your name?	wie ist Ihr Name?
	vee ist eer **nah**-me?
my name is...	mein Name ist...
	mine **nah**-me ist...
I don't understand	ich verstehe nicht
	ikh fer-**shtay**-e nikht
do you speak English?	sprechen Sie Englisch?
	shpre-khen zee **eng**-lish?
the meal was delicious	das Essen war köstlich
	das **es**-sen var **kur's**-tlich
thanks for everything	danke für alles
	dan-ke foor **a**-lez
you have a beautiful house	sie haben ein schönes Haus
	zee **hab**-ben ine **shur'**nez hows
we must stay in touch	wir müssen in Kontakt bleiben
	weer **moos**-sen een **kon**-takt **bly**ben
here is my address	hier ist meine Adresse
	heer ist **mine**-e a-**dres**-se
we'd like to come back	wir würden gerne wiederkommen
	veer **wur'd**-en **gehr**-ne **vee**-der-kom-men

Money

Money

• The euro is the currency of Germany.
• Euro is pronounced **oy**-roh and Cent as in English.
• You can use your cash card to get euros from cash machines if your card supports Maestro or Cirrus services.
• Cash machines (ATM) are called **Geldautomat** (**gelt**-owto-maht) in German.

where can I change money?	**wo kann ich Geld wechseln?** voh kan ikh gelt **vek**-seln?
where is the nearest cash machine?	**wo ist der nächste Geldautomat?** voh ist der **naykh**-ste **gelt**-owto-maht?
where is the bank?	**wo ist die Bank?** voh ist dee bank?
when does the bank open/close?	**wann macht die Bank auf/zu?** van makht dee bank owf/tsoo?
is there a bureau de change?	**gibt es einen Geldwechsel?** gipt es **ine**-nen **gelt**-veksel?
I want to cash these traveller's cheques	**ich möchte gern diese Reiseschecks einlösen** ikh **mu'rkh**-te gern **dee**-ze **ry**-ze-sheks **ine**-lur'-zen
what's the rate...?	**wie ist der Kurs...?** vee ist der koors...?
for pounds/dollars	**für Pfund Sterling/Dollars** foor pfoont **ster**-ling/**do**llars
I want to change ... pounds	**ich möchte ... Pfund** ikh **mur'kh**-te ... pfoon
I want to change ... dollars	**ich möchte ... Dollar** ikh **mur'kh**-te ... **do**llar

- Banks usually open Mon–Fri 9am to 4pm but local times may vary.
- They may open for a few hours on Saturdays, especially in larger cities.
- Credit cards are accepted for most purchases, but are not used as widely as in the UK.
- Coins are **Münzen**, notes are **Geldscheine**.

what's the commission?	**wie hoch ist die Gebühr?**
	vee hohkh ist dee ge-**boohr**?
how much is it?	**was kostet das?**
	vas **kos**tet das?
where can I pay?	**wo kann ich bezahlen?**
	voh kan ikh be**tsah**-len?
I want to pay	**zahlen, bitte**
	tsah-len, **bi**-te
we want to pay separately	**wir möchten einzeln bezahlen**
	veer **mur'kh**-ten **ine**-tseln be**tsah**-len
can I pay by credit card?	**kann ich mit Kreditkarte bezahlen?**
	kan ikh mit kre**deet**-kar-te be**tsah**-len?
do you accept traveller's cheques?	**nehmen Sie Reiseschecks?**
	naymen zee **ry**-ze-sheks?
how much is it...?	**was kostet das...?**
	vas **kos**tet das...?
per person/per night/per kilo	**pro Person/pro Nacht/pro Kilo**
	pro per-**zon**/pro nakht/pro **kee**-lo
are service and VAT included?	**sind Bedienung und Mehrwertsteuer inbegriffen?**
	zint be-**dee**noong oont **mayr**-vayrt-shtoy-er **in**-be-griffen?
I need a receipt	**ich brauche eine Quittung**
	ikh **brow**-khe **ine**-e **kvi**-toong
do you require a deposit?	**nehmen Sie eine Kaution?**
	naymen zee **ine**-e kow-**tsyohn**?
I've nothing smaller	**ich habe es nicht kleiner**
	ikh **hah**-be es nikht **kline**-er
keep the change	**stimmt so**
	shtimt zoh

Getting around

Airport

• •

- Most signs are in German and English.
- The German national airline is Lufthansa **www.lufthansa.co.uk**.
- You can find information on Swiss and Austrian airports at
www.europeforvisitors.com/switzaustria

to the airport, please	**zum Flughafen, bitte** tsoom **flook**-hafen, **bi**-te
how can I get into town?	**wie komme ich in die Stadt?** vee **kom**me ikh in dee shtat?
where do I get the bus to the town centre?	**wo fährt der Bus zum Stadtzentrum ab?** voh fayrt der boos tsoom **shtat**-tsentroom ap?
how much is it...?	**was kostet die Fahrt...?** vas **kos**tet dee fahrt...?
to the town centre	**ins Stadtzentrum** ins **shtat**-tsentroom
to the airport	**zum Flughafen** tsoom **flook**-hafen
where do I check in for...?	**wo ist der Check-in für...?** voh ist der **check**-in foor...?
which gate for the flight to...?	**welches Gate hat der Flug nach...?** **vel**-khes gate hat der flook nakh...?
boarding will take place at gate number...	**Sie steigen von Gate Nummer ... ein** zee **shty**-gen fon gate noomer ... ine
go immediately to gate number...	**gehen Sie sofort zu Gate Nummer...** **gay**en zee zo-**fort** tsoo gate noomer...
your flight is delayed	**Ihr Flug hat Verspätung** eer flook hat fer-**shpay**-toong

Customs and passports

• There is no restriction by quantity or value, on goods purchased by travellers in another EU country provided they are for their own personal use (this covers gifts). Check guidelines for travellers on **www.hmrc.gov.uk**.
• EU citizens with nothing to declare can use the blue customs channels.

I have nothing to declare	**ich habe nichts zu verzollen** ikh **hah**-be nikhts tsoo fer-**tsol**len
here is...	**hier ist...** heer ist...
my passport	**mein Pass** mine pass
my green card	**meine grüne Versicherungskarte** **mine**-e **groo**-ne fer-**zikh**-e-roongz-kar-te
do I have to pay duty on this?	**muss ich das verzollen?** moos ikh das fer-**tsol**len?
it's for my own personal use	**es ist für meinen persönlichen Gebrauch** es ist foor **mine**-en per-**zur'n**-likhen ge-**browkh**
we're on our way to...	**wir sind auf der Durchreise nach...** veer zint owf der **doorkh**-ry-ze nakh...
the children are on this passport	**die Kinder stehen in diesem Pass** dee **kin**der **shtay**-en in **dee**-zem pass
this is the baby's passport	**das is der Pass für das Baby** das ist der pas foor das **ba**by
I'm...	**Ich bin...** ikh bin...
British (m/f)	**Brite/Britin** **bree**-te/**bree**-tin
Australian (m/f)	**Australier/Australierin** ow**strah**lee-er/ow**strah**lee-er-in
I have a visa	**ich habe ein Visum** ikh **hah**-be ine **vee**zoom

Asking the way – questions

• •

- Remember to use the polite form **Sie** when addressing people.
- You can catch people's attention with **Entschuldigung!**
- Even if people don't approach you on their own initiative, don't be afraid to ask for help. Many Germans speak English and, once over any initial reserve, are very helpful.

excuse me, please	**entschuldigen Sie, bitte**
	ent**shool**-digen zee, **bi**-te
where is...?	**wo ist...?**
	voh ist...?
where is the nearest...?	**wo ist der/die/das nächste...?**
	voh ist der/dee/das **naykh**-ste...?
where are the toilets?	**wo sind die Toiletten?**
	voh zint dee twa-**let**-ten?
how do I get to...?	**wie komme ich...?**
	vee **kom**me ikh...?
to the station	**zum Bahnhof** (der/das nouns)
	tsoom **bahn**-hohf
to Heidelberg	**nach Heidelberg** (with places)
	nakh **hy**del-berk
is this the right way to...?	**bin ich hier richtig zum/zur/nach...?**
	bin ikh heer **rikh**tikh tsoom/tsoor/nakh...?
to the castle	**zur Burg** (die nouns)
	tsoor boork
is it far to the...?	**ist es weit zum/zur/nach...?**
	ist es vite tsoom/tsoor/nakh...?
is the beach far?	**ist es weit zum Strand?**
	ist es vite tsoom shtrant?
can I walk there?	**kann ich dahin laufen?**
	kan ikh da**hin low**fen?
is there a bus that goes there?	**fährt ein Bus dahin?**
	fayrt ine boos da**hin**?
I'm looking for...	**ich suche...**
	ikh **zoo**khe...

we're looking for...	**wir suchen...**
	veer **zoo**khen...
we're lost (on foot)	**wir haben uns verlaufen**
	veer **hah**-ben oons fer-**low**fen
we're lost (in car)	**wir haben uns verfahren**
	veer **hah**-ben oons fer-**fah**ren

Asking the way – answers

● It's no use being able to ask the way if you don't understand the reply. We've anticipated some likely answers so listen carefully for these.
● As in all places, policemen, taxi drivers and bus drivers are good people to ask directions from. You can get free maps from tourist offices.

keep going straight ahead	**gehen Sie immer geradeaus weiter**
	gay-en zee **i**mmer ge-**rah**-de-ows **vye**-ter
you have to turn round	**kehren Sie um**
	kehr-ren zee oom
turn...	**biegen Sie...**
	bee-gen zee...
right/left	**rechts ab/links ab**
	rekhts ap/links ap
you go... (on foot)	**gehen Sie...**
	gay-en zee...
towards...	**in Richtung...**
	in **rikh**-toong...
as far as...	**bis zu...**
	bis tsoo...
you go... (driving)	**fahren Sie...**
	fah-ren zee...
right/left	**nach rechts/nach links**
	nakh rekhts/nakh links
take...	**nehmen Sie...**
	nay-men zee...
the first road on the right	**die erste Straße rechts**
	dee **ers**-te **shtrah**-se rekhts

the second road on the left	**die zweite Straße links**
	dee **tsvye**-te **shtrah**-se links
the road to...	**die Straße nach...**
	dee shtrah-se nakh...
follow the signs for...	**folgen Sie den Schildern nach...**
	fol-gen zee den **shil**-dern nakh...

Bus

● Bus and tram tickets can be purchased from ticket machines, some tobacconists or sometimes from the driver.
● Multi-journey tickets (**Mehrfahrtenkarte**) and day tickets (**Tageskarte**) are also available.
● Central bus stations (**Busbahnhof**) are usually located near the main railway station (**Hauptbahnhof**).

where is the bus station?	**wo ist der Busbahnhof?**
	voh ist der **boos**-bahn-hohf?
where is the tram stop?	**wo ist die Straßenbahnhaltestelle?**
	voh ist dee **shtrah**senbahn-**hal**-te-shtel-le?
I want to go...	**ich möchte...**
	ikh **mur'kh**-te...
to the station	**zum Bahnhof**
	tsoom **bahn**-hohf
to the museum	**zum Museum**
	zum moo-**zay**-oom
to the art gallery	**zur Kunsthalle**
	tsoor **koonst**-hal-le
to Bonn	**nach Bonn**
	nakh bon
does this bus go to...?	**fährt dieser Bus nach...?**
	fayrt **dee**-ser boos nakh...?
which bus do I take to get there?	**mit welchem Bus komme ich dahin?**
	mit **vel**-khem boos **kom**me ikh da**hin**?
where does the bus go from?	**wo fährt der Bus ab?**
	voh fayrt der boos ap?

how often are the buses?	**wie oft fahren die Busse?**
	vee oft **fah**-ren dee **boo**-se?
when is the last bus?	**wann geht der letzte Bus?**
	van gayt der **let**-ste boos?
please tell me when to get off	**sagen Sie mir bitte, wann ich aussteigen muss**
	zahgen zee meer **bi**-te van ikh **ows**-shtygen moos

Metro

• •

• **U** is the sign for the metro (**U-Bahn**), **S** is for the suburban trains (**S-Bahn**). Parts of the **U-Bahn** can also be overground.
• In many cities you can get **eine Touristenkarte** (which covers all public transport), or **eine Familienkarte** (2 adults, 2 children). Ask for **spezielle Fahrkarten**.
• **Die Innenstadt** is the inner city.

where is the nearest metro station?	**wo ist die nächste U-Bahn-Haltestelle?**
	voh ist dee **naykh**-ste **oo**bahn-**hal**-te-shtel-le?
what special tickets are there?	**welche speziellen Fahrkarten gibt es?**
	vel-khe shpe-tsee-**el**-len **fahr**-kar-ten gipt es?
a tourist ticket, please	**eine Touristenkarte, bitte**
	ine-e too**ris**ten-karte, **bi**-te
inner zones	**die Innenstadt**
	dee **in**-nen-shtat
all zones	**alle Zonen**
	al-le **tsoh**-nen
do you have a map of the metro?	**gibt es eine Karte mit allen U-Bahn-Linien?**
	gipt es **ine**-e **kar**-te mit **al**-len **oo**-bahn-**lee**-nee-en?
I want to go to...	**ich möchte zum/zur/nach...**
	ikh **mur'kh**-te tsoom/tsoor/nakh...
can I go by metro?	**kann ich mit der U-Bahn fahren?**
	kan ikh mit der **oo**bahn **fah**-ren?
do I have to change?	**muss ich umsteigen?**
	moos ikh **oom**-shtygen?
where?	**wo?**
	voh?

which line is it for...?	**welche Linie fährt nach...?** **vel**-khe **lee**-nee-e fayrt nakh...?
what is the next stop?	**was ist der nächste Halt?** vas ist der **naykh**-ste halt?
which zones?	**welche Zonen?** **vel**-khe **tsoh**-nen?
for the inner city or all zones?	**für die Innenstadt oder für alle Zonen?** foor dee **in**nen-shtat **oh**der foor **al**-le **tsoh**-nen?

Train

••

- Buy your ticket prior to boarding the train.
- Check if a supplement, **ein Zuschlag**, is required before you board the train. It costs less if you buy it with your ticket. There is usually a surcharge for the InterCity Express (ICE).
- It is a good idea to pre-book seats on ICE trains during busy periods.

where is the station?	**wo ist der Bahnhof?** voh ist der **bahn**-hohf?
to the station, please	**zum Bahnhof, bitte** tsoom **bahn**-hohf, **bi**-te
a single to...	**einmal einfach nach...** **ine**-mal **ine**-fakh nakh...
2 singles to...	**zweimal einfach nach...** **tsvy**-mal **ine**-fakh nakh...
a return to...	**eine Rückfahrkarte nach...** **ine**-e **rook**-fahr-kar-te nakh...
2 returns to...	**zweimal hin und zurück nach...** **tsvy**-mal hin oont tsoo-**rook** nakh...
a child's return to...	**eine Kinderrückfahrkarte nach...** **ine**-e kinder-**rook**-fahr-kar-te nakh...
1st class/2nd class	**erster Klasse/zweiter Klasse** **er**-ster **kla**-se/**tsvy**-ter **kla**-se
do I have to pay a supplement?	**muss ich einen Zuschlag zahlen?** moos ikh **ine**-en **tsoo**shlak **tsah**len?

is my pass valid on this train?	**ist mein Pass für diesen Zug gültig?**
	ist mine pass foor **dee**zen tsook **gool**tikh?
I want to book...	**ich möchte ... buchen**
	ikh **mur'kh-te** ... **boo**-khen
a seat	**einen Platz**
	ine-en plats
a couchette	**einen Liegewagenplatz**
	ine-en **lee**-ge-vahgen-plats

• In Germany children under 6 always travel free, children between 6 and 14 travel free if accompanied by a parent or grandparent and are included on their tickets.
• Visit **www.bahn.de** and click on 'Internat. Guests' for lots of information in English including the timetable for Germany and many other countries. There is a booking centre in the UK at **www.bahn.co.uk**.

do you have a timetable?	**haben Sie einen Fahrplan?**
	hah-ben zee **ine**-en **fahr**-plahn?
do I need to change?	**muss ich umsteigen?**
	moos ikh **oom**-shty-gen?
where?	**wo?**
	voh?
which platform does it leave from?	**von welchem Bahnsteig fährt er ab?**
	fon **vel**-khem **bahn**-shtike fayrt er ap?
does the train to ... leave from here?	**fährt hier der Zug nach ... ab?**
	fayrt heer der tsook nakh ... ap?
is this the train for...?	**ist das der Zug nach...?**
	ist das der tsook nakh...?
where is the left-luggage?	**wo ist die Gepäckaufbewahrung?**
	voh ist dee ge**pek**-owf-bevahroong?
is there a buffet on the train?	**hat der Zug einen Speisewagen?**
	hat der tsook **ine**-en **shpy**-ze-vahgen?
is this seat free?	**ist hier noch frei?**
	ist heer nokh fry?
this is my seat	**das ist mein Platz**
	das ist mine plats

Taxi

• •

- Most German taxis are cream with a yellow sign on the roof.
- To get a taxi you have to find a taxi rank, **Taxistand**, or phone for one.
- You can often find ads for taxi firms in phoneboxes: you must give your name and the address of the phonebox which is written under the word **Standort**.

to the airport, please	**zum Flughafen, bitte** tsoom **flook**-hafen, **bi**-te
to the station, please	**zum Bahnhof, bitte** tsoom **bahn**-hohf, **bi**-te
to this address, please	**zu dieser Adresse bitte** tsoo **dee**zer a-**dre**-se **bi**-te
to hotel...	**zum Hotel...** tsoom ho**tel**...
how much will it cost?	**was wird das kosten?** vas virt das **kos**ten?
why is it so much?	**warum ist das so teuer?** vah**room** ist das zoh **toy**-er?
how much is it to the centre?	**was kostet die Fahrt ins Zentrum?** vas **kos**tet dee fahrt ins **tsen**troom?
where can I get a taxi?	**wo bekomme ich hier ein Taxi?** voh be-**kom**me ikh heer ine **ta**xi?
please order me a taxi	**bitte bestellen Sie mir ein Taxi** **bi**-te be-**shte**llen zee meer ine **ta**xi
straightaway	**sofort** zo-**fort**
for ... o'clock	**für ... Uhr** foor ... oor
I need a receipt	**ich brauche eine Quittung** ikh **brow**-khe **ine**-e **kvi**-toong
I've nothing smaller	**ich habe es nicht kleiner** ikh **hah**-be es nikht **kline**-er
keep the change	**stimmt so** shtimt zoh

Boat

• •

● The Swiss rail pass allows you reduced travel on the Swiss Lakes. They have to be purchased in your own country before arriving in Switzerland.
● A car ferry is an **Autofähre**.
● An outside cabin is **Außenkabine**, an inside cabin is an **Innenkabine** and a single cabin is a **Einzelkabine**.

1 ticket/2 tickets	**einmal/zweimal**
	ine-mal/**tsvy**-mal
single	**einfach**
	ine-fakh
round trip	**eine Rundfahrt**
	ine-e **roont**-fahrt
is there a tourist ticket?	**gibt es eine Touristenkarte?**
	gipt es **ine**-e too**ris**ten-kar-te?
are there any boat trips?	**gibt es Bootsausflüge?**
	gipt es **boats**-ows-floo-ge?
how long is the trip?	**wie lange dauert die Fahrt?**
	vee **lang**-e **dow**-ert dee fahrt?
when is the next boat?	**wann geht das nächste Schiff?**
	van gayt das **naykh**-ste shif?
when is the next ferry?	**wann geht die nächste Fähre?**
	van gayt dee **naykh**-ste **fair**-re?
when is the first boat?	**wann geht das erste Schiff?**
	van gayt das **er**-ste shif?
when is the last boat?	**wann geht das letzte Schiff?**
	van gayt das **lets**-te shif?
where does the boat leave from?	**wo fährt das Schiff ab?**
	voh fairt das shif ap?
is there a timetable?	**gibt es einen Fahrplan?**
	gipt es **ine**-en **fahr**-plahn?
can we hire a boat?	**können wir ein Boot mieten?**
	kur'-nen veer ine boat **mee**-ten?
can we eat on board?	**können wir an Bord essen?**
	kur'-nen veer an board **es**-sen?

Car

Driving

- Motorway tax (in sticker form – **vignette**) is payable in Switzerland and Austria.
- The Swiss tax is valid for one year and runs from 1 December to 31 January. It can be purchased at the border. For Austria there are stickers valid for ten days, two months or a year.
- Always have your car documents and passport with you.

can I park here?	**kann ich hier parken?**
	kan ikh heer **par**ken?
do I need a parking disk?	**brauche ich eine Parkscheibe?**
	brow-khe ikh **ine**-e **park**-shy-be?
where can I park?	**wo kann ich parken?**
	voh kan ikh **par**-ken?
is there a car park?	**gibt es einen Parkplatz?**
	gipt es **ine**-en **park**-plats?
where can I get a parking disk?	**wo kann ich eine Parkscheibe bekommen?**
	voh kan ikh **ine**-e **park**-shy-be be-**kom**men?
how long can I park here?	**wie lange kann ich hier parken?**
	vee **lang**-e kan ikh heer **par**ken?
we're going to...	**wir fahren nach...**
	veer **fah**-ren nakh...
what's the best route?	**was ist der beste Weg?**
	vas ist der **bes**-te vayk?
how do I get to the motorway?	**wie komme ich zur Autobahn?**
	vee **kom**-me ikh tsoor **ow**to-bahn?
which exit is it for...?	**welche Ausfahrt muss ich nach ... nehmen?**
	vel-khe **ows**-fahrt muss ikh nakh ... **nay**-men?

is the pass open?	ist der Pass offen?
	ist der pass **of**fen?
do I need snow chains?	brauche ich Schneeketten?
	brow-khe ikh **shnay**-ketten?

Petrol

• •

• Prices are higher at motorway filling stations in Germany.
A cheaper alternative is an **Autohof** (truck-stop) which you find
just off the motorway.
• It's against the law to run out of petrol on the **Autobahn**.
Fines are on-the-spot and high.
• It is compulsory to carry a first-aid kit and warning triangle.

is there a petrol station near here?	ist hier in der Nähe eine Tankstelle?
	ist heer in der **nay**-e **ine**-e **tank**-shte-le?
fill it up, please	voll tanken, bitte
	fol **tang**-ken, **bi**-te
...euro worth of unleaded petrol	...Euro bleifrei bitte
	...**oy**-roh **bly**-fry **bi**-te
which pump?	welche Säule?
	vel-khe **zoy**-le?
pump number...	Säule Nummer...
	zoy-le **noo**mer...
where is the air line?	wo ist die Druckluft?
	voh ist dee **drook**-looft?
where is the water?	wo ist das Wasser?
	voh ist das **vas**ser?
please check...	bitte überprüfen Sie...
	bi-te oober-**proo**fen zee...
the oil/the water	das Öl/das Wasser
	das ur'l/das **vas**ser
the tyre pressure	den Reifendruck
	den **ry**fen-drook
a token for wash number...	einen Chip für Waschprogramm Nummer...
	ine-en chip foor **vash**-pro-gram **noo**mer...

Problems/breakdown

• If you break down on the motorway in Germany you can call the roadside services from one of the orange emergency phones. Assistance is free, though any parts must be paid for.
• The police must be called to any accident whether there are injuries or not (dial 110).
• Fire and ambulance can be contacted on 112.

the road patrol, please	die **Straße**nwacht, **bi**tte
	dee **shtra**sen-vakht, **bi**-te
I've broken down	ich habe eine Panne
	ikh **hah**-be **ine**-e **pa**-ne
I'm on my own	ich bin allein
	ikh bin **al**-line
I have children in the car	ich habe Kinder dabei
	ikh **hah**-be **kin**der da-**by**
where is the nearest garage?	wo ist die nächste Werkstatt?
	voh ist dee **naykh**-ste **verk**-shtat?
something is wrong with...	es stimmt etwas nicht mit...
	es shtimt **et**vas nikht mit...
is it serious?	ist es etwas Ernstes?
	ist es **et**vas **ern**-stes?
can you repair it?	können Sie es reparieren?
	kur'n-en zee es raypa-**ree**ren?
when will it be ready?	wann wird es fertig sein?
	van virt es **fer**-tikh zine?
how much will it cost?	was wird das kosten?
	vas virt das **kos**ten?
the car won't start	das Auto springt nicht an
	das **ow**to shpringt nikht an
I have a flat tyre	ich habe einen Platten
	ikh **hah**-be **ine**-en **pla**-ten
the engine is overheating	der Motor wird zu heiß
	der **moh**tor virt tsoo hice

the battery is flat	**meine Batterie ist leer**
	mine-e ba-te**ree** ist layr
can you put in a new windscreen?	**können Sie eine neue Windschutzscheibe einsetzen?**
	kur'-nen zee **ine**-e **noy**-e **vint**shoots-shy-be **ine**-zetsen?

Car hire

• •

• You can pre-book a car prior to your trip. This means you are guaranteed the car you want.

• To rent a car from most agencies in Germany you need to be at least 21 and have had your licence for at least a year.

• Check the insurance offered. The standard one is just 3rd party. For fully comprehensive you have to pay extra.

I want to hire a car	**ich möchte ein Auto mieten**
	ikh **mur'kh**-te ine **ow**to **mee**ten
for one day	**für einen Tag**
	foor **ine**-en tahk
for ... days	**für ... Tage**
	foor ... **tah**-ge
how much is it?	**was kostet es?**
	vas **kos**tet es?
is fully comprehensive insurance included?	**ist eine Vollkaskoversicherung inbegriffen?**
	ist **ine**-e **fol**-kasko-fer-**zikh**eroong **in**-be-griffen?
do you have...?	**haben Sie...?**
	hah-ben zee...?
a larger car	**ein größeres Auto**
	ine **grur'**-ser-es **ow**to
a smaller car	**ein kleineres Auto**
	ine **kline**-e-res **ow**to
a cheaper car	**ein billigeres Auto**
	ine **bil**-ig-er-es **ow**to

an automatic	eins mit Automatik
	ines mit owto-**mah**-tik
what do we do if we break down?	was tun wir bei einem Unfall?
	vas toon veer by **ine**-em **oon**fal?
what petrol must I use?	was muss ich tanken?
	vas mus ikh **tang**-ken?
must I return the car here?	muss ich das Auto hierher zurückbringen?
	moos ikh das **ow**to **heer**-her tsoo**rook**-bringen?
by what time?	bis wann?
	bis van?
please show me the controls	bitte erklären Sie mir die Schalter
	bi-te er-**klay**-ren zee meer dee **shal**-ter
where are the documents?	wo sind die Papiere?
	vo zint dee pa**pee**re?
where is the nearest petrol station?	wo ist die nächste Tankstelle?
	voh ist dee **naykh**-ste **tank**-shtel-e?

Shopping

Shopping – holiday

• Most large shops in Germany are open all day from 9am to 6pm Monday to Friday (with the largest ones often staying open longer). On Saturday they are open until late afternoon. Shops shut on Sundays and public holidays.
• Christmas markets are great for handicrafts and culinary specialities. The most famous is in Nuremberg.

do you sell...?	**verkaufen Sie...?**
	fer-**kow**fen zee...?
stamps	**Briefmarken**
	breef-marken
batteries for this camera	**Batterien für diese Kamera**
	ba-te**ree**-en foor **dee**-ze **ka**mera
where can I buy...?	**wo bekomme ich...?**
	voh be-**kom**me ikh...?
films	**Filme**
	filme
10 stamps	**zehn Briefmarken**
	tsayn **breef**-marken
for postcards	**für Postkarten**
	foor **post**-kar-ten
to Britain	**nach England**
	nakh **eng**-lant
a colour film	**einen Farbfilm**
	ine-en **farp**-film
a memory card for my digital camera	**ein Speicherkarte für meine Digitalkamera**
	ine-e **shpaykh**er-kar-te foor **mine**-e digi-**tahl**-kamera

I'm looking for a present	**ich suche ein Geschenk**
	ikh **zook**he ine ge**shenk**
have you anything else?	**haben Sie noch etwas Anderes?**
	hah-ben zee nokh **et**vas **an**-de-res?
it's a gift	**es ist ein Geschenk**
	es ist ine ge**shenk**
please wrap it up	**bitte verpacken Sie es**
	bi-te fer-**pak**-en zee es
is there a market?	**gibt es einen Markt?**
	gipt es **ine**-en markt?
when?	**wann?**
	van?

Shopping – clothes

● Department stores such as **Karstadt** offer a wide range of clothes (**Kaufhaus** means department store). You also find familiar chains such as Gap, but there are many smaller and more individualistic shops.

● You may find clothes sizes more generous in Germany than in other European countries.

can I try this on?	**kann ich das anprobieren?**
	kan ikh das **an**proh-beeren?
where are the changing rooms?	**wo sind die Umkleidekabinen?**
	voh zint dee **oom**-kly-de-ka-**bee**nen?
it's too big	**es ist zu groß**
	es ist tsoo grohs
have you anything smaller?	**haben Sie etwas Kleineres?**
	hah-ben zee **et**vas **kline**-er-es?
it's too small	**es ist zu klein**
	es ist tsoo kline
have you anything larger?	**haben Sie etwas Größeres?**
	hah-ben zee **et**vas **grur'**-ser-es?
it's too expensive	**es ist zu teuer**
	es ist tsoo **toy**-er

have you anything cheaper?	**haben Sie etwas Billigeres?**
	hah-ben zee **et**vas **bil**-ig-er-es?
I'm just looking	**ich schaue mich nur um**
	ikh **show**-e mikh noor oom
I'll take this one	**ich nehme das hier**
	ikh **nay**-me das heer
I take size...	**ich habe Größe...**
	ikh **hah**-be **grur'**-se...
I take size ... shoe	**ich habe Schuhgröße...**
	ikh **hah**-be **shoo**-grur'-se...
what size are you?	**welche Größe haben Sie?**
	vel-khe **grur'**-se **hah**-ben zee?
does it fit?	**passt es?**
	past es?

Shopping – food

• Supermarkets are usually open from 8am till early evening Monday to Saturday, but local times may vary (closed Sundays and public holidays).
• When supermarkets are closed you can still get essentials at some petrol stations.
• You need a coin (usually a euro) to release a trolley.
• You pay for plastic bags at the checkout; nearly everyone brings their own bags.

where can I buy...?	**wo kann ich ... kaufen?**
	voh kan ikh ... **kow**fen?
bread	**Brot**
	broht
fruit	**Obst**
	ohbst
milk	**Milch**
	milkh
where is the baker's?	**wo ist die Bäckerei?**
	voh ist dee be-ke-**rye**?

where is the supermarket?	**wo ist der Supermarkt?** voh ist der **su**per-markt?
where is the market?	**wo ist der Markt?** voh ist der markt?
when is the market?	**wann ist Markt?** van ist markt?
it's my turn next	**ich bin dran** ikh bin dran
that's enough	**das reicht** das rykht
a litre of...	**einen Liter...** **ine**-en **lee**ter...
milk	**Milch** milkh
water	**Wasser** **vas**ser
beer	**Bier** beer
a bottle of...	**eine Flasche...** **ine**-e **fla**-she...
water	**Wasser** **vas**ser
wine	**Wein** vine
sparkling wine	**Sekt** sekt
a can of...	**eine Dose...** **ine**-e **doh**-ze...
coke	**Cola** **co**la
beer	**Bier** beer
tonic water	**Tonic** **to**nic
a carton of...	**einen Karton...** **ine**-en kar-tong...

orange juice	**Orangensaft**
	o**ron**jen-saft
apple juice	**Apfelsaft**
	apfel-saft

• In most German towns there are weekly markets (**Wochenmarkt**), usually held on Saturdays (and another weekday).
• Larger supermarkets often have a separate area for drinks and mineral waters (**Getränkemarkt**). Bottles and cans carry a deposit which you get back on returning them.
• Cash/debit card are the commonest ways to pay in supermarkets.

4oz/100 grams of...	**hundert Gramm...**
	hoondert gram...
cheese	**Käse**
	kay-ze
ham	**Schinken**
	shin-ken
half a pound of...	**ein halbes Pfund...**
	ine **hal**-bes pfoont...
liver sausage	**Leberwurst**
	leh-ber-voorst
minced pork	**Schweinehack**
	shvy-nehak
a kilo of...	**ein Kilo...**
	ine **kee**lo...
potatoes	**Kartoffeln**
	kar-**to**feln
apples	**Äpfel**
	epfel
8 slices of...	**acht Scheiben...**
	akht **shy**-ben...
ham	**Schinken**
	shin-ken
salami	**Salami**
	sa**la**mee

a portion of...	**eine Portion...**
	ine-e por-tsy**ohn**...
sauerkraut	**Sauerkraut**
	sauerkraut
salad	**Salat**
	za**laht**
a packet of...	**ein Päckchen...**
	ine **pek**-khen...
biscuits	**Kekse**
	kayk-se
pumpernickel bread	**Pumpernickel**
	poomper-nickel
a tin of...	**eine Dose...**
	ine-e **doh**-ze...
tomatoes	**Tomaten**
	to**mah**-ten
stew	**Eintopf**
	ine-topf
a jar of...	**ein Glas...**
	ine glahs...
jam	**Marmelade**
	mar-me**lah** de
olives	**Oliven**
	o**lee**ven
gherkins	**Gurken**
	goorken

Daylife

Sightseeing

- Tourist offices organize city walks (**Stadtrundgänge**) and city bus tours (**Stadtrundfahrten**).
- Museums and galleries are open on Sundays, but are usually closed on Mondays.
- In cities with lots of tourist attractions, you can often buy tickets that allow you multiple entry.

where is the tourist office?	**wo ist die Touristeninformation?**
	voh ist dee too**ris**ten-infor-matsy**ohn**?
we want to visit...	**wir möchten ... besuchen**
	veer **mur'kh**-ten ... be**zoo**khen
have you any leaflets?	**haben Sie Broschüren?**
	hah-ben zee bro-**shoo**ren?
when can we visit...?	**wann können wir ... besichtigen?**
	van **kur'**-nen veer ... be**zikh**-tigen?
how long is ... open?	**wie lange ist ... geöffnet?**
	vee **lan**-ge ist ... ge-**ur'f**-net?
what day does it close?	**an welchem Tag ist es zu?**
	an **vel**-khem tahk ist es tsoo?
we'd like to go to...	**wir möchten nach...**
	veer **mur'kh**-ten nakh...
are there any excursions?	**gibt es Ausflugsfahrten?**
	gipt es **ows**-flooks-fahrten?
when does it leave?	**wann ist die Abfahrt?**
	van ist dee **ap**-fahrt?
where does it leave from?	**wo ist die Abfahrt?**
	voh ist dee **ap**-fahrt?

how much is the entrance?	**was kostet der Eintritt?**
	vas **kos**tet der **ine**-trit?
are there reductions for...?	**gibt es Ermäßigung für...?**
	gipt es er-**may**-sigoong foor...?
students	**Studenten**
	shtoo-**den**ten
seniors (pl)	**Rentner**
	rentner

Beach

• In the Baltic, a red ball on top of a pole indicates that it is too dangerous to swim. If the ball is halfway down, then it's dangerous for children but OK for adult swimmers.
• In southern Germany there are many outdoor swimming pools (**Freibad**).
• Designated nudist beaches are marked **FKK**.

which is a good beach?	**welcher Strand ist gut?**
	vel-kher shtrahnt ist goot?
how do I get there?	**wie komme ich dahin?**
	vee **kom**me ikh da**hin**?
is there a swimming pool near here?	**gibt es ein Schwimmbad in der Nähe?**
	gipt es ine **shvim**-baht in der **nay**-e?
can we swim in the lake?	**können wir im See baden?**
	kur'-nen veer im zeh **bah**-den?
is the water clean?	**ist das Wasser sauber?**
	ist das **vas**ser **zow**-ber?
is the water deep?	**ist das Wasser tief?**
	ist das **vas**ser teef?
is the water cold?	**ist das Wasser kalt?**
	ist das **vas**ser kalt?
is it safe for children?	**ist es sicher für Kinder?**
	ist es **zi**kher foor **kin**der?
are there currents?	**gibt es Strömungen?**
	gipt es **shtrur'**-moong-en?

where can we...?	**wo können wir...?**
	voh **kur'**-nen veer...?
windsurf	**windsurfen**
	wint-surfen
waterski	**Wasserski fahren**
	vasser-shee **fah**-ren
can we hire...?	**können wir ... mieten?**
	kur'-nen veer ... **mee**-ten?
a jetski	**einen Jetski**
	ine-en **jet**ski
a deck chair	**einen Liegestuhl**
	ine-en **lee**-ge-shtool
how do we hire a beach hut?	**wie können wir einen Strandkorb mieten?**
	vee **kur'**-nen veer **ine**-en **shtrant**-korb **mee**-ten?

Sport

• •

• Most tourist offices will have details of local sports facilities. There are many well-marked walks (from gentle strolls to more strenuous Alpine hikes) in southern Germany. Check at local tourist offices for information and guides.

• There are over 200 signposted long-distance cycle routes throughout Germany with special bike lanes in most cities.

where can we...?	**wo können wir...?**
	voh **kur'**-nen veer...?
play tennis	**Tennis spielen**
	tennis **shpee**len
play golf	**Golf spielen**
	golf **shpee**len
go swimming	**Schwimmen gehen**
	shvim-en **gay**-en
hire bikes	**Fahrräder leihen**
	fah-rehder **lye**-en
go fishing	**angeln**
	angeln

go riding	**reiten** **ry**-ten
how much is it...?	**was kostet es...?** vas **kos**tet es...?
per hour	**pro Stunde** pro **shtoon**-de
per day	**pro Tag** pro tahk
how do I book a court?	**wie reserviere ich einen Platz?** vee ray-zer-**vee**-re ikh **ine**-en plats?
can we hire rackets?	**kann man Schläger leihen?** kan man **shlay**-ger **lye**-en?
is there a guide to local walks?	**gibt es einen Wanderführer von dieser Gegend?** gipt es **ine**-en **van**der-foorer fon **dee**zer **gay**gent?
do I need walking boots?	**brauche ich Wanderstiefel?** **brow**-khe ikh **van**der-shteefel?
how long is this walk?	**wie lange dauert diese Wanderung?** vee lang **dow**-ert **dee**-ze **van**-de-rung?

Skiing

. . . .

• Switzerland and Austria offer many opportunities for winter sports.

• Germany has a number of winter sports areas where you can enjoy anything from downhill skiing to snowboarding and cross-country skiing.

• Check out **www.bbc.co.uk/weather/sports/skiing** for snow information.

can I hire skis?	**kann ich Skier leihen?** kan ikh **shee**-er **lye**-en?
how much is a pass?	**was kostet ein Pass?** vas **kos**tet ine pass?
I'm a beginner	**ich bin Anfänger** ikh bin **an**-fenger

which is an easy run?	**welche Abfahrt ist einfach?** **vel**-khe **ap**-fahrt ist **ine**-fakh?
is it safe to ski today?	**ist das Skifahren heute ungefährlich?** ist das **shee**-fahren **hoy**-te **oon**-gefayrlikh?
what is the snow like?	**wie ist der Schnee?** vee ist der shnay?
is there a map of the ski runs?	**gibt es eine Pistenkarte?** gipt es **ine**-e **pis**ten-kar-te?
my skis are...	**meine Skier sind...** **mine**-e **shee**-er zint...
too long	**zu lang** tsoo lang
too short	**zu kurz** tsoo koorts
my bindings are...	**meine Bindungen sind...** **mine**-e **bin**-doong-en zint...
too loose	**zu locker** tsoo **lo**cker
too tight	**zu fest** tsoo fest
where can we go cross-country skiing?	**wo können wir Langlauf fahren?** voh **kur'**-nen veer **lang**-lowf **fah**-ren?
what length skis do you want?	**welche Länge brauchen Sie?** **vel**-khe **leng**-e **brow**-khen zee?
what is your shoe size?	**welche Schuhgröße haben Sie?** **vel**-khe **shoo**-grur'-se **hah**-ben zee?

Nightlife

Nightlife – popular

••

• Bars and discos in Germany are open till late. You have to be over 18 years to drink alcohol (and often to get into discos where ID card checks are common).
• Student clubs are open to the public at a slightly higher charge.
• Music festivals include the **Love Parade** in Berlin, the **Sound of Frankfurt**, and **Bochum Total**, claiming to be Europe's largest music event.

what is there to do at night?	**was kann man abends machen?** vas kan man **ah**bents **ma**khen?
are there any concerts?	**gibt es Konzerte?** gipt es kon-**tser**te?
which is a good bar?	**welche Bar ist gut?** **vel**-khe bar ist goot?
which is a good disco?	**welche Disco ist gut?** **vel**-khe **dis**co ist goot?
where can we hear live music?	**wo gibt es Livemusik?** voh gipt es **live**-moo-zeek?
is it expensive?	**ist es teuer?** ist es **toy**-er?
is there a student club?	**gibt es hier einen Studentenklub?** gipt es heer **ine**-en shtoo-**den**ten-klup?
where do local people go at night?	**wo gehen die Einheimischen abends hin?** voh **gay**-en dee **ine**-hime-mee-shen **ah**bents hin?
is it a safe area?	**ist die Gegend sicher?** ist dee **gay**gent **zi**kher?
do you want to dance with me?	**möchten Sie mit mir tanzen?** **mur'kh**-ten zee mit meer **tan**tsen?

| would you like to go out tomorrow night? | **möchten Sie morgen abend mit mir ausgehen?** |
| | mur'kh-ten zee **mor**gen **ah**bent mit meer **ows**-gay-en? |

Nightlife – cultural

• A list of cultural events should be available from tourist offices or listed in the local paper.
• Germany has many music theatres with permanent ensembles and orchestras such as the **Gewandhausorchester** in Leipzig and the **Bamberger Symphoniker**.
• Eating and drinking is not allowed in auditoriums.

is there a list of cultural events?	**gibt es einen Veranstaltungskalender?**
	gipt es **ine**-en fehr-**an**shtaltoongs-ka**len**der?
are there any festivals?	**gibt es hier Festivals?**
	gipt es heer **fes**tivals?
we'd like to go...	**wir möchten ... gehen**
	veer **mur'kh**-ten ... **gay**-en
to the theatre	**ins Theater**
	ins tay-**ah**ter
to the opera	**in die Oper**
	in dee **oh**-per
to the ballet	**ins Ballett**
	ins bahl-**let**
to a concert	**in ein Konzert**
	in ine kon-**tsert**
what's on?	**was wird gespielt?**
	vas virt ge**shpeelt**?
do I need to book?	**muss ich reservieren?**
	moos ikh ray-zer-**vee**-ren?
how much are the tickets?	**was kosten die Karten?**
	vas **kos**ten dee **kar**-ten?
row 3...	**Reihe 3...**
	rye-e dry...

55

seat number 10	**Platz 10**
	plats tsayn
2 tickets...	**zwei Karten...**
	tsvy **kar**-ten...
for tonight	**für heute Abend**
	foor **hoy**-te **ah**bent
for tomorrow night	**für morgen Abend**
	foor **mor**gen **ah**bent
for 5th August	**für den fünften August**
	foor den **foonf**-ten ow**goost**
when does the performance end?	**wann ist die Vorstellung zu Ende?**
	van ist dee **for**-shtelloong tsoo **en**-de?

Accommodation

Hotel

• •

• Tourist information offices will be able to provide a list of all the different kinds of accommodation available.
• **Urlaub auf dem Bauernhof** (holidays on farms) are popular for families.
• A **Hotel garni** is usually a smaller hotel offering bed and breakfast accommodation.

have you a room for tonight?	**haben Sie ein Zimmer für heute Nacht?** **hah**-ben zee ine **tsim**mer foor **hoy**-te nakt?
a single room	**ein Einzelzimmer** ine **ine**-tsel-tsimmer
a double room	**ein Doppelzimmer** ine **dop**pel-tsimmer
a family room	**ein Familienzimmer** ine fa**mee**lee-en-tsimmer
with bath	**mit Bad** mit baht
with shower	**mit Dusche** mit **doo**-she
how much is it per night?	**wie viel kostet es pro Nacht?** **vee**feel **kos**tet es pro nakt?
is breakfast included?	**ist das Frühstück inbegriffen?** ist das **froo**-shtook **in**-be-griffen?
I booked a room	**ich habe ein Zimmer reserviert** ikh **hah**-be ine **tsim**mer ray-zer-**veert**
my name is...	**mein Name ist...** mine **nah**-me ist...

I'd like to see the room	**ich möchte das Zimmer gern ansehen**
	ikh **mur'kh**-te das **tsim**mer gern an-**zay**en
have you anything cheaper?	**haben Sie etwas Billigeres?**
	hah-ben zee **et**vas **bi**li-ge-res?
what time is...?	**wann gibt es...?**
	van gipt es...?
breakfast	**Frühstück**
	froo-shtook
dinner	**Abendessen**
	ahbent-essen
the key, please	**den Schlüssel, bitte**
	den **shloo**-sel, **bi**-te
room number...	**Zimmer** (number)...
	tsimmer...
are there any messages for me?	**sind Nachrichten für mich da?**
	zint **nahkh**-rikhten foor mikh dah?
come in!	**herein!**
	he-**rine**!
please come back later	**bitte kommen Sie später noch einmal**
	bi-te **kom**men zee **shpay**ter nokh **ine**-mal
I'd like breakfast in my room	**ich möchte gern Frühstück auf meinem Zimmer**
	ikh **mur'kh**-te gern **froo**-shtook owf **mine**-em **tsim**mer
please bring...	**bitte bringen Sie...**
	bi-te **bring**en zee...
toilet paper	**Toilettenpapier**
	twa-**le**-ten-pa**peer**
soap	**Seife**
	zye-fe
clean towels	**saubere Handtücher**
	zow-be-re **hant**-tookher
a glass	**ein Glas**
	ine glahs
please clean...	**bitte machen Sie ... sauber**
	bi-te **ma**khen zee ... **zow**-ber

my room	**mein Zimmer**
	mine **tsim**mer
the bath	**das Bad**
	das baht
I need an alarm call	**ich brauche einen Weckruf**
	ikh **brow**-khe **ine**-en **vek**-roof
at 7 o'clock	**um sieben Uhr**
	oom **zee**ben oor
is there a laundry service?	**gibt es einen Wäschereiservice?**
	gipt es **ine**-en veshe-**rye**-service?
can I borrow an iron?	**kann ich ein Bügeleisen haben?**
	kan ikh ine **boo**gel-ize-en **hah**-ben?
I'm leaving tomorrow	**ich reise morgen ab**
	ikh **rye**-ze **mor**gen ap
please prepare the bill	**machen Sie bitte die Rechnung fertig**
	makhen zee **bi**-te dee **rekh**-noong **fer**tikh

Self-catering

• Germany, Austria and Switzerland all use 220 volts. If you plan to take any electrical appliances such as hairdryers, irons or kettles, you should make sure you have an adaptor.

• Holiday flats and cottages are normally rented out on a weekly basis (Saturday to Saturday) and you are normally expected to clean the property before you leave. You may be asked to separate your waste for recycling.

which is the key for this door?	**welcher Schlüssel ist für diese Tür?**
	vel-kher **shloo**-sel ist foor **dee**-ze toor?
where are the fuses?	**wo sind die Sicherungen?**
	voh zint dee **zikh**-eroong-en?
is there always hot water?	**gibt es ständig heißes Wasser?**
	gipt es **shten**-dikh **hy**-ses **va**sser?
please show us how this works	**bitte zeigen Sie uns, wie das funktioniert**
	bi-te **tsy**-gen zee oons vee das foonk-tsyoh-**neert**

how does ... work?	**wie funktioniert...?**	vee foonk-tsyoh-**neert**...?
the dryer	**der Wäschetrockner**	der **ve**she-trok-ner
the waterheater	**der Wasserboiler**	der **vas**ser-boy-ler
the heating	**die Heizung**	dee **hye**-tsung
the washing machine	**die Waschmaschine**	die **vash**-mah-shee-ne
the cooker	**der Herd**	der hert
whom do I contact if there are any problems?	**wen spreche ich bei Problemen an?**	vehn **shpre**khe ikh by proh**bleh**men an?
we need extra...	**wir brauchen extra...**	veer **brow**-khen **eks**tra...
keys	**Schlüssel**	**shloo**-sel
cutlery	**Besteck**	be**shtek**
sheets	**Bettwäsche**	**bet**-veshe
the gas has run out	**das Gas ist alle**	das gahs ist **al**-le
what do I do?	**was muss ich tun?**	vas moos ikh toon?

Camping and caravanning

• •

• In Germany and Switzerland the speed of a car towing a caravan must not exceed 50 kph in built-up areas and 80 kph on other roads and motorways (Austria up to 100 kph on motorways).
• Places where you can fill water tanks and empty toilets, etc, are called **Entsorgungsstation**.

have you a list of campsites?	**haben Sie eine Liste von Campingplätzen?**
	hah-ben zee **ine**-e **lis**-te fon **kam**ping-pletsen?
have you any vacancies?	**haben Sie noch Plätze frei?**
	hah-ben zee nokh **plet**-se fry?
how much is it per night?	**was kostet die Nacht?**
	vas **kos**tet dee nakht?
we'd like to stay for ... nights	**wir möchten ... Nächte bleiben**
	veer **mur'kh**-ten ... **nekh**-te **bly**-ben
where are the washrooms?	**wo sind die Waschräume?**
	voh zint dee **vash**-roy-me?
where can I empty the chemical toilet?	**wo kann ich die chemische Toilette entsorgen?**
	voh kan ikh dee **khe**-mishe twa-**le**-te ent-**zor**-gen?
is there a restaurant?	**gibt es ein Restaurant?**
	gipt es ine restoh-**rong**?
is there a shop?	**gibt es einen Laden?**
	gipt es **ine**-en **lah**-den?
can we park our caravan here overnight?	**können wir unseren Wohnwagen hier über Nacht parken?**
	kur'-nen veer **oon**seren **vohn**-vahgen heer **oo**ber nakht **par**ken?
can we camp here overnight? (for tent)	**können wir über Nacht hier zelten?**
	kur'-nen veer **oo**ber nakht heer **tsel**-ten?

Different travellers

Children

••

- In Germany children up to 4 must have their own special car seat (**Kindersitz**) and up to 12 must have booster seats (and sit in the back). In Austria and Switzerland children must travel in the back with seatbelts.
- Restaurants often have children's dishes (**Kinderteller**).
- **Europapark** in the south of Germany is a theme park.

a child's ticket	**eine Kinderkarte**
	ine-e **kin**der-kar-te
he/she is ... years old	**er/sie ist...**
	er/zee ist...
is there a reduction for children?	**gibt es Ermäßigung für Kinder?**
	gipt es er-**may**-sigoong foor **kin**der?
where can I change the baby?	**wo kann ich das Baby wickeln?**
	voh kan ikh das **ba**by **vi**-keln?
can you warm this up?	**können Sie das aufwärmen?**
	kur'-nen zee das **owf**-ver-men?
do you have a children's menu?	**haben Sie eine Kinderkarte?**
	hah-ben zee **ine**-e **kin**der-kar-te?
do you have...?	**haben Sie...?**
	hah-ben zee...?
a child's car seat	**einen Kindersitz**
	ine-en **kin**-der-zits
a high chair	**einen Kinderstuhl**
	ine-en **kin**der-shtool
a cot	**ein Kinderbett**
	ine **kin**der-bet
is it ok to bring children here?	**können wir die Kinder mitbringen?**
	kur'-nen veer dee **kin**der **mit**-bringen?

is there a playpark?	**gibt es einen Spielplatz?**
	gipt es **ine**-en **shpeel**-plats?
what's there for children to do?	**was können die Kinder hier unternehmen?**
	vas **kur'**-nen dee **kin**der heer oonter-**nay**men?
I have two children	**ich habe zwei Kinder**
	ikh **hah**-be tsvy **kin**der
do you have children?	**haben Sie Kinder?**
	hah-ben zee **kin**der?

Special needs

• •

• On all Intercity and on most Eurocity and fast trains, special wheelchair compartments are now available in second class. A wheelchair sign indicates facilities for the disabled.
• You can arrange help in advance for getting on and off trains. To book it ring the hotline 01805 512 512.
• The standard UK disabled badge is valid throughout the EU or go to **www.bahn.de**, click on **Mobilität&Service** and follow the links.

is it possible to visit ... with a wheelchair?	**kann man ... auch im Rollstuhl besuchen?**
	kan man ... aukh im **rol**-shtool be**zoo**khen?
do you have toilets for the disabled?	**haben Sie Toiletten für Behinderte?**
	hah-ben zee twa-**le**-ten foor be-**hin**-der-te?
I need a bedroom on the ground floor	**ich brauche ein Zimmer im Erdgeschoss**
	ikh **brow**-khe ine **tsim**mer im **ert**-geshos
is there a lift?	**gibt es einen Aufzug?**
	gipt es **ine**-en **owf**tsook?
where is the lift?	**wo ist der Aufzug?**
	voh ist der **owf**tsook?
I can't walk far	**ich kann nicht weit laufen**
	ikh kan nikht vite **low**-fen
are there many steps?	**sind es viele Stufen?**
	zint es **fee**le **shtoo**fen?
is there an entrance for wheelchairs?	**gibt es einen Eingang für Rollstuhlfahrer?**
	gipt es **ine**-en **ine**-gang foor **rol**-shtool-fahrer?

can I travel on this train with a wheelchair?	**kann ich als Rollstuhlfahrer in diesem Zug mitfahren?**
	kan ikh als **rol**-shtool-fahrer in **dee**zem tsook **mit**-fahren?
is there a reduction for the disabled?	**gibt es Ermäßigung für Behinderte?**
	gipt es er-**may**-sigoong foor be-**hin**-der-te?

Exchange visitors

• •

• These phrases are intended for families hosting German-speaking visitors.

• Germans usually have lunch between noon and 1pm. Normally this is their main hot meal. Dinner, a lighter meal (usually bread and cold sliced meats and cheese), is at 7pm.

what would you like for breakfast?	**was möchten Sie zum Frühstück?**
	vas **mur'kh**-ten zee tsoom **froo**-shtook?
do you eat...?	**essen Sie...?**
	es-sen zee...?
what would you like to eat?	**was möchten Sie essen?**
	vas **mur'kh**-ten zee **es**-sen?
what would you like to drink?	**was möchten Sie trinken?**
	vas **mur'kh**-ten zee **trin**ken?
did you sleep well?	**haben Sie gut geschlafen?**
	hah-ben zee goot ge**shlah**fen?
what would you like to do today?	**was möchten Sie heute unternehmen?**
	vas **mur'kh**-ten zee **hoy**-te oonter-**nay**men?
I will pick you up at...	**ich hole Sie um ... ab**
	ikh **hoh**-le zee oom ... ap
did you enjoy yourself?	**hat es Ihnen gefallen?**
	hat es **ee**nen ge**fal**len?
take care	**passen Sie auf sich auf**
	passen zee owf zikh owf
please be back no later than...	**bitte seien Sie bis spätestens ... zurück**
	bi-te **zy**-en zee bis **shpay**-testens ... tsoo**rook**

we'll be in bed when you get back	**wir werden schon schlafen, wenn Sie zurückkommen**
	veer **vehr**-den shohn **shlah**fen, ven zee tsoo**rook**-kommen

• These phrases are intended for those people staying with German-speaking families.
• You should use the polite **Sie** form with older people and those you do not know well.
• If invited to a German home, it is considered polite to take a little gift, such as a bunch of flowers.

I like...	**ich mag...**
	ikh makh...
I don't like...	**ich mag ... nicht**
	ikh makh ... nikht
that was delicious	**das war sehr gut**
	das vahr zehr goot
thank you very much	**vielen Dank**
	fee-len dank
may I phone home?	**darf ich nach Hause telefonieren?**
	darf ikh nakh **how**-ze taylay-fo-**nee**ren?
can I have a key?	**kann ich einen Schlüssel bekommen?**
	kan ikh **ine**-en **shloo**-sel be-**kom**men?
can I borrow...?	**kann ich ... borgen?**
	kan ikh ... **bohr**-gen?
a hairdryer/an iron	**einen Föhn/ein Bügeleisen**
	ine-en fur'n/ine boogel-**ize**-en
can you take me by car?	**können Sie mich mit dem Auto hinbringen?**
	kur'-nen zee mikh mit dem **ow**to **hin**-bringen?
what time do you get up?	**wann stehen Sie auf?**
	van **shtay**en zee owf?
I'm staying with...	**ich wohne bei...**
	kh **voh**-ne by...
I've had a great time	**es hat mir sehr gut gefallen**
	es haht meer zehr goot ge**fal**len

Difficulties

Problems

• •

• Germans may be slightly reserved, but they are helpful if approached.
• Many Germans speak good English (particularly the young).
• If you need to attract someone's attention, begin your request with **Entschuldigung!**

excuse me!	**Entschuldigung!**
	ent-**shool**-di-goong!
can you help me?	**können Sie mir helfen?**
	kur'-nen zee meer **hel**fen?
I don't speak German	**ich spreche kein Deutsch**
	ikh **shpre**-khe kine doytch
do you speak English?	**sprechen Sie Englisch?**
	shprekhen zee **eng**-lish?
does anyone speak English?	**spricht jemand Englisch?**
	shprikht **yay**mant **eng**-lish?
I'm lost	**ich habe mich verlaufen**
	ikh **hah**-be mikh fer-**low**fen
how do I get to...?	**wie komme ich zum/zur/nach...?**
	vee **kom**me ikh tsoom/tsoor/nakh...?
I'm late	**ich habe mich verspätet**
	ikh **hah**-be mikh vers**hpay**-tet
I need to get to...	**ich muss zum/zur/nach...**
	ikh moos tsoom/tsoor/nakh...
I've missed...	**ich habe ... verpasst**
	ikh **hah**-be ... fer-**past**
my connection	**meinen Anschluss**
	mine-en **an**-shloos

my plane	**mein Flugzeug** mine **flook**-tsoyk
I've lost...	**ich habe ... verloren** ikh **hah**-be ... fer-**loh**ren
my passport	**meinen Pass** **mine**-en pass
my money	**mein Geld** mine gelt
my suitcase...	**mein Koffer...** mine **ko**fer...
is damaged	**wurde beschädigt** **voor**-de be-**shay**-dikht
is missing	**ging verloren** geeng fer-**loh**ren
leave me alone!	**lassen Sie mich in Ruhe!** **las**sen zee mikh in **roo**-e!
go away!	**hau ab!** how ap!

Complaints

• •

• Germans usually attach great importance to quality and good service. If they are not satisfied with something, they say so.
• If you complain, you can often get compensation (**Entschädigung**), e.g. for long delays on the trains.
• Germans automatically expect to receive good service and quality.

the light	**das Licht** das likht
the lock	**das Schloss** das shlos
...doesn't work	**...funktioniert nicht** ...foonk-tsyoh-**neert** nikht
the toilet	**die Toilette** dee twa-**le**-te

the heating	**die Heizung**
	dee **hyt**-soong
the room is...	**das Zimmer ist...**
	das **tsim**mer ist...
dirty	**schmutzig**
	shmootsik
too hot	**zu warm**
	tsoo varm
too cold	**zu kalt**
	tsoo kalt
too noisy	**zu laut**
	tsoo lowt
too small	**zu klein**
	tsoo kline
this isn't what I ordered	**das habe ich nicht bestellt**
	das **hah**-be ikh nikht be**shtelt**
I want to complain	**ich möchte mich beschweren**
	ikh **mur'kh**-te mikh be**shveh**ren
the bill is not correct	**die Rechnung stimmt nicht**
	dee **rekh**-noong shtimt nikht
I want my money back	**ich möchte mein Geld zurück**
	ikh **mur'kh**-te mine gelt tsoo**rook**
we've been waiting for a very long time	**wir warten schon sehr lange**
	veer **var**-ten shohn zehr **lang**-e
this is broken	**das ist kaputt**
	das ist ka**poot**
can you repair it?	**können Sie das reparieren?**
	kur'-nen zee das raypa-**ree**ren?

Emergencies

....

- In Germany, if you don't have time to check in the local telephone directory for the emergency ambulance service, the fire brigade also has an ambulance service. Ring 112.
- The Police emergency number is 110.
- If you need urgent medical help, go to the A&E (**Notaufnahme**) of the nearest hospital.

help!	**Hilfe!** **hil**-fe!
fire!	**Feuer!** **foy**-er!
can you help me?	**können Sie mir helfen?** **kur'n**-en zee meer **hel**-fen?
there's been an accident	**ein Unfall ist passiert** ine **oon**fal ist pa**seert**
these are my insurance details	**hier sind meine Versicherungsangaben** here zint **mine**-e fer-**zikh**-e-roongs-an-**ga**ben
someone is injured	**es ist jemand verletzt worden** es ist **yay**mant fer**letst vor**den
please call...	**bitte rufen Sie**... **bi**-te **roo**fen zee...
the police	**die Polizei** dee poli-**tsye**
an ambulance	**einen Krankenwagen** **ine**-en **kran**ken-vahgen
the fire brigade	**die Feuerwehr** dee **foy**-er-vehr
where's the police station?	**wo ist die Polizeiwache?** voh ist dee poli-**tsy**-va-khe?
I want to report a theft	**ich möchte einen Diebstahl melden** ikh **mur'kh**-te **ine**-en **deep**-shtahl **mel**den
my car has been stolen	**mein Auto ist gestohlen worden** mine **ow**to ist ge**shtoh**-len **vor**den

my car has been broken into	**mein Auto ist aufgebrochen worden**
	mine **ow**to ist **owf**-gebro-khen **vor**den
I've been robbed	**ich bin beraubt worden**
	ikh bin be-**rowpt vor**den
I've been attacked	**ich bin überfallen worden**
	ikh bin oober-**fa**llen **vor**den
I've been raped	**ich bin vergewaltigt worden**
	ikh bin fer-ge**val**-tikht **vor**den
I need a report for my insurance	**ich brauche einen Bericht für meine Versicherung**
	ikh **brow**-khe **ine**-en be**rikht** foor **mine**-e ferzikh-eroong
how much is the fine?	**wie viel Strafe muss ich zahlen?**
	veefeel **shtrah**-fe moos ikh **tsah**-len?
where do I pay it?	**wo kann ich das bezahlen?**
	voh kan ikh das be-**tsah**len?
I have no money	**ich habe kein Geld**
	ikh **hah**-be kine gelt
I would like to phone my embassy	**ich möchte mit meiner Botschaft telefonieren**
	ikh **mur'kh**-te mit **mine**-er **boht**shaft taylay-fo-**nce**ren
I'm very sorry	**es tut mir sehr leid**
	es toot meer zayr lite

Health

Health

• Pharmacies will be able to provide advice on any health matters and deal with minor problems. Look out for the old fashioned 'A' sign.
• EU citizens are entitled to free emergency dental and medical care. You must have your European Health Insurance Card (available from **www.dh.gov.uk/travellers**).

have you something for...?	**haben Sie etwas gegen...?** **hah**-ben zee **et**vas **gay**-gen...?
car sickness	**Reisekrankheit** **ry**-ze-krank-hite
diarrhoea	**Durchfall** **doorkh**-fal
is it safe to give children?	**kann man es bedenkenlos auch Kindern geben?** kan man es be-**deng**-ken-lohs owkh **kin**dern **gay**ben?
I'm ill	**ich bin krank** ikh bin krank
I need a doctor	**ich brauche einen Arzt** ikh **brow**-khe **ine**-en artst
my son/my daughter has a high temperature	**mein Sohn/meine Tochter hat hohes Fieber** mine zohn / **mine**-e **tokh**ter hat **hoh**-es **fee**ber
I'm on this medication	**ich nehme dieses Medikament** ikh **nay**-me **dee**zes medeeka**ment**
I have high blood pressure	**ich habe hohen Blutdruck** ikh **hah**-be **hoh**-en **bloot**-drook

I have fallen	**ich bin hingefallen**
	ikh bin hin-ge-**fal**-en
I'm diabetic	**ich bin Diabetiker(in)**
	ikh bin dee-a-**bay**-tiker(in)
I'm pregnant	**ich bin schwanger**
	ikh bin **shvan**ger
I'm on the pill	**ich nehme die Pille**
	ikh **nay**-me dee **pi**-le
I'm allergic to penicillin	**ich bin allergisch gegen Penizillin**
	ikh bin a-ler-gish **gay**-gen peni-tsi**leen**
my blood group is...	**meine Blutgruppe ist...**
	mine-e blootgroo-pe ist...
I'm breastfeeding	**ich stille mein Baby**
	ikh **shtil**le mine **ba**by
is it safe to take?	**kann man das bedenkenlos einnehmen?**
	kan man das be-**deng**-ken-lohs **ine**-naymen?
will I/he/she have to go to hospital?	**muss ich/er/sie ins Krankenhaus?**
	moos ikh/er/zee ins **kran**ken-hows?
I need to go to casualty	**ich muss zur Notaufnahme**
	ikh moos tsoor **noht**-owf-nahme
where is the hospital?	**wo ist das Krankenhaus?**
	voh ist das **kran**ken-hows?
when are visiting hours?	**wann ist die Besuchszeit?**
	van ist dee be**zookhs**-tsite?
which ward?	**welche Station?**
	vel-khe shtah-tsee-**ohn**?
I need a dentist	**ich brauche einen Zahnarzt**
	ikh **brow**-khe **ine**-en **tsahn**artst
he/she has toothache	**er/sie hat Zahnschmerzen**
	er/zee hat **tsahn**-shmer-tsen
can you do a temporary filling?	**können Sie mir eine provisorische Plombe machen?**
	kur'-nen zee meer **ine**-e provi-**zo**rish-e **plom**-be **ma**khen?
I have an abscess	**ich habe einen Abszess**
	ikh **hah**-be **ine**-en apst**sess**

it hurts	**das tut weh**
	das toot vay
can you repair my dentures?	**können Sie mein Gebiss reparieren?**
	kur'-nen zee mine ge**biss** raypa-**ree**ren?
do I have to pay now?	**muss ich das gleich bezahlen?**
	moos ikh das **glykh** be**tsah**-len?
how much will it be?	**wie teuer wird es?**
	vee **toy**-er virt es?
I need a receipt for my insurance	**ich brauche eine Quittung für meine Krankenkasse**
	ikh **brow**-khe **ine**-e **kvi**-toong foor **mine**-e **kran**ken-ka-se

Business

Business

• Germany hosts many top international fairs such as the computer fair CeBIT in Hannover and the Frankfurt Book Fair.
• Book accommodation well in advance.
• There are a number of public holidays in Germany when all companies are closed. These include Whit Monday, Ascension Day and Reunification Day on 3 October.

my name is...	**mein Name ist...** mine **nah**-me ist...
here's my card	**hier ist meine Karte** heer ist **mine**-e **kar**-te
I work for...	**ich arbeite für...** ikh **ar**by-te foor...
I'd like to arrange a meeting	**ich möchte eine Besprechung ausmachen** ikh **mur'kh**-te **ine**-e be-**shpre**-khoong **ows**-makhen
on April 4th at 11 o'clock	**am vierten April um elf Uhr** am **feer**-ten a**pril** oom elf oor
where can I plug in my laptop?	**wo kann ich meinen Laptop anschließen?** voh kan ikh **mine**-en **lap**top **an**-schleessen?
what is your website address?	**was ist Ihre Web-Adresse?** vas ist **ee**r-e **web**-adress-e?
can we meet for lunch?	**können wir uns bei einem Mittagessen treffen?** **kur'**-nen veer oons by **ine**-em **mi**tahk-essen **tref**fen?
I'm staying at Hotel...	**ich wohne im Hotel...** ikh **voh**-ne im ho**tel**...

how do I get to your office?	**wie komme ich zu Ihrem Büro?** vee **kom**me ikh tsoo **ee**-rem boo**roh**?
here is some information about my company	**hier sind einige Informationen über meine Firma** heer zint **ine**-nee-ge infor-matsy**ohn**-en **oo**ber **mine**-e **feer**-ma
I have an appointment with...	**ich habe einen Termin mit...** ikh **hah**-be **ine**-en ter-**meen** mit...
at ... o'clock	**um ... Uhr** oom ... oor
I'm delighted to meet you at last	**schön, dass wir uns endlich persönlich kennenlernen** shur'n, das veer oons **ent**-likh per-**sur'n**-likh **ken**nen-layr-nen
my German isn't very good	**mein Deutsch ist nicht sehr gut** mine doytch ist nikht zehr goot
please speak slowly	**bitte sprechen Sie langsam** **bi**-te **shpre**-khen zee **lang**-zahm
what is the name of the managing director?	**wie ist der Name des Geschäftsführers?** vee ist der **nah**-me des ge**shefts**-foorers?
I'd like some information about the company	**ich möchte einige Informationen über die Firma** ikh **mur'kh**-te **ine**-neege infor-matsy**ohn**-en **oo**ber dee **feer**-ma
do you have a press office?	**haben Sie eine Presseabteilung?** **hah**-ben zee **ine**-e **pres**-se-ap-tye-loong?
I need an interpreter	**ich brauche einen Dolmetscher** ikh **brow**-khe **ine**-en **dol**-met-sher
can you copy this for me?	**können Sie das für mich kopieren?** **kur'**-nen zee das foor mikh ko**pee**-ren?
do you have an appointment?	**haben Sie einen Termin?** **hah**-ben zee **ine**-en ter-**meen**?
...isn't in the office at the moment	**...ist zurzeit nicht im Büro** ...ist tsoor-**tsyte** nikht im boo**roh**

he/she will be back in a few minutes	**er/sie kommt in ein paar Minuten wieder**
	er/zee kommt in ein pahr mi**noo**-ten **vee**der
I'll put you through	**ich verbinde**
	ikh fer-**bin**-de
can I take a message?	**kann ich etwas ausrichten?**
	kan ikh **et**-vas **ows**-rikh-ten?

Phoning

∙∙

- Dialling codes from the UK: Germany oo 49, Switzerland oo 41, Austria oo 43.
- Dialling code to the UK from Europe: oo 44.
- Most phoneboxes take phonecards (**Telefonkarten**) which you can buy in newsagents' and phone shops.
- Visitors from the UK should have no problems using their mobile phones but should check roaming charges beforehand.
- The word for 'phone call' is **Anruf**.

a phonecard, please	**eine Telefonkarte, bitte**
	ine-e taylay-**fon**-kar-te, **bi**-te
I want to make a phone call	**ich möchte telefonieren**
	ikh **mur'kh**-te taylay-fo-**nee**ren
Mr Braun, please	**Herr Braun, bitte**
	hayr brown, **bi**-te
extension ..., please	**Apparat ..., bitte**
	apa-**raht** ..., **bi**-te
can I speak to...?	**kann ich mit ... sprechen?**
	kan ikh mit ... **shpre**-khen?
this is Jim Brown	**hier ist Jim Brown**
	heer ist jim brown
I'll call back later	**ich rufe später wieder an**
	ikh **roo**-fe **shpay**ter **vee**der an
I'll call back tomorrow	**ich rufe morgen wieder an**
	ikh **roo**-fe **mor**gen **vee**der an
an outside line, please	**eine Amtsleitung, bitte**
	ine-e **amts**-lye-toong, **bi**-te

I can't get through	**ich komme nicht durch**
	ikh **kom**me nikht doorkh
do you have a mobile?	**haben Sie ein Handy?**
	hah-ben zee ine **han**dy?
what is your mobile number?	**wie lautet Ihre Handynummer?**
	vee **lau**-tet **ee**-re **han**dy-noomer?
my mobile number is...	**meine Handynummer ist...**
	mine-e **han**dy-noomer ist...
where can I get a SIM card for my mobile?	**wo bekomme ich eine SIM-Karte für mein Handy?**
	voh be-**ko**mme ikh **ine**-e **zim**-kar-te foor mine **han**dy?
hello	**hallo**
	ha**lo**
who is calling?	**wer spricht, bitte?**
	ver shprikht, **bi**-te?
it's engaged	**es ist besetzt**
	es ist be**zetst**
can you text me?	**können Sie mir eine SMS schicken?**
	kur-nen zee meer **ine**-e es-em-**es shi**-ken?
I'll text you	**ich schicke ihnen eine SMS**
	ikh **shi**-ke **ee**nen **ine**-e es-em-**es**

E-mail/fax

• Internet cafés are found in most cities and often have special deals. The most common internet service provider is T-Online.
• German domain names end in **.de** for **Deutschland**.
• www dot is pronounced 'veh veh veh poonkt'.
• The @ symbol is pronounced 'at', as in English.

I want to send an e-mail	**ich möchte eine E-Mail schicken**
	ikh **mur'kh**-te **ine**-e **ee**-mail **shi**-ken
my e-mail address is...	**meine E-Mail Adresse ist...**
	mine-e **ee**-mail a-**dres**-se ist...

what's your e-mail address?	**wie ist Ihre E-Mail-Adresse?**
	vee ist **ee**-re **ee**-mail-a-**dre**-se?
how do you spell it?	**wie schreibt sich das?**
	vee shrypt zikh das?
all one word	**alles in einem Wort**
	a-les in **ine**-em vort
all lower case (small letters)	**alles kleingeschrieben**
	a-les **kline**-ge-**shree**ben
did you get my e-mail?	**haben Sie meine E-Mail bekommen?**
	hah-ben zee **mine**-e **ee**-mail be-**kom**men?
the website is www.anyone.co.uk	**die Website ist www.anyone.co.uk**
	dee website ist veh veh veh poonkt anyone poonkt tseh oh poonkt oo kah
I want to send a fax	**ich möchte ein Fax schicken**
	ikh **mur'kh**-te ine fax **shi**-ken
what's your fax number?	**wie ist Ihre Faxnummer?**
	vee ist **ee**-re **fax**-noomer?
do you have a fax?	**haben Sie ein Fax?**
	hah-ben zee ine fax?

Internet/cybercafé

• •

• Most hotels provide internet access points, and public libraries, as in the UK, usually also have internet access. Libraries may require you to obtain a membership card (take your passport in case you're asked for it) but day membership, at a very cheap rate, is likely to be available as an alternative.

• German computer and internet terminology will pose very few problems as it is largely English-based (eg words like Browser, Chatroom, Homepage, Link, online etc).

I want to check my e-mail	**ich möchte meine E-Mail checken**
	ikh **mur'kh**-te **mine**-e **ee**-mail **check**-en
how much is it...	**was kostet es...**
	vas **kos**-tet es...

Internet/cybercafé

78

for 15 minutes?	**für fünfzehn Minuten?**
	foor **foonf**-tsayn mi**noo**-ten?
for one hour?	**für eine Stunde?**
	foor **ine**-e **shtoon**-de?
to print something out?	**etwas auszudrucken?**
	et-vas **ows**-tsoo-droo-ken?
I'd like to put these photos onto CD	**ich möchte diese Fotos auf CD brennen**
	ikh **mur'kh**-te **dee**ze **fo**tos owf tsy-**day bren**-en
can you print it out?	**können Sie es ausdrucken?**
	kur'-nen zee es **ows**-droo-ken?
where can I get a memory stick?	**wo bekomme ich eine Memorystick?**
	voh be-**kom**me ikh **ine**-en **me**mory-stick?
can you help me please?	**können Sie mir bitte helfen?**
	kur'-nen zee meer **bi**-te **hel**fen?
it doesn't work	**es funktioniert nicht**
	es foonk-tsyoh-**neert** nikht
my computer has crashed	**mein Computer ist abgestürzt**
	mine com**pu**ter ist **ap**-geshtoortst

Practical info

Numbers

0	null	nool
1	eins	ines
2	zwei	tsvy
3	drei	dry
4	vier	feer
5	fünf	foonf
6	sechs	zekhs
7	sieben	**zee**ben
8	acht	akht
9	neun	noyn
10	zehn	tsayn
11	elf	elf
12	zwölf	tsvur'lf
13	dreizehn	**dry**-tsayn
14	vierzehn	**feer**-tsayn
15	fünfzehn	**foonf**-tsayn
16	sechzehn	**zekh**-tsayn
17	siebzehn	**zeep**-tsayn
18	achtzehn	**akh**-tsayn
19	neunzehn	**noyn**-tsayn
20	zwanzig	**tsvan**-tsikh
21	einundzwanzig	**ine**-oont-tsvan-tsikh
22	zweiundzwanzig	**tsvy**-oont-tsvan-tsikh
30	dreißig	**dry**-sikh
40	vierzig	**feer**-tsikh
50	fünfzig	**foonf**-tsikh
60	sechzig	**zekh**-tsikh
70	siebzig	**zeep**-tsikh

80	achtzig	**akh**-tsikh
90	neunzig	**noyn**-tsikh
100	hundert	**hoon**dert
101	hunderteins	**hoon**dert-ines
250	zweihundert	**tsvy**-hoondert
	fünfzig	**foonf**-tsikh
500	fünfhundert	**foonf**-hoondert
1,000	tausend	**tow**zent
1st	erste	**er**-ste
2nd	zweite	**tsvy**-te
3rd	dritte	**drit**-te
4th	vierte	**feer**-te
5th	fünfte	**foonf**-te
6th	sechste	**zehks**-te
7th	siebte	**zeep**-te
8th	achte	**akh**-te
9th	neunte	**noyn**-te
10th	zehnte	**tsayn**-te

Days and months

. . . .

Monday	Montag	**mohn**-tahk
Tuesday	Dienstag	**deens**-tahk
Wednesday	Mittwoch	**mit**-vokh
Thursday	Donnerstag	**don**ners-tahk
Friday	Freitag	**fry**-tahk
Saturday	Samstag	**zams**-tahk
Sunday	Sonntag	**zon**-tahk
January	Januar	**yan**-ooar
February	Februar	**feb**-rooar
March	März	mehrts
April	April	ap-**reel**
May	Mai	mye
June	Juni	**yoo**-nee

July	Juli	**yoo**-lee
August	August	ow-**goost**
September	September	sep-**tem**ber
October	Oktober	ok-**to**ber
November	November	no-**vem**ber
December	Dezember	dayt-**sem**ber

what's the date?	der Wievielte ist heute?
	der **vee**-feel-te ist **hoy**-te?
which day?	welcher Tag?
	vel-kher tahk?
day	Tag
	tahk
week	Woche
	vokh-e
month	Monat
	mo-naht
year	Jahr
	yahr
it's the 5th of March 2008	heute ist der fünfte März zweitausendacht
	hoy-te ist der **foonf**-te merts **tsvy**towzent-akht
on Saturday	am Samstag
	am **zams**-tahk
on Saturdays	samstags
	zams-tahks
every Saturday	jeden Samstag
	yay-den **zams**-tahk
this Saturday	diesen Samstag
	deezen **zams**-tahk
next Saturday	nächsten Samstag
	naykh-sten **zams**-tahk
last Saturday	letzten Samstag
	lets-ten **zams**-tahk
please can you confirm the date?	können Sie bitte das Datum bestätigen?
	kur'-nen zee **bi**-te das **dah**toom be**shtay**-teegen?

Time

• Central European Time is 1 hour ahead of the UK.
• The half hour is expressed by referring forwards to the next full hour not backwards to the last full hour as in English. In Austria and eastern Germany you will also hear **viertel** (quarter) **acht** meaning 'a quarter past 7' and **drei viertel** (three quarters) **acht** meaning 'a quarter to 8'.

what time is it, please?	**wie spät ist es, bitte?** vee shpayt ist es **bi**-te?
am/pm	**morgens/nachmittags/abends** (eve) **mor**gens/**nakh**-mi-tahks/**ah**bents
it's 1 o'clock	**es ist ein Uhr** es ist ine oor
it's 6 o'clock	**es ist sechs Uhr** es ist zekhs oor
it's half past 8	**es ist halb neun** es ist halp noyn
an hour	**eine Stunde** **ine**-e **shtoon**-de
half an hour	**eine halbe Stunde** **ine**-e **hal**-be **shtoon**-de
a quarter of an hour	**eine Viertelstunde** **ine**-e **feer**tel-**shtoon**-de
three quarters of an hour	**eine Dreiviertelstunde** **ine**-e **dry**-feertel-**shtoon**-de
until 8 o'clock	**bis acht Uhr** bis akht oor
it is 10 past 9	**es ist zehn nach neun** es ist tsehn nakh noyn
at 10am	**um 10 Uhr morgens** oom tsayn oor **mor**gens
at 4pm	**um 16 Uhr** oom **zekh**-tsayn oor
soon/later	**bald/später** balt/shpay-ter

Eating out

Eating out

••

As far as cuisine is concerned, Germany can be grouped into three main regions – northern, western and southern.

The northern region is the only one with a coastline so fish, especially herring, but also fish such as sole and plaice, appears frequently on the menu. Try **Krabbensalat**, shrimp salad, and don't miss **Matjeshering** (salted herring) especially in June when the new season starts and the herring is at its freshest. However, meat is still the most important item on the menu here, as it is in the rest of the country. There is also strong influence from Polish and Scandinavian cuisines.

The western region comprises both sides of the river Rhine and its famous valley and has strong French influences. Some local specialities include the use of frogs' legs (**Froschschenkel**) and snails (**Schnecken**). **Schwarzwälder Schinken** (Black Forest ham) is not to be missed. This region is more food conscious and is said to have the best German restaurants.

The southern region is dominated by Bavaria. Here veal is popular, the main speciality is **Kalbshaxe** (knuckles of veal). Other specialities are **Eisbein**, knuckle of pork, and **Leberkäse,** a sausage made from pork, beef and seasonings. Pasta is also popular especially in Swabia where **Spätzle** (noodles) are popular. **Sauerkraut** is a favourite, served with pork. This region is rich in dairy products. Try **Kaiserschmarren** (pancakes with a rich filling) and **Strudel**, normally filled with apples.

In Germany the main meal of the day is usually **Mittagessen**, lunch. It starts with soup, followed by the main dish (meat with vegetables or salad and potato or rice, etc) and an optional dessert or fruit. Dinner (**Abendessen**) consists of platters of cold meats and cheeses. On occasions Germans also have a hot meal, but not a heavy one. Breakfast (**Frühstück**) generally consists of a variety of cold meats and cheeses, with different kinds of bread and jam and fresh coffee.

Ordering drinks

• •

• There are many cafés and confectioners' shops (**Konditoreien**) where coffee and cakes are served. Some bakeries also have a small café, usually standing. These normally open very early and are good places for breakfast.
• Tea is also available, especially in northern Germany, particularly Frisia where it is more popular.

a black coffee	**einen schwarzen Kaffee**
	ine-en **shvar**-tsen ka**fay**
a white coffee	**einen Kaffee mit Sahne**
	ine-en ka**fay** mit **zah**-ne
a tea	**einen Tee**
	ine-en tay
with milk	**mit Frischmilch**
	mit **frish**-milkh
with lemon	**mit Zitrone**
	mit tsi**troh**-ne
a lager	**ein helles Bier**
	ine **he**-les beer
a bitter	**ein Altbier**
	ine **alt**-beer
a half pint	**ein Kleines**
	ine **kli**ne-es
a pint	**ein Großes**
	ine **groh**-ses

a bottle of mineral water	**eine Flasche Mineralwasser**
	ine-e **fla**-she mi-ne**rahl**-vasser
sparkling	**mit Kohlensäure**
	mit **kohl**en-zoy-re
still	**still**
	shtill
the wine list, please	**die Weinkarte, bitte**
	dee **vine**kar-te, **bi**-te
a bottle of house wine	**eine Flasche Hauswein**
	ine-e **fla**-she **hows**vine
a glass of white wine/red wine	**ein Glas Weißwein/Rotwein**
	ine glahs **vice**vine/**roht**vine
a bottle of red wine	**eine Flasche Rotwein**
	ine-e **fla**-she **roht**vine
a bottle of white wine	**eine Flasche Weißwein**
	ine-e **fla**-she **vice**vine
would you like a drink?	**möchten Sie etwas trinken?**
	mur'kh-ten zee **et**vas **trin**ken?
what will you have?	**was möchten Sie?**
	vas **mur'kh**-ten zee?

Ordering food

• Many restaurants in Germany close one day a week (**Ruhetag**, or 'rest day'), often Mondays.
• If all you want is a quick snack, you can get things like sausages and hamburgers at an **Imbiss**.
• Eating places must display prices outside.
• Restaurants usually offer set-price meals.

I'd like to book a table	**ich möchte einen Tisch reservieren**
	ikh **mur'kh**-te **ine**-en tish ray-zer-**vee**ren
for ... people	**für ... Personen**
	foor ... per-**zoh**nen
for tonight	**für heute Abend**
	foor **hoy**-te **ah**bent

at 8pm	**um zwanzig Uhr**
	oom **tsvan**-tsikh oor
the menu, please	**die Speisekarte, bitte**
	dee **shpy**-ze-kar-te, **bi**-te
is there a dish of the day?	**gibt es ein Tagesgericht?**
	gipt es ine **tah**ges-gerikht?
have you a set-price menu?	**haben Sie eine Tageskarte?**
	hah-ben zee **ine**-e **tah**ges-kar-te?
I'll have this	**ich nehme das**
	ikh **nay**-me das
what do you recommend?	**was können Sie empfehlen?**
	vas **kur'**-nen zee emp-**fay**len?
I don't eat meat	**ich esse kein Fleisch**
	ikh **es**-se kine flysh
do you have any vegetarian dishes?	**haben Sie vegetarische Gerichte?**
	hah-ben zee vaygay-**ta**rish-e ge-**rikh**-te?
excuse me, please!	**Entschuldigung, bitte!**
	ent**shool**-digoong, **bi**-te!
more bread	**noch Brot**
	nokh broht
more water	**noch Wasser**
	nokh **vas**ser
the bill, please	**zahlen, bitte**
	tsah-len, **bi**-te
enjoy your meal!	**guten Appetit!**
	goo-ten apay-**teet**!
cheers!	**prost!**
	prohst!

Special requirements

• •

• Although meat is an important part of the traditional German diet, more and more restaurants are now offering vegetarian alternatives.

• Hygiene and quality control standards are very high and many restaurants try to use organic produce wherever possible.

are there any vegetarian restaurants here?	**gibt es hier vegetarische Restaurants?**
	gipt es heer vaygay-**ta**rish-e restoh-**rongs**?
I'm vegetarian	**ich bin Vegetarier(in)**
	ikh bin vaygay-**ta**ree-er(in)
I don't eat meat/ pork	**ich esse kein Fleisch/Schweinefleisch**
	ikh **es**-se kine flysh/**shvy**-ne-flysh
I don't eat fish/ shellfish	**ich esse keinen Fisch/keine Meeresfrüchte**
	ikh **es**-se **kine**-en fish/**kine**-e **meh**res-frur'kh-te
I'm allergic to shellfish	**ich bin allergisch gegen Meeresfrüchte**
	ikh bin a-**ler**-gish **gay**-gen **meh**res-frur'kh-te
I am allergic to peanuts	**ich bin allergisch gegen Erdnüsse**
	ikh bin a-**ler**-gish **gay**-gen **ert**-noos-se
I can't eat raw eggs	**ich kann kein rohes Ei essen**
	ikh kan kine **roh**-es eye **es**-sen
I can't eat liver	**ich kann keine Leber essen**
	ikh kan **kine**-e **lay**-ber **es**-sen
I am on a diet	**ich bin auf Diät**
	ikh bin owf dee-**ayt**
I don't drink alcohol	**ich trinke keinen Alkohol**
	ikh **trin**-ke **kine**-en **al**ko-hol
what is in this?	**was ist darin enthalten?**
	vas ist da-**rin** ent-**hal**ten?
is it raw?	**ist das roh?**
	ist das roh?

Eating photoguide

Eating places

IMBISS Germans are fond of snacks and there are numerous roadside stalls. There should be no worries over trying the food, as there are strict hygiene laws governing the operation of stalls.

Typical snack food is **Bratwurst** (fried sausage), **Bockwurst** (boiled sausage) and **Frikadelle** (thick hamburger, but without the roll).

A huge variety of sausages is served at all times of the day. All are 100% meat.

Stehcafé
An den Römersteinen

A **Stehcafé** is a good place for coffee and cake. Often attached to a baker's and open from 7am.

BIERGARTEN
auf der Mole

A **Biergarten** is an open-air pub serving a selection of hearty meals. They are particularly popular in Bavaria where you can often bring your own picnic and spend the evening in a beer garden with the whole family.

In smaller towns restaurants tend to shut for one day – generally Mondays (**Montag Ruhetag** = closed Monday). As a rule, eating places (including restaurants) have a menu with prices outside, so you will see the cost before going in. Restaurants frequently offer set-price meals.

There is a wide variety of Chinese and Italian restaurants.

Some hotels have special offers. Here it is a Summer buffet. It includes aperitif and parking (**inkl. Aperitif u. Parken**). The price is for two people.

You can find a great variety of cakes at a **Café Konditorei**, served with cream (**mit Sahne**) and very good coffee.

Turkish food (such as doner kebabs) tends to be sold in snackbars rather than restaurants.

Ratskeller One of the unusual places where one can eat in Germany (and eat well) is the town hall (**Rathaus**), which often has a restaurant open to the public (usually in the basement), called the **Ratskeller** (council's cellar).

Fleischer

Butcher's

Metzgerei is a southern German term for butcher's.

In butcher's shops there is often an area for a quick meal (generally eaten standing) such as this dish: **Wiener Würstchen mit Kartoffelsalat** (boiled frankfurter with potato salad).

durchgehend warme Küche

Hot meals served all day

Bistro

A good place for breakfast, snacks, coffee and cakes.

Germany has a huge variety of bread and rolls. It is generally served at breakfast or with a light evening meal. Butter is usually served with bread. German butter is unsalted.

Reading the menu

Don't be overwhelmed by German words – they may be long, but they are made up of smaller bits of words. Try to work out what the item is by identifying what makes up the long word. So **Tomatencremesuppe** is cream of tomato soup. You will also come across English terms such as **Snacks**. There are also usually children's menus. Remember, German portions are quite large!

Speisekarte	Menu
Vorspeisen	**Starters**
Suppen • Salate • Knoblauchbrot	Soups • Salads • Garlic Bread
Fleisch, Wild & Geflügel, Fisch	**Meat, Game & Poultry, Fish**
Meeresfrüchte	Seafood
Gemüse	**Vegetables**
Käse	**Cheeses**
Dessert	**Dessert**
Getränke	**Drinks**

Unsere
Augebote :

Sandwich
Bel. Brötchen
Suppen
Süßwaren

Snack Board
Our offers
Sandwich
Roll with meat or cheese. **Bel.** is short for **belegtes** 'filled'
Soups
Sweets

BIS 15 Uhr
MITTAGS MENUE

Until 3pm
Mittags menue = lunch menu.
It's normally spelt **Mittagsmenü**.

heiß
Hot

kalt
Cold

Look out for restaurant offers in local newspapers.

Post theatre menu

from 10pm
ab 22.00 Uhr

vegetarian dishes on request
auf Wunsch auch vegetarisch

home delivery and party service
Außer Haus & Partyservice

Tagesgericht
für 12 € 50
Fisch
oder Fleisch
oder Geflügel

Dish of the day
12 € 50
fish
or meat
or poultry

Mittagsmenü
Vorspeise +
Hauptgericht
+ Kaffee

Lunchtime menu
starter + main
course
+ coffee

KLEINE SPEISEKARTE   Snack Menu

Drinks

Beer There are over 1,000 breweries in Germany with more than half of them in Bavaria. Many cities have at least one brewpub. Wheat beers are a speciality of Bavaria along with smoked beer. It is best to sample the local beer in the place it has been brewed. In Cologne you should try the pale refreshing **Kölsch** and in Düsseldorf sample the darkish malty **Altbier**.

Weißbier

The Bavarians also brew dark versions of their wheat beers. These may contain some malted wheat that has been darkened by roasting. **Dunkel** means dark.

Pilsner A typical lager available all over Germany.

Hefe-Weißbier
Beer from Bavaria with a fruity, slightly smoked aroma.

Kölsch
A pale-coloured, light-textured, fruity-flavoured beer brewed in Cologne. Best drunk in a brewpub.

Wine Wines are usually categorised according to three criteria: the growing area, the village/vineyard where they are produced, and the type of grape. Major grape varieties include **Riesling**, **Edelzwicker**, **Gewürztraminer** and **Müller-Thurgau**. The names of the villages and vineyards producing wines are innumerable. The name of the wine is often the name of the village (e.g. **Nierstein**) plus the name of the particular vineyard (e.g. **Gutes Domtal**) which combined become **Niersteiner Gutes Domtal**.

Qualitätswein mit Prädikat This is the mark of the highest quality wine. If you want a good German wine, choose this rather than **Tafelwein**, **Landwein** or **QbA** (wine from a specified region).

A service charge is generally included in the bill, so tipping is discretionary.

Getränke nicht inklusive

Drinks not included

Weinkarte	Wine List
Weißwein	**trocken**
vice-vine	**tro**-ken
white wine	dry
Roséwein	**halbtrocken**
roh**zay**-vine	**halp**-tro-ken
rosé wine	medium dry
Rotwein	**lieblich**
rohtvine	**leep**-likh
red wine	sweet
Sekt	**Tafelwein**
zekt	**tah**fel-vine
sparkling wine	table wine

Menu reader

∙∙

Aal eel

Aalsuppe eel soup

Allgäuer Emmentaler whole-milk hard cheese from the Allgäu

Allgäuer Käsespätzle cheese noodles from the Allgäu

Alpzirler cow's milk cheese from Austria

Alsterwasser lager shandy

Altbier top-fermented beer from the lower Rhine

Ananas pineapple

Apfel apple

Apfelkorn apple brandy

Apfelkuchen apple cake

Apfelmus apple puree

Apfelsaft apple juice

Apfelsalami salami with apple

Apfelstrudel flaky pastry filled with apples and spices

Apfelwein cider (apple wine)

Aprikose apricot

Arme Ritter French toast

Art style or fashion of e.g. '**nach Art des Hauses**' = à la maison

Artischocken artichokes

Aubergine aubergine

Auflauf baked dish, can be sweet or savoury

Aufschnitt sliced cold meats

Austern oysters

Bäckerofen 'baker's oven', pork and lamb bake from Saarland

Backpflaumen prunes

Banane banana

Bandnudeln ribbon pasta

Barack apricot brandy

Barsch perch

Bauernfrühstück scrambled eggs, bacon, cooked diced potatoes, onions, tomatoes

Baunzerl little bread roll with distinctive cut on top (Austria)

Bayrisch Kraut shredded cabbage cooked with sliced apples, wine and sugar

Beilage side dish

Bereich Bernkastel area along the Moselle producing crisp white wines

Bergkäse cheese from the Alps

Berliner doughnut filled with jam

Berliner Weiße fizzy beer with fruit syrup added

Berner Erbsensuppe soup made of dried peas with pig's trotters

Bienenstich type of cake, baked on a tray with a coating of almonds and sugar and a cream filling

Bierschinken ham sausage

Bierteig pastry made with beer

Bierwurst ham sausage

Birchermüsli muesli with yoghurt (Switzerland)

Birne pear

Birne Helene dessert with vanilla ice cream, pear and chocolate sauce

Birnen, Bohnen und Speck (Northern Germany) pears, green beans and bacon

Birnenmost pear wine

Birnensekt sparkling pear wine

Blätterteig puff pastry

Blätterteigpastete vol-au-vent

Blattsalat green salad

blau rare (meat); poached (fish)

Blauschimmelkäse blue cheese

Blumenkohl cauliflower

Blunz'n black pudding (South Germany and Austria)

Blutwurst black pudding

Bockbier strong beer (light or dark), drunk especially in Bavaria

Bockwurst boiled sausage. A popular snack served with a bread roll

Böhmische Knödel sliced dumplings

Bohnen beans

Bohnensalat bean salad

Bohnensuppe thick bean and bacon soup

Bosniakerl wholemeal roll with caraway seeds

Brathähnchen roast chicken

Brathering fried herring (eaten cold)

Bratkartoffeln fried potatoes

Bratwurst fried sausage. A popular snack served with a bread roll

Brauner strong black coffee with a little milk

Bremer Kükenragout Bremen chicken fricassée

Brezel (or in Bavaria: **Brezn**) pretzel

Broiler spit-roasted chicken (East Ger.)

Brombeeren blackberries

Bröselknödel soup with little dumplings prepared with bone

marrow and breadcrumbs

Brot bread

Brötchen bread roll

Brühe clear soup

Brühwurst thick frankfurter

B'soffene pudding soaked in mulled wine

Buletten thick hamburgers (but without the bread)

Buletten mit Kartoffelsalat thick hamburgers with potato salad

Bündnerfleisch raw beef smoked and dried, served thinly sliced

Burgenländische Krautsuppe thick cabbage and vegetable soup

Butter butter

Butterbrot open sandwich

Butterkäse high-fat cheese

Cervelat fine beef and pork salami

Chindbettering ring of bread

Champagner champagne

Champignons button mushrooms

Cordon bleu veal cutlet filled with boiled ham and cheese, covered in breadcrumbs

Cremeschnitten cream slices

Currywurst sausage served with a spicy sauce. A popular snack originally from Berlin

Damenkäse mild buttery cheese

Dampfnudeln hot yeast dumplings with vanilla sauce

Danziger Goldwasser schnapps containing tiny bits of gold leaf

Datteln dates

Deutsches Beefsteak thick hamburger (but without the bread)

dicke Bohnen broad beans

Doppelbockbier like **Bockbier**, but still stronger

Dorsch cod

Dresdner Suppentopf Dresden vegetable soup with dumplings (East Ger.)

Dunkles dark beer

Ei egg

Eier im Glas soft boiled eggs served in a glass

Eierkuchen pancakes

Eierschwammerln chanterelles

Eierspeispfandl special Viennese omelette

eingelegt pickled

Einmachsuppe chicken or veal broth with cream and egg

Einspänner coffee with whipped cream served in a glass (Austria)

Eintopf stew

Eis ice cream

Eisbecher knickerbocker glory

Eisbein boiled pork knuckle often served with sauerkraut

Eiskaffee iced coffee served with vanilla ice cream

Eiswein a rich, naturally sweet, white wine made from grapes which are harvested only after a period of frost

Emmentaler Swiss Emmental, whole-milk hard cheese

Ennstaler blue cheese from mixed milk

Ente duck

Erbach area producing scented white wines mainly from Riesling grape

Erbsen peas

Erbsenpüree green pea purée

Erbsensuppe pea soup

Erdäpfel potatoes (Austria)

Erdäpfelgulasch spicy sausage and potato stew

Erdäpfelknödel potato and semolina dumplings

Erdäpfelkren relish with potato and horseradish (Austria)

Erdäpfelnudeln fried, boiled potato balls tossed in fried breadcrumbs

Erdbeeren strawberries

Erdnüsse peanuts

erster Gang first course

Essig vinegar

Export Bier premium beer

Falscher Hase baked mince meatloaf

Fasan pheasant

Feigen figs

Fenchel fennel

fettarm low in fat

Fisch fish

Fischfilet fish fillet

Fischgerichte fish and seafood

Fischklöße fish dumplings

Fischsuppe fish soup

flambiert flambé

Fledermaus boiled beef in horse-radish cream browned in the oven

Fleisch meat

Fleischgerichte meat dishes

Fleischklößchen meatballs

Fleischlaberln highly seasoned meat cake (Austria)

Fleischpflanzerl thick hamburger (without the bread)

Fleischsalat sausage salad with onions

Fleischsuppe meat soup served with dumplings

Flunder flounder

Fondue melted cheese with wine and bread for dipping

Forelle trout

Forelle blau steamed trout with potatoes and vegetables

Forelle Müllerin trout fried in batter with almonds

Forelle Steiermark trout fillet with bacon in white sauce

Frikadelle thick hamburger (without the bread)

frisch fresh

Frittatensuppe beef broth with strips of pancake (Austria)

frittiert fried

Froschschenkel frogs' legs

Frucht fresh fruit

Früchtetee fruit tea

Fruchtsaft fruit juice

Fünfkernbrot wholemeal bread made with five different cereals

Gang course

Gans goose

Gänseleber foie gras

Gänseleberpastete goose liver pâté

Gebäck pastries

gebacken baked

gebackene Leber liver fried in breadcrumbs

gebraten roasted/fried

gedämpft steamed

Geflügel poultry

gefüllt stuffed/filled

gefüllte Kalbsbrust stuffed breast of veal

gefüllte Paprika peppers filled with mince

gegrillt grilled

gegrillter Lachs grilled salmon

Gehacktes mince

gekocht boiled

gekochtes Rindfleisch mit grüner Soße boiled beef with green sauce

gemischter Salat mixed salad

Gemüse vegetables

Gemüse und Klöße vegetables and dumplings

Gemüselasagne vegetable lasagne

Gemüseplatte mixed vegetables

Gemüsesuppe vegetable soup

geräuchert smoked

Gericht dish

geschmort braised

Geschnetzeltes thinly sliced meat in sauce served with potatoes or rice

Geselchtes smoked meats (Austria)

Gespritzter spritzer, white wine and soda water

Gewürzgurken gherkins

Gitziprägel baked rabbit in batter (a Swiss dish)

Glühwein mulled wine

Goldbarsch redfish

Graf Görz Austrian soft cheese

Grammeln croissant stuffed with bacon

Grießklößchensuppe soup with semolina dumplings

Grießtaler gnocchi
Grog hot rum
grüne Bohnen green beans
grüne Veltlinersuppe green wine soup
grüner Salat green salad
Grünkohl kale
Gruyère gruyère cheese
Güggeli roast chicken with onions and mushrooms in white wine sauce (Switzerland)
Gulasch stewed diced beef and pork with paprika served with dumplings and red cabbage
Gulaschsuppe spicy meat soup with paprika
Gulyas beef stew with paprika
Gumpoldskirchner spicy white wine from Austria
Gurke cucumber
Gurkensalat cucumber salad
gutbürgerliche Küche traditional German cooking
Gyros kebab
Hackbraten mincemeat roast
Hackepeter auf Schrippen mit Zwiebeln spiced minced pork on rolls, with onions
Hackfleisch mince
Hähnchen chicken
Hähnchenbrust chicken breast
halbtrocken medium-dry
Hamburger Rundstück Hamburg meat roll
Hammel mutton
Hartkäse hard cheese
Hase hare

Hasenbraten roast hare
Hasenpfeffer peppered rabbit stew
Hauptgericht main course
Hausbrauerei house brewery
hausgemacht home-made
Hausmannskost good traditional home cooking
Hawaiitoast toast with cooked ham, pineapple slice and melted cheese
Hecht pike
Hefeweizen wheat beer
Heidschnuckenragout lamb stew
heiß hot
Helles light beer
Hering herring
Heringsschmaus herring in creamy sauce
Herz heart
Heuriger new wine
Himbeeren raspberries
Himbeergeist raspberry brandy
Hirn brain
Hirsch venison
Honig honey
Hühnchen chicken
Hühnerfrikasse chicken fricassée
Hühnerschenkel chicken drumsticks
Hühnerleber chicken liver
Hummer lobster
Ingwer ginger
Jägerschnitzel cutlet served with mushrooms and wine sauce
Joghurt yoghurt
Johannisbeeren currants (can be red, black or white)
Jura Omelette bacon, potato and onion omelette

Kabeljau cod
Kaffee coffee
Kaffee komplett coffee with milk and sugar
Kaffee mit Milch coffee with milk
koffeinfreier Kaffee decaf
Kaisermelange black coffee with an egg yolk
Kaiserschmarren strips of pancake served with raisins, sugar and cinnamon
Kakao cocoa
Kalb veal
Kalbsbraten roast veal
Kalbshaxe knuckle of veal
Kalbskoteletts veal cutlets
Kalbsleber calf's liver
Kalbsschnitzel veal escalope
kalt cold
kalte Platte cold meat platter
Kaninchen rabbit
Kapuziner Austrian equivalent to a cappuccino which is black coffee with a drop of milk
Karotten carrots
Karpfen carp
Karpfen blau poached carp
Karpfen in Bier carp poached in beer with herbs
Kartoffeln potatoes
Kartoffelklöße potato dumplings
Kartoffelpuffer potato pancakes
Kartoffelpüree mashed potatoes
Kartoffelsalat potato salad
Kartoffelsuppe potato soup
Käse cheese
Käsebrötchen roll with small bacon pieces in the dough and melted cheese on top
Käsefondue dish made from melted cheese and flavoured with wine and kirsch into which you dip bread
Käsekuchen cheesecake
Käsenudeln noodles served with cheese
Käseplatte cheese platter with various cheeses
Käsesuppe cheese soup
Kasseler smoked pork
Kasseler Rippe mit Sauerkraut smoked pork rib with sauerkraut
Kastanienroulade roulade with chestnut filling
Katenspeck streaky bacon
Kaviar caviar
Kekse biscuits
Kirschen cherries
Kirschwasser cherry schnapps
Kirtagssuppe soup with caraway seed thickened with potato (Austria)
Klops rissole
Klöße dumplings
Knackwurst hot spicy sausage. A popular snack served with bread
Knoblauch garlic
Knödel dumpling
Knödelbeignets fruit dumplings
Knöderl dumplings (Austria)
Kohl cabbage
Kohlrouladen stuffed cabbage
Kohlsprossen Brussels sprouts
Kölsch top-fermented beer from Cologne
Kompott stewed fruit
Konfitüre jam

Königsberger Klopse meatballs served in thick white sauce with capers
Kopfsalat lettuce salad
Korn rye spirit
Kotelett pork chop/cutlet dipped in breadcrumbs and deep fried
Krabben prawns
Krabbencocktail prawn cocktail
Kraftbrot wheatgerm bread
Kraftfleisch corned beef
Kraftsuppe consommé
Krapfen doughnut
Kräuter herbs
Kräutertee herbal tea
Krautwickerl stuffed cabbage
Krebs crawfish, crab
Kren horseradish
Kristallweizen a kind of sparkling beer
Kroketten croquettes
Kuchen cake
Kürbis pumpkin
Labskaus cured pork, herring and potato stew
Lachs salmon
Lachsbrot smoked salmon with bread
Lamm lamb
Lammkeule leg of lamb
Languste spiny lobster
Lasagne lasagne
Lauch leeks
Leber liver
Leberkäse pork liver meatloaf
Leberknödelsuppe light soup with chicken liver dumplings
Leberpastete liver paté
Leberwurst liver sausage

Lebkuchen gingerbread
Leinsamenbrot wholemeal bread with linseed
Leipziger Allerlei vegetable dish made from peas, carrots, cauliflower and cabbage (East German)
Lendenbraten roast loin
lieblich sweet (wine)
Likör liqueur
Limburger strong cheese flavoured with herbs
Limonade lemonade
Linsen lentils
Linsenspecksalat lentil salad with bacon
Linsensuppe lentil and sausage soup
Linzer Torte latticed tart with jam topping
Liptauer Quark cream cheese with paprika and herbs
Lunge lungs
Mais sweetcorn
Maiskolben corn on the cob
Makrele mackerel
Malzbier dark malt beer
Mandarine tangerine
Mandeln almonds
Marillenknödel apricot dumplings (Austria)
Marmelade jam
Maronitorte chestnut tart
Märzenbier stronger beer brewed for special occasions
Mastochsenhaxe knuckle of beef (with sauce) from Sachsen-Anhalt (East German)
Maß a litre of beer

Matjes herring
Maultaschen ravioli-like pasta filled with pork, veal and spinach mixture
Meeresfrüchte seafood
Meerrettich horseradish
Mehrkornbrötchen rolls made with several kinds of wholemeal flour
Melange milky coffee
Melone melon
Menü combination of items from the menu at a special price, usually consisting of three courses
Mettenden sausage with a filling similar to mince
Milch milk
Milchrahmstrudel strudel filled with egg custard and soft cheese
Milchreis rice pudding
Milchshake milk shake
Mineralwasser mineral water **mit/ohne Kohlensäure** carbonated/non-carbonated
Mirabellen small yellow plums
Mischbrot grey bread made with rye and wheat flour
Mittagstisch lunch menu
Mohn poppy seed
Mohnnudeln noodles with poppy seeds, cinnamon, sugar and butter
Mohntorte gâteau with poppy seeds
Möhren carrots
Möhrensalat carrot salad
Mohr im Hemd chocolate pudding
Most fruit juice; (in the South) fruit wine
Münchener a kind of dark lager from Munich

Muscheln mussels
Nachspeisen desserts
Nachtisch dessert
Nieren kidneys
Nierstein village on the Rhine producing medium to sweet white Rheinwein
Nockerln small dumplings
Nudeln noodles
Nudelsuppe noodle soup
Nüsse nuts
Nusskuchen nut cake
Nusstorte nut gâteau
Obst fruit
Obstkuchen fruit cake
Obstsalat fruit salad
Ochsenschwanz oxtail
Ochsenschwanzsuppe oxtail soup
Öl oil
Oppenheim village on the Rhine producing fine white wines
Orange orange
Orangensaft orange juce
Palatschinken pancakes filled with curd mixture or jam or ice cream
Pampelmuse grapefruit
paniert coated with breadcrumbs
Paprika peppers
Pellkartoffeln small jacket potatoes served with their skins, often accompanied by Quark
Peperoni hot chilli pepper
Petersilie parsley
Pfannkuchen pancakes
Pfeffer pepper
Pfefferkäse mit Schinken ham and pepper cheese log

Pfifferlinge chanterelles
Pfirsich peach
Pflaumen plums
Pflaumenkuchen plum tart
Pils, Pilsner a strong, slightly bitter lager
Pilze mushrooms
Pilzsuppe mushroom soup
Pommes frites chips
Portion portion, serving
Powidltascherl ravioli-like pasta filled with plum jam (Austria)
Preiselbeeren cranberries
Pumpernickel very dark bread made with wholemeal coarse rye flour
Punschpudding pudding containing alcohol
Pute turkey
Putenschnitzel turkey breast in breadcrumbs
Quark curd cheese
Raclette melted cheese and potatoes
Radieschen radish(es)
Radler beer with lemonade (Bavaria)
Ragout stew
Rahm sour cream
Rahmschnitzel cutlet with a creamy sauce
Rahmsuppe creamy soup
Räucherkäse mit Schinken smoked cheese with bacon pieces
Räucherkäse mit Walnüssen smoked cheese with pieces of walnut
Räucherlachs smoked salmon
Räucherspeck smoked bacon
Reh venison
Rehrücken roast saddle of venison

Reibekuchen potato cakes
Reis rice
Remoulade, Remouladensoße tartar sauce
Rhabarber rhubarb
Riesling Riesling wine
Rieslingsuppe wine soup made with Riesling
Rind(fleisch) beef
Rinderbraten roast beef
Rinderrouladen rolled beef (beef olives)
Rippenbraten roast spare ribs
Risi lisi, Risipisi rice with peas
roh raw
Rollmops marinated herring fillet rolled up with small pieces of onion, gherkins and white peppercorns
Rosenkohl Brussels sprouts
Roséwein rosé wine
Rosinen raisins
Rösti fried diced potatoes, onions and bacon
Rotbarsch rosefish
rote Bete beetroot
rote Grütze raspberry, red currant and wine jelly served with fresh cream
Rote Rübe beetroot
Rotkohl red cabbage
Rotwein red wine
Roulade beef olive
Rübe turnip
Rührei scrambled eggs
Sachertorte rich chocolate gâteau
Saft juice
Sahne cream
Saison season e.g. **je nach Saison**

depending on the season
Salat salad
 gemischter Salat mixed salad
Salatbeilage side salad
Salz salt
Salzkartoffeln boiled potatoes
Sardellen anchovies
Sardinen sardines
Sauerbraten braised pickled beef
served with dumplings and vegetables
Sauerkraut shredded pickled white
cabbage
Scampi scampi
Schafskäse ewe's milk cheese
scharf spicy
Schaschlik shish kebab
Schellfisch haddock
Schnaps strong spirit
Schinken ham
Schinkenkipferl ham-filled
croissant
Schinkenwurst ham sausage
Schlachtplatte mixture of cold
sausages and meat
Schlagsahne whipped cream
Schmelzkäse cheese spread
Schmorgurken hotpot with
cucumber and meat
Schnecke snail
Schnittlauch chives
Schnittlauchbrot chives on bread
Schnitzel escalope served with
potatoes and vegetables
Schokolade chocolate
Schokoladentorte chocolate
gateaux
Scholle plaice

Schorle wine and sparkling water
Schwäbischer Apfelkuchen
apple cake from Swabia
Schwammerlgulasch mushroom
stew
Schwarzbrot rye bread
Schwarze Johannisbeeren
blackcurrants
schwarzer Tee black tea
Schwarzwälder Kirschtorte
Black Forest cherry gâteau
Schwarzwälder Schinken Black
Forest ham
Schwarzwälder Torte fruit
compote flan with cream
Schwein pork
Schweinebraten roast pork
Schweinefleisch pork
Schweinehaxe knuckle of pork
Schweinekotelett pork chop
Schweinsrostbraten roast pork
Schwertfisch swordfish
Seezunge sole
Sekt sparkling wine like champagne
Selters(wasser) sparkling mineral
water
Semmeln bread rolls
Semmelknödel whole roll dumpling
Senf mustard
Seniorenteller small portion of a
dish for senior citizens
Sesam sesame
Slibowitz plum schnapps
Sonnenblumenbrot wholemeal
bread with sunflower seeds
Soße sauce
Spanferkel suckling pig

Spargel asparagus
Spargelcremesuppe cream of asparagus soup
Spargelsalat asparagus salad
Spätzle home-made noodles
Speck bacon (fat)
Speisekarte (printed) menu
Spezialität des Hauses speciality of the house/chef's special
Spiegelei fried egg, sunny side up
Spieß kebab style
Spinat spinach
Sprudel sparkling mineral water
Stachelbeeren gooseberries
Stachelbeertorte gooseberry tart
Stangl croissant covered with cheese
Starkbier strong beer
Steinbutt turbot
Steinpilze wild mushroom found in the woods
Steirischer Selchkäse ewe's milk cheese (Austria)
Steirisches Lammkarree mit Basilikum lamb baked with basil (Austria)
Sterz Austrian polenta
Stollen spiced loaf with candied peel traditionally eaten at Christmas
Strudel strudel
Sulz/Sülze meat in aspic
Suppe soup
süß sweet
süßsauer sweet-and-sour
Tafelspitz boiled beef of various cuts
Tafelspitzsulz beef in aspic
Tagesgericht dish of the day
Tagessuppe soup of the day

Tee tea
Tee mit Milch tea with milk
Tee mit Zitrone tea with lemon
ein Kännchen Tee a (little) pot of tea
eine Tasse Tee a cup of tea
Thunfisch tuna fish
Thüringer Rostbratwurst sausages from Thuringia, grilled or fried
Tilsiter savoury cheese with sharpish taste
Tintenfisch squid
Tomaten tomatoes
Tomatensaft tomato juice
Tomatensoße tomato sauce
Topf stew
Topfen curd cheese (Austria)
Topfenknödel curd cheese dumplings
Topfennudeln pasta with cheese
Topfenstrudel flaky pastry strudel with curd-cheese filling
Torte gateau
Trauben grapes
Traubensaft grape juice
trocken dry (wine)
Truthahn turkey
Türkischer Turkish coffee
überbacken baked in the oven with cheese on top
vegetarische Gerichte vegetarian dishes
Vollkorn wholemeal
Vollkornbrot wholemeal bread
Vorspeisen starters
Wacholder juniper

Waldpilze wild mushrooms
Walnüsse walnuts
warm warm
warmer Krautsalat salad with warm cabbage and crunchy bacon
Wasser water
Weichkäse cream cheese
Wein wine
Weinbrand brandy
Weinkarte wine list
Weißbrot white bread
Weiße golden wheat beer
Weißkohl white cabbage
Weißwein white wine
Weißwurst white sausage (veal and pork with herbs)
Weizenbier wheat beer
Wels catfish
Westfälischer Schinken Westphalian ham
Wiener frankfurters
Wiener Backhendl roast chicken covered in breadcrumbs
Wiener Fischfilets fish fillets baked in sour cream sauce
Wiener Hofburgtorte chocolate gâteau
Wiener Kartoffelsuppe potato soup with mushrooms
Wiener Sachertorte Viennese chocolate cake
Wiener Schnitzel veal escalope fried in breadcrumbs
Wiener Würstchen frankfurter
Wild game
Wildbraten roast venison
Wildgulasch game stew

Wildschwein wild boar
Wirsingkohl Savoy cabbage
Wurst sausage
Würstchen frankfurter
Würzfleisch strips of meat roasted in a spicy sauce
Zander pike-perch
Ziegenkäse goat's milk cheese
Ziegett mixed milk cheese
Zigeunerschnitzel cutlet in paprika sauce
Zillertaler cow's cheese from the Zillertal
Zimt cinnamon
Zitrone lemon
Zitronentee lemon tea
Zopf braided bread loaf
Zucchini courgette
Zucker sugar
Zuger Köteli baked dace with herbs and wine
Zunge tongue
Zürcher Geschnetzeltes thinly sliced meat (veal or turkey), served with a wine sauce and mushrooms (and side dish such as Rösti) (Switzerland)
Zwetsch(g)en plums
Zwetsch(g)endatschi damson tart
Zwetsch(g)enknödel plum dumplings
Zwiebeln onions
Zwiebelkuchen onion flan
Zwiebelrostbraten large steak with onions
Zwiebelsalami salami with onion
Zwiebelsuppe onion soup

Grammar

Nouns

....

All German nouns begin with a capital letter and are either masculine (der), feminine (die) or neuter (das). The words for 'the' and 'a(n)' must agree with the noun they accompany.

	masculine	feminine	neuter
the	der Mann	die Frau	das Licht
a, an	ein Mann	eine Frau	ein Licht

The plural form varies from noun to noun – there is no universal plural as in English (cat – cats, dog – dogs).

singular	plural
Mann	Männer
Frau	Frauen
Licht	Lichter

The plural for 'the' for all forms is die. There's no plural for the ein form. The plural noun is used on its own.

die Männer   die Frauen   die Lichter

From the phrases in this book you'll see that the endings for the word for 'the' vary according to what part the noun plays in the sentence. If the noun is the subject of the sentence, i.e. carrying out the action, then it is in the nominative case (the one found in dictionaries), e.g. der Mann steht auf (the man stands up). The subject der Mann comes before the verb.

If the noun is the direct object of the sentence, i.e. the action of the verb is being carried out on the noun, then the noun is in the accusative case, e.g. ich sehe den Mann (I see the man). Note how der has changed to den. The same applies to ein, e.g. ich sehe einen Mann (I see a man).

If you see 'of' in front of the English noun, or 's or s' at the end, then the noun is in the genitive case (it belongs to someone or something), e.g. das Haus der Frau (the woman's house). Note how die has changed to der. The same applies to ein, e.g. das Haus einer Frau (a woman's house).

If you see 'to the' or 'to a' in front of the English noun, then the noun is in the dative case, e.g. ich gebe es der Frau (I give it to the woman). Note how die has changed to der. The same applies to ein, e.g. ich gebe es einer Frau (I give it to a woman).

Other words used before nouns have similar endings to der and ein. Those like der are: dieser (this); jener (that); jeder (each); welcher (which).

	masculine	feminine	neuter	plural
nominative	der Mann	die Frau	das Licht	die Frauen
accusative	den Mann	die Frau	das Licht	die Frauen
genitive	des Mannes	der Frau	des Lichtes	der Frauen
dative	dem Mann	der Frau	dem Licht	den Frauen

Those like ein are: mein (my); dein (your – familiar singular); Ihr (your – polite singular and plural); sein (his); ihr (her); unser (our); euer (your – familiar plural); ihr (their).

	masculine	feminine	neuter
nominative	ein Mann	eine Frau	ein Licht
accusative	einen Mann	eine Frau	ein Licht
genitive	eines Mannes	einer Frau	eines Lichtes
dative	einem Mann	einer Frau	einem Licht

Grammar

The word kein (no, not any) also has the same endings as for ein, except that it can be used in the plural.

nominative keine Männer   genitive keiner Männer
accusative keine Männer   dative keinen Männern

My, your, his, her, our, its, their

These words all take the same endings as for ein and agree with the noun they accompany whether masculine, feminine, etc and according to the noun's function (nominative, accusative, etc).

mein Mann kommt (my husband is coming) (nominative)
ich liebe meinen Mann (I love my husband) (accusative)
das Auto meines Mannes (my husband's car) (genitive)
ich gebe es meinem Mann (I give it to my husband) (dative)
meine Kinder kommen (my children are coming) (nominative plural)
ich liebe meine Kinder (I love my children) (accusative plural)
die Spielsachen meiner Kinder (my children's toys) (genitive plural)
ich gebe es meinen Kindern (I give it to my children) (dative plural)

Other words which take these endings are: dein (your – familiar singular); sein (his); ihr (her); unser (our); euer (your – familiar plural); Ihr (your – polite singular and plural); ihr (their).

Adjectives

When adjectives are used before a noun, their endings vary like the words for der and ein, depending on the gender (masculine, feminine or neuter) and whether the noun is plural, and how the noun is used in the sentence (whether it is the subject, object, etc). Here are examples using the adjective klug – 'clever':

	masculine	feminine
nominative	der kluge Mann	die kluge Frau
	ein kluger Mann	eine kluge Frau
accusative	den klugen Mann	die kluge Frau
	einen klugen Mann	eine kluge Frau
genitive	des klugen Mannes	der klugen Frau
	eines klugen Mannes	einer klugen Frau
dative	dem klugen Mann	der klugen Frau
	einem klugen Mann	einer klugen Frau
	neuter	plural
nominative	das kluge Kind	die klugen Männer
	ein kluges Kind	kluge Frauen
accusative	das kluge Kind	die klugen Männer
	ein kluges Kind	kluge Frauen
genitive	des klugen Kindes	der klugen Männer
	eines klugen Kindes	kluger Frauen
dative	dem klugen Kind	den klugen Männern
	einem klugen Kind	klugen Frauen

When the adjective follows the verb there is no agreement.

der Mann ist klug / die Frau ist klug / das Kind ist klug

Pronouns

subject		direct object	
I	ich	me	mich
you (fam. sing.)	du	you (fam. sing.)	dich
he/it (masc.)	er	him/it (masc.)	ihn
she/it (fem.)	sie	her/it (fem.)	sie
it (neut.)	es	it (neut.)	es
we	wir	us	uns
you (fam. pl.)	ihr	you (fam. pl.)	euch
you (polite sing. & pl.)	Sie	you (polite sing. & pl.)	Sie
they (all genders)	sie	them (all genders)	sie

Indirect object pronouns are: mir (to me); dir (to you) (fam. sing.); ihm (to him/it); ihr (to her/it); ihm (to it: neut.); uns (to us); euch (to you: fam. pl.); Ihnen (to you: polite sing. & pl.); ihnen (to them).

In German there are two ways of addressing people: the familiar form – du (when talking to just one person you know well), ihr (when talking to more than one person you know well), and the polite form – Sie (always written with a capital letter), which can be used for one or more people.

Verbs

There are two main types of verb in German – 'weak' verbs (which are regular) and 'strong' verbs (which are irregular).

	weak	strong
	spielen (to play)	helfen (to help)
ich	spiele	helfe
du	spielst	hilfst
er/sie/es	spielt	hilft
wir	spielen	helfen
ihr	spielt	helft
Sie	spielen	helfen
sie	spielen	helfen

Other examples of 'strong' verbs are:

	sein (to be)	haben (to have)
ich	bin	habe
du	bist	hast
er/sie/es	ist	hat
wir	sind	haben
ihr	seid	habt
Sie	sind	haben
sie	sind	haben

To make a verb negative, add nicht:

ich verstehe nicht I don't understand
das funktioniert nicht it doesn't work

Past tense

Here are a number of useful past tenses:

ich war	I was
wir waren	we were
Sie waren	you were (polite)
ich hatte	I had
wir hatten	we had
Sie hatten	you had (polite)
ich/er/sie/es spielte	I/he/she/it played
Sie/wir/sie spielten	you/we/they played
ich/er/sie/es half	I/he/she/it helped
Sie/wir/sie halfen	you/we/they helped

Another past form corresponds to the English 'have ...ed' and uses the verb haben (to have).

ich habe gespielt I have played
wir haben geholfen we have helped

In German the present tense is very often used where we would use the future tense in English.

ich schicke eine E-Mail I will send an e-mail
ich schreibe einen Brief I will write a letter

Dictionary

• •

A

a (with das words) ein
(with der words) ein
(with die words) eine
abbey die Abtei
able: to be able können
abortion die Abtreibung
about (concerning) über
about 4 o'clock ungefähr vier Uhr
above (overhead) oben
(higher than) über
abroad im Ausland
abscess der Abszess
accelerator das Gaspedal
to accept akzeptieren
accident der Unfall
**accident and emergency
  department** die Notaufnahme
accommodation die Unterkunft
to accompany begleiten
account (bill) die Rechnung
(in bank) das Konto
account number die Kontonummer
to ache: it aches es tut weh
acid die Säure
actor der Schauspieler
adaptor der Adapter
address die Adresse
what is the address? wie lautet
  die Adresse?
address book das Adressbuch
adhesive tape das Klebeband
admission fee der Eintrittspreis
adult der/die Erwachsene
for adults für Erwachsene
advance: in advance im Voraus
advertisement (in paper) die Anzeige
to advise raten
A&E die Notaufnahme
aerial die Antenne
aeroplane das Flugzeug
aerosol die Spraydose
afraid: to be afraid of Angst haben vor

after (afterwards) danach
after lunch nach dem Mittagessen
afternoon der Nachmittag
in the afternoon am Nachmittag
this afternoon heute Nachmittag
tomorrow afternoon morgen
  Nachmittag
aftershave das Rasierwasser
again wieder
against gegen
age das Alter
agency die Agentur
ago: a week ago vor einer Woche
to agree vereinbaren
agreement die Vereinbarung
AIDS das Aids
air die Luft
air ambulance (helicopter) der
  Rettungshubschrauber
airbag der Airbag
airbed die Luftmatratze
air conditioning die Klimaanlage
air-conditioning unit die
  Klimaanlage
air freshener der Lufterfrischer
airline die Fluggesellschaft
air mail: by air mail per Luftpost
airplane das Flugzeug
airport der Flughafen
airport bus der Flughafenbus
air ticket das Flugticket
aisle der Gang
alarm die Alarmanlage
alarm call der Weckruf
alarm clock der Wecker
alcohol der Alkohol
alcohol-free alkoholfrei
alcoholic alkoholisch
all alle
allergic: to be allergic to allergisch
  sein gegen
I'm allergic to... ich bin allergisch
  gegen...

allergy die Allergie
to allow erlauben
to be allowed dürfen
all right (agreed) in Ordnung
are you all right? geht es Ihnen gut?
almost fast
alone allein
Alps die Alpen
already schon
also auch
altar der Altar
aluminium foil die Alufolie
always immer
a.m. vormittags
am: *I am* ich bin
amber (traffic lights) gelb
ambulance der Krankenwagen
America Amerika
American *adj* amerikanisch
   m/f der/die Amerikaner(in)
amount: *total amount* die
   Gesamtsumme
anaesthetic die Narkose
general anaesthetic die Vollnarkose
local anaesthetic die örtliche
   Betäubung
anchor der Anker
and und
angina die Angina Pectoris
angry zornig
animal das Tier
ankle der Knöchel
anniversary der Jahrestag
to announce bekannt geben
announcement die Bekanntmachung
annual jährlich
another (additional) noch ein/noch
   eine/noch ein
   (different) ein anderer/eine andere/
   ein anderes
another beer please noch ein Bier
   bitte
answer die Antwort
to answer antworten
answerphone der Anrufbeantworter
antacid das säurebindende Mittel
antenna die Antenne

antibiotic das Antibiotikum
antifreeze das Frostschutzmittel
antihistamine das Antihistamin
anti-inflammatory das
   entzündungs-hemmende Mittel
antiques die Antiquitäten
antique shop der Antiquitätenladen
antiseptic das Antiseptikum
any jegliche(r/s)
have you any apples? haben Sie
   Äpfel?
anybody jeder
anything irgendetwas
anywhere irgendwo
apartment das Appartement
appendicitis die
   Blinddarmentzündung
apple der Apfel
appointment der Termin
I have an appointment ich habe
   einen Termin
approximately ungefähr
apricot die Aprikose
April der April
apron die Schürze
architect der/die Architekt(in)
are sind; seid
arm der Arm
armbands (to swim) die
   Schwimmflügel
armchair der Sessel
to arrange vereinbaren
to arrest verhaften
arrival die Ankunft
to arrive ankommen
art die Kunst
art gallery die Kunsthalle
arthritis die Arthritis
artichokes die Artischocken
artificial künstlich
artist der/die Künstler(in)
ashtray der Aschenbecher
to ask (question) fragen
   (for something) bitten
asleep: *to be asleep* schlafen
to fall asleep einschlafen
asparagus der Spargel

aspirin das Aspirin
asthma das Asthma
I have asthma ich habe Asthma
at: *at the hotel* im Hotel
at 8 o'clock um acht Uhr
at home zu Hause
at night am Abend
at once sofort
at (@) at
to attack angreifen
attractive attraktiv
aubergine die Aubergine
auction die Auktion
audience das Publikum
August der August
aunt die Tante
au pair das Au-pair-Mädchen
Australia Australien
Australian *adj* australisch
m/f der/die Australier(in)
Austria Österreich
Austrian *adj* österreichisch
m/f der/die Österreicher(in)
author der/die Autor(in)
automatic automatisch
automatic car das Automatikauto
autumn der Herbst
available erhältlich
avalanche die Lawine
avenue die Allee
average der Durchschnitt
to avoid (obstacle) ausweichen
(person) meiden
awake wach
away weg
awful schrecklich
awning (caravan) das Vorzelt
(on house) die Markise
axe die Axt
axle (car) die Achse

B

baby das Baby
baby food die Babynahrung
baby milk die Babymilch
baby's bottle die Babyflasche
baby seat (in car) der Kindersitz

babysitter der/die Babysitter(in)
baby wipes die Babytücher
back (of body, hand) der Rücken
backpack der Rucksack
bacon der Speck
bad (weather, news) schlecht
(fruit, vegetables) verdorben
bag die Tasche
baggage das Gepäck
baggage allowance das Freigepäck
baggage reclaim die Gepäckausgabe
bait (for fishing) der Köder
baked gebacken
baker's die Bäckerei
balcony der Balkon
ball der Ball
ballet das Ballett
balloon der Ballon
Baltic Sea die Ostsee
banana die Banane
band (musical) die Band
bandage der Verband
bank die Bank
(river) das Ufer
bank account das Bankkonto
banknote der Geldschein
bar die Bar
barbecue der Grill
to have a barbecue eine Grillparty
geben
barber der Herrenfriseur
to bark bellen
barn die Scheune
basement das Untergeschoss
basket der Korb
basketball der Basketball
Basle Basel
bat (racquet) der Schläger
bath das Bad
tub die Badewanne
to have a bath ein Bad nehmen
bathing cap die Badekappe
bathroom das Badezimmer
with bathroom mit Bad
battery die Batterie
bay (along coast) die Bucht
B&B Übernachtung mit Frühstück

to be sein
beach der Strand
nudist beach der FKK-Strand
private beach der Privatstrand
sandy beach der Sandstrand
beach hut der Strandkorb
beans die Bohnen
beard der Bart
beautiful schön
because weil
to become werden
bed das Bett
double bed das Doppelbett
single bed das Einzelbett
twin beds zwei Einzelbetten
bed and breakfast Übernachtung
  mit Frühstück
bedclothes die Bettwäsche
bedroom das Schlafzimmer
bee die Biene
beef das Rindfleisch
beer das Bier
before vor
before breakfast vor dem Frühstück
to begin beginnen
behind hinter
beige beige
to believe glauben
bell (church) die Glocke
(door) die Klingel
to belong to gehören zu
below unterhalb
belt der Gürtel
bend (in road) die Kurve
berth (train, ship) die Kabine
beside (next to) neben
best: *the best* der/die/das beste
bet die Wette
to bet on wetten auf
better besser
better than besser als
between zwischen
bib (baby's) das Lätzchen
bicycle das Fahrrad
by bicycle mit dem Fahrrad
bicycle pump die Luftpumpe
bicycle repair kit das

Fahrradflickzeug
big groß
bigger than größer als
bike (push bike) das Fahrrad
(motorbike) das Motorrad
bike lock das Fahrradschloss
bikini der Bikini
bill (account) die Rechnung
bin (dustbin) der Mülleimer
bin liner der Müllbeutel
binoculars das Fernglas
bird der Vogel
biro der Kugelschreiber
birth die Geburt
birth certificate die Geburtsurkunde
birthday der Geburtstag
happy birthday! alles Gute zum
  Geburtstag!
my birthday is on... ich habe am ...
  Geburtstag
birthday card die Geburtstagskarte
birthday present das
  Geburtstagsgeschenk
biscuits die Kekse
bit (piece) das Stück
a bit (a little) ein bisschen
bite (by insect) der Biss
(of food) der Bissen
to bite beißen
(insect) stechen
bitten (by insect) gestochen
I've been bitten ich bin gestochen
  worden
bitter (taste) bitter
black schwarz
black ice das Glatteis
blank (disk, tape) leer
blank CD or DVD der Rohling
bleach das Bleichmittel
to bleed bluten
blender der Mixer
blind (person) blind
(for window) das Rollo
blister die Blase
blocked (pipe, road) verstopft
blond (person) blond
blood das Blut

blood group die Blutgruppe
blood pressure der Blutdruck
blood test der Bluttest
blouse die Bluse
to blow-dry föhnen
blowout (tyre) die Reifenpanne
(bicycle) der Platte
blue blau
dark blue dunkelblau
light blue hellblau
blunt (knife, blade) stumpf
BMX das BMX-Rad
boar das Wildschwein
to board (plane, train, etc) einsteigen
boarding card/pass die Bordkarte
boarding house die Pension
boat (large) das Schiff
(small) das Boot
boat trip die Bootsfahrt
body der Körper
(dead) die Leiche
to boil kochen
boiled gekocht
boiler der Boiler
bomb die Bombe
bone der Knochen
fish bone die Gräte
bonnet (car) die Motorhaube
book das Buch
book of tickets die Mehrfahrtenkarte
to book buchen
booking (in hotel, train, etc) die
   Reservierung
booking office (train) der
   Fahrkartenschalter
bookshop die Buchhandlung
booster seat die Sitzerhöhung
boot (car) der Kofferraum
boots (long) die Stiefel
(ankle) die Schnürschuhe
border (country) die Grenze
boring langweilig
born: *I was born in 1980* ich bin
   neunzehn-hundertachtzig geboren
to borrow borgen
boss der/die Chef(in)
both beide

bottle die Flasche
a bottle of wine eine Flasche Wein
a half-bottle eine kleine Flasche
bottle opener der Flaschenöffner
bowl (soup, etc) die Schüssel
bow tie die Fliege
box (of wood) die Kiste
(of cardboard) der Karton
box office die Kasse
boy der Junge
boyfriend der Freund
bra der BH
bracelet das Armband
to brake bremsen
brake cable (bicycle) der Bremszug
(car) das Bremsseil
brake fluid die Bremsflüssigkeit
brake light das Bremslicht
brake pads die Bremsbeläge
brakes die Bremsen
branch (of tree) der Ast
(of bank, etc) die Filiale
brand (make) die Marke
brass das Messing
brave mutig
bread das Brot
brown bread das Granbrot
French bread das Baguette
sliced bread geschnittenes Brot
white bread das Weißbrot
bread roll das Brötchen
to break (object) zerbrechen
breakable zerbrechlich
breakdown (car) die Panne
breakdown van die Pannenhilfe
breakfast das Frühstück
when is breakfast? wann gibt es
   Frühstück?
breast die Brust
to breast-feed stillen
to breathe atmen
brick der Ziegel
bride die Braut
bridegroom der Bräutigam
bridge die Brücke
briefcase die Aktentasche
to bring bringen

Britain Großbritannien
British britisch
broadband das Breitband
broadband connection die Breitband-Verbindung
brochure die Broschüre
broken gebrochen
broken down (car, etc) kaputt
bronchitis die Bronchitis
bronze die Bronze
brooch die Brosche
broom der Besen
brother der Bruder
brother-in-law der Schwager
brown braun
bruise der Bluterguss
brush die Bürste
(for floor) der Besen
bubble bath das Schaumbad
bucket der Eimer
buffet das Buffet
buffet car der Speisewagen
to build bauen
building das Gebäude
bulb (electric) die Glühbirne
bumbag die Gürteltasche
bumper die Stoßstange
bunch (flowers) der Blumenstrauß
(grapes) die Weintraube
bureau de change die Wechselstube
burger der Hamburger
burglar der/die Einbrecher(in)
burn die Brandwunde
to burn verbrennen
bus der Bus
bus station der Busbahnhof
bus stop die Bushaltestelle
bus ticket der Busfahrschein
bus tour die Busfahrt
business das Geschäft
on business geschäftlich
business address die Geschäftsadresse
business card die Visitenkarte
business centre das Geschäftszentrum
businessman/woman der Geschäftsmann/die Geschäftsfrau
business trip die Dienstreise; die Geschäftsreise
busy beschäftigt
but aber
butcher's die Fleischerei
butter die Butter
button der Knopf
to buy kaufen
by (beside) bei
(via) über
by bus mit dem Bus
by car mit dem Auto
by ship mit dem Schiff
by train mit dem Zug
bypass die Umgehungsstraße

C

cab (taxi) das Taxi
cabaret das Varieté
cabin (on ship) die Kabine
inside cabin Innenkabine
outside cabin Außenkabine
cabin crew die Besatzung
cable car die Seilbahn
café das Café
internet café das Internetcafé
cake der Kuchen
cake shop die Konditorei
calculator der Taschenrechner
calendar der Kalender
call (on phone) der Anruf
to call (on phone) anrufen
calm (person) ruhig
(weather) windstill
camcorder der Camcorder
camera die Kamera
camera phone das Fotohandy
camera shop das Fotogeschäft
to camp campen
camping gas das Campinggas
camping mat die Isomatte
camping stove der Campingkocher
campsite der Campingplatz
can die Dose
can opener der Dosenöffner
can (to be able) können

I can/we can ich kann/wir können
Canada Kanada
Canadian *adj* kanadisch
m/f der/die Kanadier(in)
canal der Kanal
to cancel stornieren
cancellation die Stornierung
cancer der Krebs
candle die Kerze
canoe das Kanu
cap (hat) die Mütze
(diaphragm) das Diaphragma
capital (city) die Hauptstadt
cappuccino der Cappuccino
car das Auto
car alarm die Autoalarmanlage
car ferry die Autofähre
car hire die Autovermietung
car insurance die Kfz-Versicherung
car keys die Autoschlüssel
car park der Parkplatz
car parts die Ersatzteile
car port der Einstellplatz
car radio das Autoradio
car seat (children's) der Kindersitz
car wash die Waschanlage
caravan der Wohnwagen
carburettor der Vergaser
card (greetings) die (Glückwunsch)karte
(playing) die Spielkarte
cardboard die Pappe
cardigan die Strickjacke
careful vorsichtig
be careful! passen Sie auf!
carpet der Teppich
carriage (railway) der Wagen
carrot die Karotte
to carry tragen
carton der Karton
case (suitcase) der Koffer
cash das Bargeld
to cash (cheque) einlösen
cash desk die Kasse
cash machine der Geldautomat
cashier der/die Kassierer(in)
casino das Kasino
casserole dish die Kasserolle

cassette die Kassette
castle das Schloss
(medieval fortress) die Burg
casualty department die Unfallstation
cat die Katze
catalogue der Katalog
catalytic converter (car) der Katalysator
to catch (bus, train) nehmen
cat food das Katzenfutter
cathedral der Dom
Catholic katholisch
cauliflower der Blumenkohl
cave die Höhle
cavity (in tooth) das Loch
CD die CD
CD-ROM die CD-ROM
CD player der CD-Spieler
CD writer der CD-Brenner
ceiling die Decke
celery der Sellerie
cellar der Keller
cellphone das Handy
cemetery der Friedhof
cent (euro) der Cent
centimetre der Zentimeter
central zentral
central heating die Zentralheizung
central locking (car) die Zentralverriegelung
centre das Zentrum
century das Jahrhundert
ceramic die Keramik
cereal (breakfast) die Zerealien
certain (sure) sicher
certificate die Bescheinigung
chain die Kette
chair der Stuhl
chairlift der Sessellift
chambermaid das Zimmermädchen
champagne der Champagner
change (money) das Wechselgeld
to change (to alter) ändern
(bus, train, etc) umsteigen
to change clothes sich umziehen
to change money Geld wechseln

changing room die Umkleidekabine
Channel (English) der Kanal
chapel die Kapelle
charcoal die Holzkohle
charge (fee) die Gebühr
(prepaid phone time) das Gesprächsguthaben
(electrical) die Ladung
I've run out of charge (phone) mein Akku ist leer
to charge (battery) aufladen
I need to charge my phone ich muss mein Handy aufladen
to charge (money) berechnen
please charge it to my account bitte setzen Sie es auf meine Rechnung
charge card (for mobile phone) die Guthabenkarte
(store card) die Kundenkarte
charger (for battery, etc) das Ladegerät
charter flight der Charterflug
chatroom (internet) der Chatroom
cheap billig
cheap rate der Billigtarif
to check überprüfen
(passports) kontrollieren
to check in einchecken
(at hotel) sich an der Rezeption anmelden
check-in der Check-in
cheers! (toast) Prost!
cheese der Käse
chef der Koch/die Köchin
chemical toilet die chemische Toilette
chemist's die Drogerie
(for medicines) die Apotheke
cheque der Scheck
cheque book das Scheckheft
cheque card die Scheckkarte
cherry die Kirsche
chest (body) die Brust
chewing gum der Kaugummi
chicken das Hühnchen
chickenpox die Windpocken
child das Kind
children die Kinder

for children für Kinder
chilli (spice) der Chili
(vegetable) die Peperoni
chimney der Schornstein
chin das Kinn
china das Porzellan
chips (French fries) die Pommes frites
chiropodist der/die Fußpfleger(in)
chocolate die Schokolade
chocolates die Pralinen
choir der Chor
to choose auswählen
chopping board das Küchenbrett
Christian name der Vorname
Christmas Weihnachten
merry Christmas! frohe Weihnachten!
Christmas card die Weihnachtskarte
Christmas Eve der Heiligabend
church die Kirche
cigar die Zigarre
cigarette die Zigarette
cigarette lighter das Feuerzeug
cigarette papers das Zigarettenpapier
cinema das Kino
circle (theatre) der Rang
circuit breaker der Unterbrecher
(for protection) der Schutzschalter
cistern (of toilet) der Spülkasten
city die Stadt
city centre das Stadtzentrum
class: *first class* erste Klasse
second class zweite Klasse
clean sauber
to clean säubern
cleaning lady die Putzfrau
clear klar
client der Kunde/die Kundin
cliff (along coast) die Klippe
(in mountains) der Felsen
to climb (mountains) klettern
climbing boots die Bergschuhe
clingfilm® die Frischhaltefolie
clinic die Klinik
cloakroom die Garderobe
clock die Uhr
to close schließen
closed geschlossen

cloth (rag) der Lappen
(fabric) der Stoff
clothes die Kleider
clothes line die Wäscheleine
clothes peg die Wäscheklammer
clothes shop das Bekleidungsgeschäft
cloudy bewölkt
club der Klub
clutch (car) die Kupplung
clutch fluid die Kupplungsflüssigkeit
coach (bus) der Bus
coach station der Busbahnhof
coach trip die Busreise
coal die Kohle
coast die Küste
coastguard die Küstenwache
coat der Mantel
coat hanger der Kleiderbügel
cocktail bar die Cocktailbar
cockroach die Kakerlake
cocoa der Kakao
code der Code
coffee der Kaffee

black coffee schwarzer Kaffee
decaffeinated coffee koffeinfreier
  Kaffee
white coffee Kaffee mit Milch
coffee shop das Café
coil (IUD) die Spirale
coin die Münze
Coke® die Cola
colander das Sieb
cold kalt
I'm cold mir ist kalt
it's cold es ist kalt
cold (illness) die Erkältung
I have a cold ich habe mich erkältet
cold sore der Ausschlag
collar der Kragen
collar bone das Schlüsselbein
colleague der Kollege/die Kollegin
to collect (person) abholen
(something) sammeln
collection die Sammlung
Cologne Köln
colour die Farbe
colour-blind farbenblind

colour film der Farbfilm
comb der Kamm
to come kommen
(to arrive) ankommen
to come back zurückkommen
to come in hereinkommen
come in! herein!
comedy die Komödie
comfortable bequem
company (firm) die Firma
compartment (in train) das Abteil
compass der Kompass
to complain sich beschweren
complaint die Klage
complete vollständig
to complete vervollständigen
compulsory obligatorisch
computer der Computer
computer disk (floppy) die Diskette
computer game das Computerspiel
computer program das
  Computerprogramm
concert das Konzert
concert hall die Konzerthalle
concession die Ermäßigung
concussion die Gehirnerschütterung
conditioner (hair) die Pflegespülung
condom das Kondom
conductor der Schaffner/die
  Schaffnerin
conference die Konferenz
to confirm bestätigen
please confirm bitte bestätigen Sie
confirmation (flight, etc) die
  Bestätigung
confused verwirrt
congratulations! herzlichen
  Glückwünsch!
connection (train, etc) die Verbindung
constipated verstopft
consulate das Konsulat
contact (person) der/die
  Ansprechpartner(in)
to contact kontaktieren
contact details die Kontaktdaten
contact lens cleaner der
  Kontaktlinsenreiniger

contact lenses die Kontaktlinsen
to continue weitermachen
contraceptive das Verhütungsmittel
contract der Vertrag
convenient: *is it convenient?* passt es Ihnen?
convulsions die Krämpfe
to cook kochen
cooked gekocht
cooker der Herd
cookies die Kekse
cool kühl
cool-box (for picnic) die Kühlbox
copy (duplicate) die Kopie
to copy kopieren
cordless phone das schnurlose Telefon
cork der Korken
corkscrew der Korkenzieher
corner die Ecke
cornflakes die Cornflakes
corridor der Flur
cosmetics die Kosmetikartikel
cost (price) die Kosten
to cost kosten
how much does it cost? wie viel kostet es?
costume (swimming) der Badeanzug
cot das Kinderbett
cottage das Ferienhäuschen
cotton die Baumwolle
cotton bud das Wattestäbchen
cotton wool die Watte
couchette der Liegewagen
cough der Husten
to cough husten
cough sweets die Hustenbonbons
counter (shop, bar) die Theke
country das Land
countryside die Landschaft
couple (two people) das Paar
a couple of... ein paar...
courgettes die Zucchini
courier service der Kurierdienst
course (of study) der Kurs
(of meal) der Gang
cousin der Cousin/die Cousine

cover charge (in restaurant) die Gedeckkosten
cow die Kuh
craft fair der Kunsthandwerksmarkt
crafts das Kunsthandwerk
cramps die Krämpfe
cranberry juice der Preiselbeersaft
crash (collision) der Zusammenstoß
to crash einen Unfall haben (computer) abstürzen
crash helmet der Sturzhelm
cream (lotion) die Creme
(on milk) die Sahne
soured cream saure Sahne
whipped cream Schlagsahne
cream cheese der Frischkäse
crèche die Kinderkrippe
credit (on mobile phone) das Gesprächsguthaben
credit card die Kreditkarte
crime das Verbrechen
crisps die Chips
to cross (road) überqueren
cross-channel ferry die Kanalfähre
cross-country skiing der Skilanglauf
crossing (sea) die Überfahrt
crossroads die Kreuzung
crossword puzzle das Kreuzworträtsel
crowd die Menge
crowded überfüllt
crown die Krone
cruise die Kreuzfahrt
crutches die Krücken
to cry (weep) weinen
crystal das Kristall
cucumber die Gurke
cufflinks die Manschettenknöpfe
cul-de-sac die Sackgasse
cup die Tasse
cupboard der Schrank
curlers die Lockenwickler
currency die Währung
current (electric) der Strom
(water) die Strömung
curtains die Vorhänge
cushion das Kissen

custom (tradition) der Brauch
customer der Kunde/die Kundin
customs (duty) der Zoll
cut die Schnittwunde
to cut schneiden
cutlery das Besteck
cutlet das Schnitzel
cybercafé das Internetcafé
to cycle Rad fahren
cycle track der Radweg
cycling das Radfahren
cyst die Zyste
cystitis die Blasenentzündung

D

daily (each day) täglich
dairy products die Milchprodukte
dam der Damm
damage der Schaden
damp feucht
dance der Tanz
to dance tanzen
danger die Gefahr
dangerous gefährlich
dark dunkel
after dark nach Einbruch der
  Dunkelheit
date das Datum
date of birth das Geburtsdatum
daughter die Tochter
daughter-in-law die
  Schwiegertochter
dawn die Morgendämmerung
day der Tag
every day jeden Tag
per day pro Tag
dead tot
deaf taub
dear (in letter) liebe(r/s)
(expensive) teuer
debit card die Debitkarte
debts die Schulden
decaffeinated coffee der koffeinfreie
  Kaffee
December der Dezember
deckchair der Liegestuhl
to declare erklären

nothing to declare nichts zu verzollen
deep tief
deep freeze die Tiefkühltruhe
deer das Reh
to defrost entfrosten
to de-ice enteisen
delay die Verspätung
delayed verspätet
delicatessen das Feinkostgeschäft
delicious köstlich
demonstration die Demonstration
dental floss die Zahnseide
dentist der Zahnarzt/die Zahnärztin
dentures das Gebiss
deodorant das Deo
to depart abfahren
department die Abteilung
department store das Kaufhaus
departure die Abfahrt
(plane) der Abflug
departure lounge die Abflughalle
deposit die Anzahlung
to describe beschreiben
description die Beschreibung
desk der Schreibtisch
dessert der Nachtisch
details die Details
detergent das Waschmittel
detour der Umweg
to develop (photos) entwickeln
diabetes der Diabetes
diabetic (person) der Diabetiker/
  die Diabetikerin
to dial wählen
dialling code die Vorwahl
dialling tone der Wählton
diamond der Diamant
diarrhoea der Durchfall
diapers die Windeln
diaphragm (contraception) das
  Diaphragma
diary der Terminkalender
dice der Würfel
dictionary das Wörterbuch
to die sterben
diesel der Diesel
diet die Diät

I'm on a diet ich muss eine Diät einhalten
special diet spezielle Diät
different verschieden
difficult schwierig
digital camera die Digitalkamera
digital radio das Digitalradio
to dilute verdünnen
dinghy (rubber) das Schlauchboot
dining room das Esszimmer
dinner (evening meal) das Abendessen
to have dinner zu Abend essen
diplomat der Diplomat/die Diplomatin
direct (route) direkt
(train, etc) durchgehend
directions: *to ask for directions* nach dem Weg fragen
directory (phone) das Telefonbuch
directory enquiries die Auskunft
dirty schmutzig
disability die Behinderung
disabled (person) behindert
to disagree nicht zustimmen
to disappear verschwinden
disco die Disco
discount der Rabatt
to discover entdecken
disease die Krankheit
dish die Schale
(food) das Gericht
dishtowel das Geschirrtuch
dishwasher die Geschirrspülmaschine
disinfectant das Desinfektionsmittel
disk die Diskette
to dislocate auskugeln
disposable wegwerfbar
distance die Entfernung
distilled water das destillierte Wasser
district der Bezirk
to disturb stören
to dive tauchen
diversion die Umleitung
diving das Tauchen
divorced geschieden
DIY shop der Baumarkt
dizzy schwindelig
to do machen

doctor der Arzt/die Ärztin
documents die Dokumente
dog der Hund
dog food das Hundefutter
dog lead die Hundeleine
doll die Puppe
dollar der Dollar
domestic (flight) Inlands-
donor card der Organspenderausweis
door die Tür
doorbell die Klingel
dormitory (in hostel) der Schlafsaal
(student residence) das Studentenwohnheim
double Doppel-
double bed das Doppelbett
double room das Doppelzimmer
doughnut der Berliner
down: *to go down* nach unten gehen
download *n* der Download
to download herunterladen, downloaden
Down's syndrome das Downsyndrom
downstairs unten
drain der Abfluss
draught (of air) der Durchzug
there's a draught hier zieht es
draught beer das Fassbier
drawer die Schublade
drawing die Zeichnung
dress das Kleid
to dress (get dressed) sich anziehen
dressing (for food) die Soße
(for wound) das Verbandsmaterial
dressing gown der Morgenmantel
drill (tool) der Bohrer
drink das Getränk
to drink trinken
drinking water das Trinkwasser
to drive fahren
driver (of car) der Fahrer/die Fahrerin
driving licence der Führerschein
to drown ertrinken
drug das Medikament
(narcotic) die Droge
drunk betrunken
dry trocken

to dry trocknen
dry cleaner's die Reinigung
dryer der Wäschetrockner
due: *when's he due?* wann soll er ankommen?
dummy (for baby) der Schnuller
during während
dust der Staub
duster das Staubtuch
dustpan and brush Schaufel und Handfeger
duty-free zollfrei
duvet die Bettdecke
duvet cover der Bettbezug
DVD die DVD
DVD drive das DVD-Laufwerk
DVD player der DVD-Spieler
DVD writer der DVD-Brenner
to dye färben
dynamo (car) die Lichtmaschine (bike) der Dynamo

E

each jede(r/s)
ear das Ohr
earache die Ohrenschmerzen
I have earache ich habe Ohrenschmerzen
earlier früher
early früh
to earn verdienen
earphones die Kopfhörer
earrings die Ohrringe
earth die Erde
earthquake das Erdbeben
east der Osten
Easter Ostern
easy leicht
to eat essen
ecological ökologisch
economy class die Touristenklasse
eco-tourism der Ökotourismus
egg das Ei
fried egg das Spiegelei
hard-boiled egg das hart gekochte Ei
scrambled egg das Rührei
soft-boiled egg das weich gekochte Ei

either ... or entweder ... oder
elastic band das Gummiband
Elastoplast® das Pflaster
elbow der Ellbogen
electric elektrisch
electric blanket die Heizdecke
electric razor der Elektrorasierer
electric shock der elektrische Schlag
electric toothbrush die elektrische Zahnbürste
electrician der Elektriker
electricity meter der Stromzähler
electronic elektronisch
electronic organizer der (elektronische) Organizer
elevator der Fahrstuhl
e-mail die E-Mail
to e-mail e-mailen
e-mail address die E-Mail-Adresse
embassy die Botschaft
emergency der Notfall
emergency exit der Notausgang
emery board die Nagelfeile
empty leer
end das Ende
engaged (to marry) verlobt (toilet, telephone) besetzt
engine der Motor
engineer der Ingenieur/die Ingenieurin
England England
English *adj* englisch
Englishman/woman der Engländer/die Engländerin
to enjoy (to like) mögen
enjoy your meal! guten Appetit!
enough genug
that's enough das reicht
enquiry desk die Auskunft
to enter eintreten
entertainment das Entertainment
entrance der Eingang
entrance fee der Eintrittspreis
envelope der Umschlag
epileptic der Epileptiker/die Epileptikerin
epileptic fit der epileptische Anfall
equal gleich

equipment die Ausrüstung
eraser der Radiergummi
error der Fehler
escalator die Rolltreppe
to escape entkommen
essential wesentlich
estate agent's der
  Grundstücksmakler
estate car der Kombi
euro der Euro
euro cent der Eurocent
Europe Europa
European europäisch
European Union die Europäische
  Union
evening der Abend
this evening heute Abend
tomorrow evening morgen Abend
in the evening am Abend
evening dress das Abendkleid
evening meal das Abendessen
every (each) jede(r/s)
everyone jeder
everything alles
everywhere überall
examination (medical) die
  Untersuchung
(school) die Prüfung
example: *for example* zum Beispiel
excellent ausgezeichnet
except außer
excess baggage das Übergepäck
exchange der Austausch
to exchange tauschen
(money) wechseln
exchange rate der Wechselkurs
exciting aufregend
excursion der Ausflug
excuse me! (sorry) Entschuldigung!
exhaust der Auspuff
exhibition die Ausstellung
exit der Ausgang
expense account das Spesenkonto
expenses die Spesen
expensive teuer
expert der Experte/die Expertin
to expire (ticket, etc) ungültig werden

to explain erklären
explanation die Erklärung
explosion die Explosion
export der Export
to export exportieren
express (train) der Schnellzug
express (parcel, etc) per Express
extension lead das
  Verlängerungskabel
extra (spare) übrig
(more) noch ein(e)
an extra towel ein zusätzliches
  Handtuch
eye das Auge
eyebrows die Augenbrauen
eye drops die Augentropfen
eye liner der Eyeliner
eye shadow der Lidschatten

F
fabric der Stoff
face das Gesicht
face cloth der Waschlappen
facial die Gesichtspflege
facilities die Einrichtungen
factor (sunblock) der
  (Lichtschutz)faktor
factor 25 (Lichschutz)faktor 25
factory die Fabrik
to faint ohnmächtig werden
fainted ohnmächtig
fair (hair) blond
(just) gerecht
fair (trade fair) die Messe
(funfair) der Jahrmarkt
fake unecht
fall (autumn) der Herbst
to fall fallen
I have fallen ich bin hingefallen
false teeth das Gebiss
family die Familie
famous berühmt
fan (electric) der Ventilator
(football, music) der Fan
fan belt der Keilriemen
fancy dress die Verkleidung
far weit

how far is it? wie weit ist es?
fare (train, bus, etc) der Fahrpreis
farm der Bauernhof
to fill füllen
farmer der Bauer/die Bäuerin
farmers' market der Wochenmarkt;
 der Bauernmarkt
farmhouse das Bauernhaus
fashionable modern
fast schnell
too fast zu schnell
to fasten: to fasten the seatbelt
 sich anschnallen
fat (big) dick
fat das Fett
saturated fat gesättigte Fettsäure
unsaturated fat ungesättigte
 Fettsäure
father der Vater
father-in-law der Schwiegervater
fault (defect) der Fehler
it wasn't my fault das war nicht
 meine Schuld
favour der Gefallen
favourite Lieblings-
fax das Fax
by fax per Fax
to fax faxen
fax number die Faxnummer
February der Februar
to feed füttern
feeding bottle die Babyflasche
to feel fühlen
I don't feel well ich fühle mich nicht
 wohl
I feel sick mir ist schlecht
feet die Füße
female weiblich
ferry die Fähre
festival das Festival
to fetch (bring) holen
fever das Fieber
few: a few ein paar
fiancé(e) der/die Verlobte
field das Feld
fig die Feige
to fight kämpfen
file (nail) die Feile

(computer) die Datei
(for papers) der Ordner
to fill füllen
to fill in (form) ausfüllen
to fill up (tank) volltanken
fillet das Filet
filling (in tooth) die Plombe
film der Film
Filofax® der Terminplaner
filter der Filter
to find finden
fine (to be paid) die Geldstrafe
finger der Finger
to finish beenden
fire das Feuer
fire alarm der Feuermelder
fire brigade die Feuerwehr
fire engine das Feuerwehrauto
fire escape die Feuertreppe
fire exit der Notausgang
fire extinguisher der Feuerlöscher
fireplace der Kamin
fireworks das Feuerwerk
firm (company) die Firma
first erste(r/s)
first aid die Erste Hilfe
first class (travel) erste Klasse
first name der Vorname
fish der Fisch
to fish angeln
fishing permit der Angelschein
fishing rod die Angel
fishmonger's die Fischhandlung
fit (seizure) der Anfall
to fit passen
it doesn't fit es passt nicht
to fix reparieren
can you fix it? können Sie es
 reparieren?
fizzy sprudelnd
flag die Fahne
flames die Flammen
flash das Blitzlicht
flashlight (torch) die Taschenlampe
flask (thermos) die Thermosflasche
flat (level) flach
flat die Wohnung

flat battery die leere Batterie
flat tyre die Reifenpanne
flavour der Geschmack
what flavour? welchen Geschmack?
flaw der Defekt
fleas die Flöhe
fleece das Vlies
flesh das Fleisch
flex die Verlängerungsschnur
flight der Flug
flip-flops die Badelatschen
flippers die Schwimmflossen
flood die Flut
flash flood die Überschwemmung
floor (of building) die Etage
(of room) der Boden
which floor? auf welcher Etage?
on the ground floor im Erdgeschoss
on the first floor in der ersten Etage
floorcloth der Scheuerlappen
floppy disk die Diskette
flour das Mehl
flowers die Blumen
flu die Grippe
fly die Fliege
to fly fliegen
fly sheet das Überzelt
fog der Nebel
foggy neblig
foil die Folie
to fold falten
to follow folgen
food das Essen
food poisoning die Lebensmittelvergiftung
foot der Fuß
on foot zu Fuß
football der Fußball
football match das Fußballspiel
football player der Fußballer
footpath der Fußweg
for für
for me für mich
for him/her für ihn/sie
forbidden verboten
forehead die Stirn
foreign ausländisch

foreigner der Ausländer/
die Ausländerin
forest der Wald
forever für immer
to forget vergessen
fork (for eating) die Gabel
(in road) die Gabelung
form (document) das Formular
fortnight zwei Wochen
forward vorwärts
fountain der Brunnen
4x4 der Geländewagen
fox der Fuchs
fracture der Bruch
fragile zerbrechlich
fragrance das Parfüm
frame (picture) der Rahmen
France Frankreich
free (not occupied) frei
(costing nothing) umsonst
free-range- Freiland-
free-range eggs Eier aus
Freilandhaltung
freezer die Tiefkühltruhe
French *adj* französisch
French beans die grünen Bohnen
French fries die Pommes frites
Frenchman/woman der Franzose/
die Französin
frequent häufig
fresh frisch
freshwater das Süßwasser
Friday der Freitag
fridge der Kühlschrank
fried gebraten
friend der Freund/die Freundin
friendly freundlich
frog der Frosch
from von
from England aus England
from Scotland aus Schottland
front die Vorderseite
in front of vor
front door die Eingangstür
frost der Frost
frozen gefroren
fruit das Obst

dried fruit das Trockenobst
fruit juice der Fruchtsaft
to fry braten
frying pan die Bratpfanne
fuel (petrol) das Benzin
fuel gauge die Tankanzeige
fuel pump (in car) die Benzinpumpe
(at petrol station) die Zapfsäule
fuel tank der Tank
full voll
(occupied) besetzt
I'm full ich bin satt!
full board die Vollpension
fumes die Abgase
fun der Spaß
funeral die Beerdigung
funfair der Jahrmarkt
funny (amusing) komisch
fur der Pelz
furnished möbliert
furniture die Möbel
fuse die Sicherung
fuse box der Sicherungskasten

future die Zukunft

G

gallery die Galerie
game das Spiel
(meat) das Wild
garage (private) die Garage
(for repairs) die Werkstatt
(petrol station) die Tankstelle
garden der Garten
garlic dcr Knoblauch
gas das Gas
gas cooker der Gasherd
gastritis die Gastritis
gate (airport) das Gate
gay (person) der/die Homosexuelle
gearbox das Getriebe
gear cable (bike) der Schaltzug
gear lever der Schaltknüppel
gears das Getriebe
first gear der erste Gang
second gear der zweite Gang
third gear der dritte Gang
fourth gear der vierte Gang

neutral gear der Leerlauf
reverse gear der Rückwärtsgang
generous großzügig
genetically modified genmanipuliert
gents' (toilet) die Herrentoilette
genuine echt
German *adj* deutsch
   m/f der/die Deutsche
German measles die Röteln
Germany Deutschland
to get (to obtain) bekommen
(to fetch) holen
to get in(to) (bus, etc) einsteigen
to get off (bus, etc) aussteigen
gift das Geschenk
gift shop der Geschenkeladen
gigabyte das Gigabyte
gigahertz das Gigahertz
girl das Mädchen
girlfriend die Freundin
to give geben
to give back zurückgeben
glacier der Gletscher
glass das Glas
a glass of water ein Glas Wasser
glasses (spectacles) die Brille
glasses case das Brillenetui
gloves die Handschuhe
glue der Klebstoff
gluten das Gluten
gluten-free glutenfrei
GM-free genfrei
to go (on foot) gehen
(in car) fahren
I'm going to... ich fahre nach...
we're going to... wir fahren nach...
to go home nach Hause fahren
to go on foot zu Fuß gehen
to go back zurückgehen
to go in hineingehen
to go out ausgehen
God Gott
goggles (swimming) die Taucherbrille
(skiing) die Schneebrille
gold das Gold
golf das Golf
golf ball der Golfball

golf clubs die Golfschläger
golf course der Golfplatz
good gut
(pleasant) schön
good afternoon guten Tag
goodbye auf Wiedersehen
good day guten Tag
good evening guten Abend
good morning guten Morgen
good night gute Nacht
goose die Gans
GPS (global positioning system) das GPS
grandchild das Enkelkind
granddaughter die Enkelin
grandfather der Großvater
grandmother die Großmutter
grandparents die Großeltern
grandson der Enkel
grapefruit die Grapefruit
grapes die Trauben
grass das Gras
grated (cheese) gerieben
gram(me) das Gramm
grater die Reibe
great (big) groß
(wonderful) großartig
Great Britain Großbritannien
green grün
greengrocer's der Gemüseladen
greetings card die Grußkarte
grey grau
grill der Grill
to grill grillen
grilled gegrillt
grocer's der Lebensmittelladen
ground der Boden
ground floor das Erdgeschoss
on the ground floor im Erdgeschoss
groundsheet der Zeltboden
group die Gruppe
guarantee die Garantie
guard *m/f* (on train) der Schaffner/die Schaffnerin
guava die Guave
guest der Gast
guesthouse die Pension
guide *m/f* (tour guide) der

Fremdenführer/die Fremdenführerin
guidebook der Reiseführer
guided tour die Führung
guitar die Gitarre
gun die Waffe
gym das Fitnesscenter
gym shoes die Turnschuhe
gynaecologist der Gynäkologe/die Gynäkologin, der Frauenarzt/die Frauenärztin

H

haemorrhoids die Hämorrhoiden
hail der Hagel
hair die Haare
hairbrush die Haarbürste
haircut der Haarschnitt
hairdresser der Friseur
hairdryer der Föhn
hair dye die Tönung
hair gel das Haargel
hairgrip die Haarklemme
hair spray das Haarspray
half halb
a half bottle eine kleine Flasche
half an hour eine halbe Stunde
half board die Halbpension
half fare der halbe Fahrpreis
half price der halbe Preis
ham der Schinken
(cooked) der Kochschinken
(cured) der geräucherte Schinken
hamburger der Hamburger
hammer der Hammer
hand die Hand
handbag die Handtasche
handbrake die Handbremse
hand-made handgearbeitet
handicapped behindert
handkerchief das Taschentuch
handle der Griff
handlebars der Lenker
hand luggage das Handgepäck
hands-free kit (for phone) die Freisprecheinrichtung
hands-free phone das Telefon mit Freisprechanlage

handsome gut aussehend
hang gliding das Drachenfliegen
hangover der Kater
to hang up auflegen
to happen passieren
what happened? was ist passiert?
happy glücklich
happy birthday! alles Gute zum Geburtstag!
harbour der Hafen
hard (difficult) schwierig
(not soft) hart
hard drive die Festplatte
to harm schädigen
harvest die Ernte
hat der Hut
to have haben
I have... ich habe...
we have... wir haben...
do you have...? haben Sie...?
to have to müssen
hay fever der Heuschnupfen
he er

head der Kopf
headache die Kopfschmerzen
I have a headache ich habe Kopfschmerzen
headlights die Scheinwerfer
headphones die Kopfhörer
health die Gesundheit
health food shop das Reformhaus
healthy gesund
to hear hören
hearing aid das Hörgerät
heart das Herz
heart attack der Herzinfarkt
heartburn das Sodbrennen
to heat up (food, milk) aufwärmen
heater das Heizgerät
(radiator) der Heizkörper
heating die Heizung
heavy schwer
heel der Absatz
heel bar der Schuhreparatur-Service
(shoemaker) der Schuster
height die Höhe
helicopter der Hubschrauber

hello hallo
helmet (for bike) der Schutzhelm
help! Hilfe!
to help helfen
hem der Saum
hepatitis die Hepatitis
her (with der words) ihr
(with das words) ihr
(with die words) ihre
to her zu ihr
herbal tea der Kräutertee
herbs die Kräuter
here hier
here is... hier ist...
hernia der Eingeweidebruch
hi! hallo!
to hide verstecken
high hoch
(number, speed) groß
high blood pressure der hohe Blutdruck
high chair der Kinderstuhl
high tide die Flut
hill der Hügel
hill-walking das Bergwandern
him ihm
hip die Hüfte
hip replacement die künstliche Hüfte
hire die Vermietung
bike hire die Fahrradvermietung
boat hire der Bootsverleih
car hire die Autovermietung
ski hire der Skiverleih
to hire mieten
hire car das Mietauto
his (with der words) sein
(with das words) sein
(with die words) seine
historic historisch
history die Geschichte
to hit schlagen
to hitchhike trampen
hobby das Hobby
to hold halten
to contain enthalten
hold-up (traffic jam) der Stau
hole das Loch

holiday der Feiertag
holidays der Urlaub
on holiday in den Ferien
home das Zuhause
at home zu Hause
homeopathic (remedy, etc)
 homöopathisch
homeopathy die Homöopathie
homepage die Homepage
homesick (to be) Heimweh haben
I'm homesick ich habe Heimweh
homosexual homosexuell
honest ehrlich
honey der Honig
honeymoon die Flitterwochen
hood (of jacket) die Kapuze
hook der Haken
to hope hoffen
I hope so hoffentlich
I hope not hoffentlich nicht
horn (car) die Hupe
hors d'œuvre die Vorspeise
horse das Pferd
horse racing das Pferderennen
to horse ride reiten
hosepipe der Schlauch
hospital das Krankenhaus
hostel das Wohnheim
(youth hostel) die Jugendherberge
hot heiß
I'm hot mir ist heiß
it's hot (weather) es ist heiß
hot-water bottle die Wärmflasche
hotel das Hotel
hour die Stunde
1 hour eine Stunde
2 hours zwei Stunden
half an hour eine halbe Stunde
house das Haus
housewife/-husband die Hausfrau/
der Hausmann
house wine der Hauswein
housework die Hausarbeit
how wie
how are you? wie geht es Ihnen?
how many? wie viele?
how much? wie viel?

hungry hungrig
to hunt jagen
hunting permit die Jagderlaubnis
hurry: *I'm in a hurry* ich habe es eilig
to hurt (be painful) wehtun
my back hurts mir tut der Rücken weh
that hurts das tut weh
husband der Mann
hut (beach) der Strandkorb
(mountain) die Hütte
hypodermic needle die Spritze

I

I ich
ice das Eis
with/without ice mit/ohne Eis
ice box die Kühlbox
ice cream das Eis
ice cube der Eiswürfel
ice rink die Eisbahn
to ice-skate Schlittschuh laufen
ice skates die Schlittschuhe
iced: *iced coffee* der Eiskaffee
iced tea der Eistee
idea die Idee
identity card der Personalausweis
if wenn
ignition die Zündung
ignition key der Zündschlüssel
ill krank
I'm ill ich bin krank
illness die Krankheit
immediately sofort
immersion heater der Boiler
immobilizer (on car) die
 Wegfahrsperre
immunisation die Immunisierung
to import importieren
important wichtig
impossible unmöglich
to improve verbessern
in in
in 2 hours in zwei Stunden
in Vienna in Wien
included inbegriffen
inconvenient unpassend
to increase vergrößern

indicator (in car) der Blinker
indigestion die Magenverstimmung
indigestion tablets die Magentabletten
indoors drinnen
infection die Infektion
infectious ansteckend
information die Auskunft
information desk der Informationsschalter
information office das Informationsbüro
ingredients die Zutaten
inhaler (for medication) der Inhalationsapparat
injection die Spritze
to injure verletzen
injured (person) verletzt
injury die Verletzung
ink die Tinte
inn das Gasthaus
inner tube der Schlauch
inquiries die Auskunft
134 **inquiry desk** der Auskunftsschalter
insect das Insekt
insect bite der Insektenstich
insect repellent das Insektenschutzmittel
inside in
instant coffee der Pulverkaffee
instead of anstelle von
insulin das Insulin
insurance die Versicherung
to insure versichern
insured versichert
to intend to vorhaben
interesting interessant
international international (arrivals, departures) Ausland
internet das Internet
internet access: do you have internet access? haben Sie Internetanschluss?
internet café das Internetcafé
interpreter der Dolmetscher/ die Dolmetscherin
interval die Pause

into in
into town in die Stadt
into the centre ins Zentrum
to introduce vorstellen
invitation die Einladung
to invite einladen
invoice die Rechnung
iPod® der iPod
Ireland Irland
Irish adj irisch
Irishman/woman der Ire/die Irin
iron (for clothes) das Bügeleisen (metal) das Eisen
to iron bügeln
ironing board das Bügelbrett
ironmonger's die Eisenwarenhandlung
is ist
island die Insel
it er/sie/es
Italian adj italienisch m/f der Italiener/die Italienerin
Italy Italien
to itch jucken
item das Ding
IUD das Intrauterinpessar; die Spirale

J

jack (for car) der Wagenheber
jacket die Jacke
jacuzzi der Whirlpool
jam (food) die Marmelade
jammed blockiert
January der Januar
jar (honey, jam, etc) das Glas
jaundice die Gelbsucht
jaw der Kiefer
jealous eifersüchtig
jeans die Jeans
jellyfish die Qualle
jet ski der Jetski
jetty die Mole
Jew der Jude/die Jüdin
jeweller's der Juwelier
jewellery der Schmuck
Jewish jüdisch
job (employment) die Stelle

to jog joggen
to join (club) beitreten
to join in mitmachen
joint (of body) das Gelenk
to joke scherzen
joke der Witz
journalist der Journalist/die Journalistin
journey die Reise
judge der Richter/die Richterin
jug der Krug
juice der Saft
carton of juice der Saftkarton
July der Juli
to jump springen
jumper der Pullover
jump leads (for car) das Starthilfekabel
junction (road) die Kreuzung
June der Juni
just: *just two* nur zwei
I've just arrived ich bin gerade angekommen

K

to keep (retain) behalten
kettle der Wasserkocher
key der Schlüssel
keycard die Schlüsselkarte
keyring der Schlüsselring
to kick (ball) schießen
(person) treten
kidneys die Nieren
to kill töten
kilo das Kilo
kilometre der Kilometer
kind (person) nett
(sort) die Art
kiosk der Kiosk
kiss der Kuss
to kiss küssen
kitchen die Küche
kitchen paper das Küchenpapier
kite der Drachen
kiwi fruit die Kiwi
knee das Knie
kneehighs die Kniestrümpfe
knickers der Slip

knife das Messer
to knit stricken
to knock stoßen
to knock down (in car) überfahren
to knock over (object) umstoßen
knot der Knoten
to know (facts) wissen
(be acquainted with) kennen
I don't know ich weiß nicht
to know how to können
kosher koscher

L

label das Schild
lace (shoe) der Schnürsenkel
ladder die Leiter
ladies' (toilet) die Damentoilette
lady die Dame
lager das helle Bier
bottled lager das Flaschenbier
draught lager das Fassbier
lake der See
lamb das Lammfleisch
lamp (for table) die Lampe
to land landen
landlady die Vermieterin
landline (phone) das Festnetz
landlord der Vermieter
landslide der Erdrutsch
lane die Gasse
(of motorway/road) die Spur
language die Sprache
language school die Sprachenschule
laptop der Laptop
laptop bag die Laptop-Tasche
large groß
last (final) letzte(r/s)
last night gestern Abend
last time letztes Mal
the last bus der letzte Bus
late spät
the train is late der Zug hat Verspätung
later später
to laugh lachen
launderette der Waschsalon
laundry service der Wäschereiservice

lavatory die Toilette
law das Gesetz
lawn der Rasen
lawyer der Rechtsanwalt/die
  Rechtsanwältin
laxative das Abführmittel
layby die Haltebucht
lazy faul
lead (metal) das Blei
to lead führen
lead-free bleifrei
leaf das Blatt
leak (of gas, liquid) das Leck
to leak: *it's leaking* es hat ein Leck
to learn lernen
**learning disability: *he/she has a
  learning disability*** er/sie hat eine
  Lernschwäche
lease (rental) der Mietvertrag
leather das Leder
to leave (a place)
  weggehen/wegfahren
when does the train leave? wann
  fährt der Zug ab?
leek der Lauch
left: *on the left* links
to the left nach links
left-luggage locker das Schließfach
left-luggage office die
  Gepäckaufbewahrung
leg das Bein
lemon die Zitrone
lemongrass das Zitonengras
lemon tea der Zitronentee
lemonade die Limonade
to lend leihen
length (size) die Länge
  (duration) die Dauer
lens die Linse
lenses (contact) die Kontaktlinsen
lesbian lesbisch
less weniger
less than weniger als
lesson die Unterrichtsstunde
to let (to allow) erlauben
  (room, house) vermieten
letter (written) der Brief

(of alphabet) der Buchstabe
letterbox der Briefkasten
lettuce der Kopfsalat
library die Bibliothek
lid der Deckel
lie (untruth) die Lüge
to lie down sich hinlegen
lifebelt der Rettungsring
lifeboat das Rettungsboot
lifeguard der Rettungsschwimmer/
  die Rettungsschwimmerin
life insurance die Lebensversicherung
life jacket die Schwimmweste
life raft die Rettungsinsel
lift (elevator) der Aufzug
can I have a lift? können Sie mich
  mitnehmen?
lift pass der Liftpass
light (not heavy) leicht
light das Licht
have you a light? haben Sie Feuer?
light bulb die Glühbirne
lighter das Feuerzeug
lighthouse der Leuchtturm
lightning der Blitz
like (preposition) wie
to like mögen
I don't like... ich mag ... nicht
I like coffee ich trinke gern Kaffee
we'd like... wir möchten...
lilo® die Luftmatratze
lime (fruit) die Limone
line (row, of railway) die Linie
  (telephone) die Leitung
linen das Leinen
lingerie die Unterwäsche
lips die Lippen
lip-reading das Lippenlesen
lipstick der Lippenstift
liqueur der Likör
list die Liste
to listen to zuhören
litre der Liter
litre of milk ein Liter Milch
litter (rubbish) der Abfall
little (small) klein
a little... ein bisschen...

to live (exist) leben
(reside) wohnen
I live in London ich wohne in London
liver die Leber
living room das Wohnzimmer
loaf of bread das Brot
local (wine, speciality) hiesig
lock das Schloss
to lock zuschließen
locker (luggage) das Schließfach
locksmith der Schlosser
log (for fire) der Holzscheit
log book (car) die Zulassung
(vehicle registration document) die (Kfz)
  Zulassung
long lang
for a long time lange Zeit
long-sighted weitsichtig
to look after sich kümmern um
to look at anschauen
to look for suchen
loose (screw, tooth) locker
it's come loose es hat sich gelockert
lorry der Lastwagen
to lose verlieren
lost (object) verloren
I've lost my wallet ich habe meine
  Brieftasche verloren
I'm lost (on foot) ich habe mich
  verlaufen
(in car) ich habe mich verfahren
lost property office das Fundbüro
lot: *a lot* viel
lotion die Lotion
lottery das Lotto
loud laut
loudspeaker der Lautsprecher
lounge (hotel/airport) die Lounge
(in house) das Wohnzimmer
love die Liebe
to love lieben
I love you ich liebe dich
I love swimming ich schwimme gern
lovely schön
low niedrig
low-alcohol alkoholarm
low-fat fettarm

low tide die Ebbe
luck das Glück
lucky glücklich
luggage das Gepäck
luggage rack die Gepäckablage
luggage tag der Kofferanhänger
luggage trolley der Gepäckwagen
lump (swelling) die Beule
lunch das Mittagessen
lunch break die Mittagspause
lung die Lunge
luxury der Luxus

M

machine die Maschine
mad verrückt
magazine die Zeitschrift
magnet der Magnet
magnifying glass die Lupe
maid (in hotel) das Zimmermädchen
maiden name der Mädchenname
mail die Post
by mail per Post
main (principal) Haupt-
main course (of meal) das
  Hauptgericht
main road die Hauptstraße
to make machen
(meal) zubereiten
make-up das Make-up
male männlich
man der Mann
men die Männer
manager der Geschäftsführer/die
  Geschäftsführerin
mango die Mango
manicure die Maniküre
manual (gear change) das
  Schaltgetriebe
many viele
map die Karte
(of region, country) die Landkarte
(of town) der Stadtplan
March der März
margarine die Margarine
marina der Jachthafen
mark (stain) der Fleck

market der Markt
market place der Marktplatz
marmalade die Orangenmarmelade
married verheiratet
are you married? sind Sie verheiratet?
I'm married ich bin verheiratet
to marry heiraten
mascara die Wimperntusche
mass (in church) die Messe
massage die Massage
mast der Mast
matches die Streichhölzer
material das Material
matter: *it doesn't matter* das macht nichts
what's the matter? was ist los?
mattress die Matratze
May der Mai
mayonnaise die Mayonnaise
maximum das Maximum
Mb (megabyte) MB
me (direct object) mich
(indirect object) mir

meal das Essen
to mean bedeuten
what does this mean? was bedeutet das?
measles die Masern
to measure messen
meat das Fleisch
I don't eat meat ich esse kein Fleisch
mechanic der Mechaniker/die Mechanikerin
medical insurance die Krankenversicherung
medical treatment die medizinische Behandlung
medicine die Medizin
medieval mittelalterlich
medium rare (meat) halb durch
to meet (by chance) treffen
(arranged) sich treffen mit
pleased to meet you! sehr erfreut!
meeting das Treffen
(business) die Besprechung
megabyte das Megabyte
128 megabytes 128 Megabyte

megahertz das Megahertz
melon die Melone
to melt schmelzen
member (of club, etc) das Mitglied
memory das Gedächtnis
memory card die Speicherkarte
memory stick der Memorystick
men die Männer
to mend reparieren
meningitis die Hirnhautentzündung
menu die Speisekarte
set menu die Tageskarte
message die Nachricht
metal das Metall
meter der Zähler
metre der Meter
metro die U-Bahn
metro station die U-Bahn-Station
micro-brewery die Hausbrauerei
microphone das Mikrofon
microwave oven die Mikrowelle
midday der Mittag
at midday am Mittag
middle die Mitte
middle-aged in den mittleren Jahren
midge die Mücke
midnight die Mitternacht
at midnight um Mitternacht
migraine die Migräne
I have a migraine ich habe Migräne
mile die Meile
milk die Milch
fresh milk die Frischmilch
full cream milk die Vollfettmilch
hot milk heiße Milch
long-life milk die H-Milch
powdered milk das Milchpulver
semi-skimmed milk die Halbfettmilch
skimmed milk die Magermilch
soya milk die Sojamilch
with/without milk mit/ohne Milch
millimetre der Millimeter
mince (meat) das Hackfleisch
mind: *do you mind if...?* haben Sie etwas dagegen, wenn...?
I don't mind es ist mir egal
mineral water das Mineralwasser

minibar die Minibar
minidisk die Minidisk
minimum das Minimum
minister (church) der Pfarrer/die Pfarrerin
(political) der Minister/die Ministerin
mint (herb) die Minze
(sweet) das Pfefferminzbonbon
minute die Minute
mirror der Spiegel
miscarriage die Fehlgeburt
to miss (train, etc) verpassen
Miss Fräulein
missing (object) verschwunden
my son's missing mein Sohn ist weg
mistake der Fehler
misty dunstig
misunderstanding das Missverständnis
to mix mischen
mixer der Mixer
mobile (phone) das Handy
mobile number die Handynummer
mobile phone charger das Handy-Ladegerät
modem das Modem
modern modern
moisturizer die Feuchtigkeitscreme
mole (on skin) das Muttermal
moment: *just a moment* einen Moment, bitte
monastery das Kloster
Monday der Montag
money das Geld
I have no money ich habe kein Geld
moneybelt die Gürteltasche
money order die Postanweisung
monitor der Monitor
month der Monat
last month letzten Monat
next month nächsten Monat
this month diesen Monat
monthly monatlich
monument das Denkmal
moon der Mond
mooring der Anlegeplatz
mop (floor) der Mopp

moped das Moped
more mehr
more than mehr als
more wine noch etwas Wein
morning der Morgen
in the morning am Morgen
this morning heute Morgen
morning-after pill die Pille danach
mosque die Moschee
mosquito die Stechmücke
mosquito net das Moskitonetz
mosquito repellent das Insektenschutzmittel
most: *most of* das meiste von
moth (clothes) die Motte
mother die Mutter
mother-in-law die Schwiegermutter
motor der Motor
motorbike das Motorrad
motorboat das Motorboot
motorway die Autobahn
mould der Schimmel
mountain der Berg
mountain bike das Mountainbike
mountain biking das Mountainbiking
mountain rescue die Bergwacht
mountaineering das Bergsteigen
mouse (also computer) die Maus
moustache der Schnurrbart
mouth der Mund
to move bewegen
it isn't moving es bewegt sich nicht
movie der Kinofilm
to mow mähen
MP3 player der MP3-Spieler
Mr Herr
Mrs Frau
Ms Frau
much viel
too much zu viel
muddy schlammig
mugging der Überfall
mumps der Mumps
Munich München
muscle der Muskel
museum das Museum
mushrooms die Pilze

music die Musik
musical das Musical
mussel die Muschel
must müssen
I must ich muss
we must wir müssen
you musn't du darfst nicht
mustard der Senf
my (with der words) mein
(with das words) mein
(with die words) meine

N

nail (fingernail) der Fingernagel
(metal) der Nagel
nailbrush die Nagelbürste
nail file die Nagelfeile
nail polish/varnish der Nagellack
nail polish remover der
  Nagellackentferner
nail scissors die Nagelschere
name der Name
what is your name? wie ist Ihr Name?
nanny das Kindermädchen
napkin die Serviette
nappy die Windel
narrow eng
national national
nationality die Nationalität
natural natürlich
nature die Natur
nature reserve das Naturschutzgebiet
navy blue marineblau
near (place, time) nahe
near the bank in der Nähe der Bank
is it near? ist es in der Nähe?
necessary notwendig
neck der Hals
necklace die Halskette
nectarine die Nektarine
to need brauchen
I need... ich brauche...
we need... wir brauchen...
I need to go ich muss gehen
needle die Nadel
needle and thread Nadel und Faden
neighbour der Nachbar/die Nachbarin

nephew der Neffe
net das Netz
the Net das Internet
neutral (car) der Leerlauf
in neutral im Leerlauf
never nie
I never drink wine Wein trinke ich nie
new neu
news die Nachrichten
newsagent's der Zeitungsladen
newspaper die Zeitung
newsstand der Zeitungskiosk
New Year (1 Jan) Neujahr
happy New Year! ein gutes neues Jahr!
New Year's Eve Silvester
New Zealand Neuseeland
next nächste(r/s)
next to neben
next week nächste Woche
the next bus der nächste Bus
nice (person) nett
(place, holiday) schön
niece die Nichte
night die Nacht
at night am Abend
last night gestern Abend
per night pro Nacht
tonight heute Abend
night club der Nachtklub
nightdress das Nachthemd
no nein
no problem kein Problem
no thanks nein danke
(without) ohne
no ice ohne Eis
no sugar ohne Zucker
nobody niemand
noise der Lärm
noisy laut
it's very noisy es ist sehr laut
non-alcoholic alkoholfrei
none keine(r/s)
non-smoker der Nichtraucher
non-smoking Nichtraucher-
north der Norden
Northern Ireland Nordirland
North Sea die Nordsee

nose die Nase
not nicht
I do not know ich weiß nicht
note (banknote) der Geldschein
(written) die Notiz
note pad der Notizblock
nothing nichts
nothing else nichts weiter
notice (sign) das Schild
novel der Roman
November der November
now jetzt
nowhere nirgends
nuclear nuklear
nudist beach der FKK-Strand
number die Zahl
number plate das Nummernschild
nurse die Krankenschwester/
der Krankenpfleger
nursery die Kinderbetreuung
nursery school die Vorschule
nut (to eat) die Nuss
(for bolt) die Schraubenmutter

O

oar das Ruder
oats der Hafer
to obtain erhalten
occupation (work) der Beruf
ocean der Ozean
October der Oktober
odd (strange) seltsam
of von
a glass of water ein Glas Wasser
made of... aus...
off (light, radio, etc) aus
(rotten) schlecht
office das Büro
off-season die Nebensaison
often oft
how often? wie oft?
oil das Öl
oil filter der Ölfilter
ointment die Salbe
OK okay
old alt
how old are you? wie alt sind Sie?

I'm... years old ich bin... Jahre alt
old-age pensioner der Rentner/
die Rentnerin
on (light, radio, etc) an
on auf
on the table auf dem Tisch
on time pünktlich
once einmal
at once sofort
onion die Zwiebel
only nur
open geöffnet
to open öffnen
opera die Oper
operation (surgical) die Operation
operator (phone) die Vermittlung
opposite gegenüber
opposite the bank gegenüber der
Bank
quite the opposite ganz im Gegenteil
optician's der Optiker
or oder
orange (colour) orange
orange (fruit) die Orange
orange juice der Orangensaft
orchestra das Orchester
order (in restaurant) die Bestellung
to order (food) bestellen
organic organisch
to organize organisieren
other: the other one der/die/das
andere
have you got any others? haben Sie
noch andere?
our (with der words) unser
(with das words) unser
(with die words) unsere
out (light, etc) aus
she's out sie ist nicht da
out of order kaputt
outdoor (pool, etc) im Freien
outside draußen
oven der Herd
ovenproof dish die feuerfeste Form
over (on top of, above) über
to overbook überbuchen
to overcharge zu viel berechnen

overdone (food) verkocht
overdose die Überdosis
to overheat überhitzen
to overload überladen
to oversleep verschlafen
to overtake überholen
to owe schulden
I owe you... ich schulde Ihnen...
you owe me... Sie schulden mir...
owner der Besitzer/die Besitzerin
oxygen der Sauerstoff

P

pace das Tempo
pacemaker der Herzschrittmacher
to pack (luggage) packen
package das Paket
package tour die Pauschalreise
packet das Paket
padded envelope der gefütterte
  Umschlag
paddling pool das Planschbecken
padlock das Vorhängeschloss

page die Seite
paid bezahlt
I've paid ich habe bezahlt
pain der Schmerz
painful schmerzhaft
painkiller das Schmerzmittel
to paint malen
painting (picture) das Bild
pair das Paar
palace der Palast
pale blass
palmtop computer der Palmtop
pan (saucepan) der Kochtopf
(frying pan) die Bratpfanne
pancake der Pfannkuchen
panniers (for bike) die Satteltaschen
panties die Unterhose
pants (underwear) der Slip
panty liner die Slipeinlage
paper das Papier
paper hankies die
  Papiertaschentücher
paper napkins die Papierservietten
paralysed gelähmt

paramedic (in ambulance) der
  Sanitäter/die Sanitäterin
parcel das Paket
pardon? wie bitte?
I beg your pardon! Entschuldigung!
parents die Eltern
park der Park
to park parken
parking disk die Parkscheibe
parking fine der Strafzettel
parking meter die Parkuhr
parking ticket (fine) der Strafzettel
(to display) der Parkschein
partner (business) der Geschäftspartner/
  die Geschäftspartnerin
(boy/girlfriend) der Partner/die Partnerin
party (celebration) die Party
(political) die Partei
pass der Pass
passenger der Passagier
passionfruit die Passionsfrucht
passport der Reisepass
passport control die Passkontrolle
password das Passwort
pasta die Nudeln
pastry der Teig
(cake) das Gebäck
path der Weg
patient (in hospital) der Patient/
  die Patientin
pavement der Bürgersteig
to pay zahlen
I'd like to pay ich möchte zahlen
where do I pay? wo kann ich
  bezahlen?
payment die Bezahlung
payphone das Münztelefon
PDA (Personal Digital Assistant) der
  PDA; der (elektronische) Organizer
peace der Frieden
peach der Pfirsich
peak rate der Höchsttarif
peanut allergy die Erdnussallergie
pear die Birne
pearls die Perlen
peas die Erbsen
pedal das Pedal

pedalo (pedal boat) das Tretboot
pedestrian der Fußgänger/
die Fußgängerin
pedestrian crossing der
Fußgängerübergang
to pee austreten
to peel (fruit) schälen
peg (clothes) die Wäscheklammer
(tent) der Hering
pen der Stift
pencil der Bleistift
penfriend der Brieffreund/die
Brieffreundin
penicillin das Penizillin
penis der Penis
penknife das Taschenmesser
pension die Rente
pensioner der Rentner/die Rentnerin
people die Leute
people carrier der Van
pepper (spice) der Pfeffer
(vegetable) die Paprikaschote
per pro
per day pro Tag
per hour pro Stunde
per person pro Person
perfect perfekt
performance die Vorstellung
perfume das Parfüm
perhaps vielleicht
period (menstruation) die Periode
perm die Dauerwelle
permit die Genehmigung
person die Person
personal organizer der Terminplaner
personal stereo der Walkman®
pet das Haustier
pet food das Tierfutter
pet shop die Zoohandlung
petrol das Benzin
petrol cap der Tankdeckel
petrol pump (at petrol station) die
Tanksäule
(in car) die Benzinpumpe
petrol station die Tankstelle
petrol tank der Tank
pharmacist der Apotheker/die

Apothekerin
pharmacy die Apotheke
to phone telefonieren
phone das Telefon
by phone per Telefon
phonebook das Telefonbuch
phonebox die Telefonzelle
phone call der Anruf
phonecard die Telefonkarte
photocopy die Fotokopie
I need a photocopy ich brauche eine
Fotokopie
to photocopy fotokopieren
photocopier das Kopiergerät
photograph das Foto
to take a photograph fotografieren
phrase book der Sprachführer
piano das Klavier
to pick (choose) auswählen
(pluck) pflücken
pickpocket der Taschendieb
picnic das Picknick
to have a picnic ein Picknick machen
picture (painting) das Bild
(photo) das Foto
pie (sweet) der Obstkuchen
(savoury) die Pastete
piece das Stück
pier die Pier
pig das Schwein
pill die Pille
to be on the Pill die Pille nehmen
pillow das Kopfkissen
pillowcase der Kopfkissenbezug
pilot der Pilot/die Pilotin
pin die Stecknadel
PIN number die Geheimzahl
pineapple die Ananas
pink rosa
pipe (smoker's) die Pfeife
(drain, etc) das Rohr
pitch (for tent/caravan) der Stellplatz
pity: *what a pity* wie schade
pizza die Pizza
place der Platz
place of birth der Geburtsort
plain (unflavoured) einfach

plait der Zopf
plane (airplane) das Flugzeug
plant die Pflanze
plaster (sticking) das Pflaster
(for broken limb) der Gips
plastic (made of) Plastik-
plastic bag der Plastikbeutel
plate der Teller
platform (at station) der Bahnsteig
which platform? welcher Bahnsteig?
play (theatre) das Stück
to play spielen
play area die Spielecke
playground der Spielplatz
play park der Spielplatz
playroom das Spielzimmer
please bitte
pleased erfreut
pleased to meet you sehr erfreut
pliers die Zange
plug (electrical) der Stecker
(in sink) der Stöpsel
to plug in einstecken
plum die Pflaume
plumber der Klempner
plumbing die Installationen
(water pipes) die Wasserleitungen
p.m. nachmittags
poached (egg, fish) pochiert
pocket die Tasche
points (in car) die
Unterbrecherkontakte
poison das Gift
poisonous giftig
police (force) die Polizei
policeman/woman der Polizist/
die Polizistin
police station das Polizeirevier
polish (shoe) die Schuhcreme
(furniture) die Möbelpolitur
pollen der Pollen
polluted verschmutzt
pony das Pony
pony trekking das Ponyreiten
pool der Swimmingpool
pool attendant der Bademeister
poor arm

pop socks die Kniestrümpfe
popular beliebt
pork das Schweinefleisch
port (seaport) der Hafen
porter (for door) der Portier
(station) der Gepäckträger
portion die Portion
portrait das Portrait
possible möglich
post: *by post* per Post
to post aufgeben
postbox der Briefkasten
postcard die Ansichtskarte
postcode die Postleitzahl
postman der Briefträger/die
Briefträgerin
post office das Postamt
poster das Poster
to postpone verschieben
pot (cooking) der Topf
potato die Kartoffel
baked potato die Folienkartoffel
boiled potatoes die Salzkartoffeln
fried potatoes die Bratkartoffeln
mashed potatoes das Kartoffelpüree
roast potatoes die Bratkartoffeln
sautéed potatoes die Röstkartoffeln
potato peeler der Kartoffelschäler
potato salad der Kartoffelsalat
pothole das Schlagloch
pottery die Töpferwaren
pound das Pfund
to pour eingießen
powder: *in powder form*
pulverförmig
powdered milk die Trockenmilch
power (electricity) der Strom
power cut der Stromausfall
pram der Kinderwagen
to pray beten
to prefer vorziehen
pregnant schwanger
I'm pregnant ich bin schwanger
to prepare vorbereiten
to prescribe verschreiben
prescription das Rezept
present (gift) das Geschenk

president der Präsident
pressure: *tyre pressure* der Reifendruck
blood pressure der Blutdruck
pretty hübsch
price der Preis
price list die Preisliste
priest der Priester
print (photo) der Abzug
printer der Drucker
printout der Ausdruck
to print out ausdrucken
prison das Gefängnis
private privat
prize der Preis
probably wahrscheinlich
problem das Problem
professor der Professor/die Professorin
programme das Programm
prohibited verboten
to promise versprechen
to pronounce aussprechen
how's it pronounced? wie spricht man das aus?
protein das Eiweiß
Protestant protestantisch
to provide zur Verfügung stellen
public öffentlich
public holiday der gesetzliche Feiertag
pudding die Nachspeise
to pull ziehen
to pull a muscle sich einen Muskel zerren
to pull over (car) anhalten
pullover der Pullover
pump (bike, etc) die Luftpumpe (in petrol station) die Tanksäule
puncture die Reifenpanne
puncture repair kit das Reifenflickzeug
puppet die Puppe
puppet show das Puppenspiel
purple violett
purpose der Zweck
on purpose absichtlich
purse der Geldbeutel
to push stoßen

pushchair der Kinderwagen
to put (place) stellen
to put back verschieben
pyjamas der Pyjama

Q

quality die Qualität
quantity die Quantität
quarantine die Quarantäne
to quarrel streiten
quarter das Viertel
quay der Kai
queen die Königin
query die Frage
question die Frage
queue die Schlange
to queue anstehen
quick(ly) schnell
quiet ruhig
quilt die Bettdecke
quite (rather) ziemlich
it's quite expensive es ist ziemlich teuer
it's quite good es ist ganz gut
quiz show das Quiz

R

rabbit das Kaninchen
rabies die Tollwut
race das Rennen
race course die Rennbahn
racquet der Schläger
radiator (car) der Kühler (heater) der Heizkörper
radio das Radio
radishes die Radieschen
raft das Floß
railcard die Bahncard
railway die Eisenbahn
railway station der Bahnhof
rain der Regen
to rain regnen
it's raining es regnet
raincoat der Regenmantel
raisins die Rosinen
rake die Harke
rape die Vergewaltigung

to rape vergewaltigen
rare (unique) selten
(steak) blutig
raspberry die Himbeere
rash (skin) der Ausschlag
rate (price) der Preis
rate of exchange der Wechselkurs
raw roh
razor der Rasierapparat
razor blades die Rasierklingen
to read lesen
ready fertig
to get ready sich fertig machen
real echt
to realize erkennen
rearview mirror der Rückspiegel
receipt die Quittung
receiver der Hörer
reception (desk) der Empfang;
die Rezeption
receptionist der Empfangschef/
die Empfangsdame
to recharge (battery) wieder aufladen
recipe das Rezept
to recognize erkennen
to recommend empfehlen
to record aufnehmen
to recover genesen
to recycle recyceln
red rot
to reduce reduzieren
reduction die Ermäßigung
refund die Rückerstattung
to refund rückerstatten
to refuse ablehnen
region das Gebiet
to register (at hotel) sich anmelden
registered letter das Einschreiben
registration form das
Anmeldeformular
to reimburse entschädigen
relation (family) der/die Verwandte
to remain (to stay) bleiben
to remember sich erinnern
I don't remember ich kann mich nicht
erinnern
remote control die Fernbedienung

to remove entfernen
rent die Miete
to rent mieten
repair die Reparatur
to repair reparieren
to repeat wiederholen
to reply antworten
report der Bericht
to report berichten
request die Bitte
to request erbitten
to require benötigen
to rescue retten
reservation die Reservierung; die
Buchung
to reserve reservieren; buchen
reserved reserviert
residence permit die
Aufenthaltsgenehmigung
rest (repose) die Ruhe
(remainder) der Rest
to rest ruhen
restaurant das Restaurant
restaurant car der Speisewagen
retired pensioniert
to return (in car) zurückfahren
(on foot) zurückgehen
(return something) zurückgeben
return ticket (train) die Rückfahrkarte
(plane) das Rückflugticket
to reverse (car) rückwärts fahren
to reverse the charges ein
R-Gespräch führen
reverse charge call das R-Gespräch
reverse gear der Rückwärtsgang
rheumatism der Rheumatismus
rib die Rippe
ribbon das Band
rice der Reis
rich (person) reich
(food) reichhaltig
to ride (horse) reiten
right (correct) richtig
right: on the right rechts
to the right nach rechts
right of way die Vorfahrt
ring der Ring

to ring klingeln
it's ringing es klingelt
to ring someone jemanden anrufen
ripe reif
river der Fluss
road die Straße
road map die Straßenkarte
road sign das Straßenschild
roast der Rostbraten
roll (bread) das Brötchen
roller blades die Rollerblades
romantic romantisch
roof das Dach
roof-rack der Dachgepäckträger
room (in house, hotel) das Zimmer
(space) der Platz
double room das Doppelzimmer
family room das Familienzimmer
single room das Einzelzimmer
room number die Zimmernummer
room service der Zimmerservice
root die Wurzel
rope das Seil
rose (flower) die Rose
rotten (fruit, etc) verfault
round rund
roundabout (traffic) der Kreisverkehr
row (in theatre, etc) die Reihe
to row (boat) rudern
rowing (sport) das Rudern
rubber (eraser) der Radiergummi
(material) das Gummi
rubber gloves die Gummihandschuhe
rubbish der Abfall
rubella die Röteln
rucksack der Rucksack
ruin (eg castle) die Ruine
ruler (measuring) das Lineal
to run rennen
rush hour die Hamptverkehrszeit
rusty rostig
rye bread das Roggenbrot

S

sad traurig
saddle der Sattel
safe (for valuables) der Safe

safe ungefährlich
is it safe? ist das ungefährlich?
safety die Sicherheit
safety belt der Sicherheitsgurt
safety pin die Sicherheitsnadel
sail das Segel
to sail segeln
sailboard das Segelbrett
sailing (sport) das Segeln
sailing boat das Segelboot
salad der Salat
green salad grüner Salat
mixed salad gemischter Salat
potato salad der Kartoffelsalat
tomato salad der Tomatensalat
salad dressing die Salatsoße
salary das Gehalt
sale (in general) der Verkauf
(seasonal bargains) der Schlussverkauf
salesperson der Verkäufer/die
  Verkäuferin
salt das Salz
salt water das Salzwasser
salty salzig
same gleich
sand der Sand
sandals die Sandalen
sandwich das Sandwich
sanitary pad die Damenbinde
satellite dish die Satellitenschüssel
satellite TV das Satellitenfernsehen
satnav (satellite navigation system, for
  car) das Satnav
Saturday der Samstag
sauce die Soße
tomato sauce die Tomatensoße
saucepan der Kochtopf
sauna die Sauna
sausage die Wurst
to save (person) retten
(money) sparen
savoury pikant
to say sagen
scales die Waage
to scan einscannen
scarf (headscarf) das Kopftuch
(round neck) das Halstuch

scenery die Landschaft
schedule der Plan
school die Schule
primary school die Grundschule
secondary school die Oberschule
scissors die Schere
score der Endstand
Scot der Schotte/die Schottin
Scotland Schottland
Scottish schottisch
screen der Bildschirm
screen wash das Scheibenputzmittel
screw die Schraube
screwdriver der Schraubenzieher
search engine die Suchmaschine
security die Sicherheit
security check die Sicherheitskontrolle
sedative das Beruhigungsmittel
to see sehen
to select auswählen
selection die Auswahl
self-catering für Selbstversorger
self-employed freiberuflich
self-service die Selbstbedienung
to sell verkaufen
do you sell...? verkaufen Sie...?
sell-by date das Haltbarkeitsdatum
Sellotape® der Tesafilm®
to send schicken
senior citizen der Rentner/die Rentnerin
separated (couple) getrennt
September der September
septic tank die Klärgrube
serious schlimm
to serve (dish) servieren
service (in shop, etc) die Bedienung
is service included? ist die Bedienung inbegriffen?
service station die Raststätte
set menu die Tageskarte
settee das Sofa
several verschiedene
to sew nähen
sex das Geschlecht
(intercourse) der Sex

shade der Schatten
in the shade im Schatten
to shake schütteln
shallow (water) seicht
shampoo das Shampoo
shampoo and set Waschen und Föhnen
to share teilen
sharp scharf
to shave rasieren
shaver der Rasierapparat
she sie
sheep das Schaf
sheet (on bed) das Betttuch
shell (seashell) die Muschel
(egg, nut) die Schale
sheltered geschützt
to shine scheinen
shingles die Gürtelrose
ship das Schiff
shirt das Hemd
shock der Schock
shock absorber der Stoßdämpfer
shoe der Schuh
shoelaces die Schnürsenkel
shoe polish die Schuhcreme
shoe shop der Schuhladen
shop der Laden
to shop einkaufen
shop assistant der Verkäufer/die Verkäuferin
shopping das Einkaufen
to go shopping einkaufen gehen
shopping centre das Einkaufszentrum
shore das Ufer
short kurz
shortage der Mangel
short circuit der Kurzschluss
shortcut die Abkürzung
shorts die Shorts
short-sighted kurzsichtig
shoulder die Schulter
to shout rufen
show (theatrical) die Aufführung
to show zeigen
shower (bath) die Dusche

(of rain) der Schauer
shower cap die Duschhaube
shower gel das Duschgel
to shrink einlaufen
shut (closed) geschlossen
to shut schließen
shutter (on window) der Fensterladen
sick (ill) krank
(nauseous) übel
I feel sick mir ist schlecht
sick bag die Spucktüte
side die Seite
side dish die Beilage
sidelight das Standlicht
sidewalk der Bürgersteig
sight die Sehenswürdigkeit
sightseeing tour die Besichtigungstour
sign (notice) das Schild
to sign unterschreiben
signal das Signal
there's no signal (mobil phone) ich bekomme kein Signal
signature die Unterschrift
signpost der Wegweiser
silk die Seide
silver das Silber
to sing singen
single (unmarried) ledig
(not double) Einzel
(ticket) einfach
single bed das Einzelbett
single room das Einzelzimmer
sink (kitchen) das Spülbecken
sister die Schwester
sister-in-law die Schwägerin
to sit sitzen
sit down please! bitte setzen Sie sich!
site (website) die Website
SIM card die SIM-Karte
size (clothes, shoes) die Größe
to skate (on ice) Schlittschuh laufen
skates (ice) die Schlittschuhe
(roller) die Rollschuhe
skateboard das Skateboard
skating rink die Eisbahn
ski der Ski

to ski Ski fahren
ski boots die Skistiefel
skiing das Skilaufen
ski instructor der Skilehrer/die Skilehrerin
ski jump die Sprungschanze
ski lift der Skilift
ski pants die Skihose
ski pass der Skipass
ski run/piste die Abfahrt
ski stick/pole der Skistock
ski suit der Skianzug
skin die Haut
skirt der Rock
sky der Himmel
sledge der Schlitten
to sleep schlafen
to sleep in verschlafen
to sleep late ausschlafen
sleeper (on train) der Schlafwagen
sleeping bag der Schlafsack
sleeping car der Schlafwagen
sleeping mat die Isomatte
sleeping pills die Schlaftabletten
slice die Scheibe
slide (photograph) das Dia
to slip rutschen
slippers die Hausschuhe
slow(ly) langsam
to slow down langsamer werden
small klein
smaller than kleiner als
smell der Geruch
(unpleasant) der Gestank
to smell riechen
smile das Lächeln
to smile lächeln
smoke der Rauch
to smoke rauchen
I don't smoke ich bin Nichtraucher(in)
smoke alarm der Feuermelder
smoked (food) geräuchert
smokers (sign) Raucher
smooth weich
SMS message die SMS
snack der Snack
to have a snack einen Imbiss essen

snack bar die Snackbar
snake die Schlange
snake bite der Schlangenbiss
to sneeze niesen
snorkel der Schnorchel
snorkelling des Schnorcheln
snow der Schnee
to snow: *it's snowing* es schneit
to snowboard Snowboard fahren
snow chains die Schneeketten
snow tyres die Winterreifen
snowed up eingeschneit
soap die Seife
soap powder das Waschmittel
socket die Steckdose
socks die Socken
soda water das Soda
sofa das Sofa
sofa bed das Sofabett
soft weich
soft drink das alkoholfreie Getränk
soldier der Soldat
sole (of shoe) die Sohle

150 **soluble** löslich
some einige
someone irgendjemand
something etwas
son der Sohn
son-in-law der Schwiegersohn
song das Lied
soon bald
as soon as possible so bald wie
  möglich
sore throat die Halsschmerzen
sorry: *I'm sorry!* tut mir leid!
sort die Sorte
what sort? welche Sorte?
soup die Suppe
sour sauer
soured cream die saure Sahne
south der Süden
souvenir das Souvenir
spa das Bad
space der Platz
spade der Spaten
Spain Spanien
spam (e-mail) der Spam

Spanish *adj* spanisch
spanner der Schraubenschlüssel
spare parts die Ersatzteile
spare room das Gästezimmer
spare tyre der Ersatzreifen
spare wheel das Ersatzrad
sparkling perlend
sparkling water das Sprudelwasser
sparkling wine der Sekt
spark plugs die Zündkerzen
to speak sprechen
do you speak English? sprechen Sie
  Englisch?
speaker (loudspeaker) der
  Lautsprecher; die Box
special speziell
special needs: *people with special
  needs* Behinderte
special offer das Sonderangebot
specialist der Spezialist/die Spezialistin
speciality die Spezialität
speed die Geschwindigkeit
speed limit die Geschwindigkeitsbegrenzung
to exceed the speed limit die
  Geschwindigkeitsbegrenzung
  überschreiten
speedometer der Tachometer
to spell: *how's it spelt?* wie
  buchstabiert man das?
to spend ausgeben
SPF (sun protection factor) LSF (or SF)
SPF 30 LSF (or SF) 30
spice das Gewürz
spicy würzig
to spill verschütten
spinach der Spinat
spin dryer die Wäscheschleuder
spine das Rückgrat
splinter der Splitter
spoilt (child) verwühnt
sponge der Schwamm
spoon der Löffel
sport der Sport
sports centre das Fitnesscenter
sports shop das Sportgeschäft
spot der Fleck

sprain die Verstauchung
spring (season) der Frühling
(metal) die Feder
spring onions die Frühlingszwiebeln
square (in town) der Platz
squash (drink, game) das Squash
stadium das Stadion
staff das Personal
stain der Fleck
stairs die Treppe
stale (bread) trocken
stalls (in theatre) das Parkett
stamp die Briefmarke
to stand stehen
star der Stern
(film) der Star
to start (begin) anfangen
starter (in meal) die Vorspeise
(in car) der Anlasser
station der Bahnhof
stationer's die Schreibwarenhandlung
statue die Statue
stay der Aufenthalt
enjoy your stay! angenehmen
  Aufenthalt!
to stay (to remain) bleiben
steak das Steak
to steal stehlen
steamed gedünstet
steel der Stahl
steep steil
steeple der Kirchturm
step der Schritt
stepdaughter die Stieftochter
stepfather der Stiefvater
stepmother die Stiefmutter
stepson der Stiefsohn
stereo die Stereoanlage
sterling das Pfund Sterling
steward/stewardess der Steward/
die Stewardess
to stick (with glue) kleben
sticking plaster das Heftpflaster
still (yet) noch
(motionless) still
still water stilles Wasser
sting der Stachel

to sting stechen
stitches: *the wound needs stitches*
  die Wunde muss genäht werden
stock cube der Brühwürfel
stockings die Strümpfe
stolen gestohlen
stomach der Magen
stomach ache die Magenschmerzen
stone der Stein
stop (sign) das Stoppschild
to stop halten
stopover die Zwischenlandung
store (shop) das Geschäft
storey das Geschoss
storm der Sturm
story die Geschichte
straight away sofort
straight on geradeaus
strange (odd) seltsam
straw (for drinking) der Strohhalm
strawberries die Erdbeeren
stream der Bach
street die Straße
street map der Stadtplan
strength die Stärke
stress der Stress
strike (of workers) der Streik
string die Schnur
striped gestreift
stroke der Schlaganfall
to have a stroke einen Schlaganfall
  haben
strong stark
strong coffee starker Kaffee
strong tea starker Tee
stuck: *it's stuck* es klemmt
student der Student/die Studentin
student discount die
  Studentenermäßigung
stuffed gefüllt
stung gestochen
stupid dumm
subscription (fee) der Beitrag
subsidiary die Tochtergesellschaft
subtitles die Untertitel
subway (metro) die U-Bahn
suddenly plötzlich

suede das Wildleder
sugar der Zucker
sugar-free zuckerfrei
to suggest vorschlagen
suit (man's) der Anzug
(woman's) das Kostüm
suitcase der Koffer
sum die Summe
summer der Sommer
summer holidays die Sommerferien
summit der Gipfel
sun die Sonne
to sunbathe sonnenbaden
sunblock die Sonnencreme
sunburn der Sonnenbrand
suncream die Sonnencreme
Sunday der Sonntag
sunglasses die Sonnenbrille
sunny sonnig
sunrise der Sonnenaufgang
sunroof das Sonnendach
sunscreen das Sonnenschutzmittel
sunset der Sonnenuntergang
152 **sunshade** der Sonnenschirm
sunstroke der Sonnenstich
suntan die Sonnenbräune
suntan lotion das Sonnenöl
supermarket der Supermarkt
supper das Abendessen
supplement (to pay) der Zuschlag
to supply zur Verfügung stellen
sure: *I'm sure* ich bin mir sicher
to surf surfen
to surf the Net im Internet surfen
surfboard das Surfbrett
surgery die Operation
surname der Nachname
surprise die Überraschung
to survive überleben
suspension (in car) die Aufhängung
to swallow verschlucken
to sweat schwitzen
sweater der Pullover
sweatshirt das Sweatshirt
sweet (not savoury) süß
sweetener der Süßstoff
sweets die Süßigkeiten

to swell anschwellen
to swim schwimmen
swimming costume der Badeanzug
swimming pool das Schwimmbad
swimsuit der Badeanzug
swing (for children) die Schaukel
swipecard die Magnetkarte
Swiss *adj* schweizerisch
m/f der Schweizer/die Schweizerin
switch der Schalter
to switch off (light) ausschalten
(machine) abschalten
(gas, water) abstellen
to switch on (light, machine) einschalten
(gas, water) anstellen
Switzerland die Schweiz
swollen geschwollen
synagogue die Synagoge
syringe die Spritze

T

table der Tisch
tablecloth die Tischdecke
tablet (pill) die Tablette
table tennis das Tischtennis
table wine der Tafelwein
to take nehmen
(medicine) einnehmen
how long does it take? wie lange dauert es?
take-away food das Essen zum Mitnehmen
to take off abfliegen
talc der Körperpuder
to talk to sprechen mit
tall groß
tampons die Tampons
tangerine die Mandarine
tank (petrol) der Tank
(fish) das Aquarium
tap der Wasserhahn
tap water das Leitungswasser
tape die Kassette
tape measure das Maßband
target das Ziel
taste der Geschmack

to taste probieren
can I taste it? darf ich es probieren?
tax die Steuer
taxi das Taxi
taxi driver der Taxifahrer/die Taxifahrerin
taxi rank der Taxistand
tea der Tee
herbal tea Kräutertee
tea with milk Tee mit Milch
tea bag der Teebeutel
teapot die Teekanne
teaspoon der Teelöffel
tea towel das Geschirrtuch
to teach unterrichten
teacher der Lehrer/die Lehrerin
team das Team
tear (in material) der Riss
teat (on bottle) der Sauger
teenager der Teenager
teeth die Zähne
telegram das Telegramm
telephone das Telefon
to telephone telefonieren
telephone box die Telefonzelle
telephone call der Anruf
telephone card die Telefonkarte
telephone directory das Telefonbuch
telephone number die Telefonnummer
television das Fernsehen
to tell erzählen
temperature die Temperatur
to have a temperature Fieber haben
temporary provisorisch
tenant der Mieter
tendon die Sehne
tennis das Tennis
tennis ball der Tennisball
tennis court der Tennisplatz
tennis racket der Tennisschläger
tent das Zelt
tent peg der Hering
terminal das Terminal
terrace die Terrasse
to test testen

testicles die Hoden
tetanus injection die Tetanusimpfung
text message die SMS
to text eine SMS schreiben
I'll text you ich schreibe Ihnen/dir eine SMS
than als
to thank danken
thank you danke
thanks very much vielen Dank
that das
that one das dort
the der, die, das
theatre das Theater
theft der Diebstahl
their (with der words) ihr
(with das words) ihr
(with die words) ihre
them ihnen
there (over there) dort
there is/there are es gibt
these diese
these ones diese hier
they sie
thick (not thin) dick
thief der Dieb
thigh der Oberschenkel
thin dünn
thing das Ding
my things meine Sachen
to think denken
thirsty durstig
to be thirsty Durst haben
this dies
this one das hier
thorn der Dorn
those jene
those ones jene dort
thread der Faden
throat die Kehle
throat lozenges die Halspastillen
through durch
to throw away wegwerfen
thumb der Daumen
thunder der Donner
thunderstorm das Gewitter

Thursday der Donnerstag
ticket die Karte
(train, bus, etc) die Fahrkarte
(entrance fee) die Eintrittskarte
a return ticket eine Rückfahrkarte
a single ticket eine einfache Fahrkarte
ticket inspector der Schaffner/
die Schaffnerin
ticket office der Fahrkartenschalter
tide die Gezeiten
high tide die Flut
low tide die Ebbe
tidy ordentlich
to tidy up aufräumen
tie die Krawatte
tight eng
tights die Strumpfhose
tile die Fliese
till (cash desk) die Kasse
(until) bis
till 2 o'clock bis zwei Uhr
time (of day) die Zeit
what time is it? wie spät ist es?
timer die Schaltuhr
timetable der Fahrplan
tin (can) die Dose
tinfoil die Alufolie
tin-opener der Dosenöffner
to tip Trinkgeld geben
tip (to waiter, etc) das Trinkgeld
tipped (cigarettes) Filter-
tired müde
tissues die Papiertaschentücher
to zu (zum/zur)
(with names of places) nach
to London nach London
to the airport zum Flughafen
toadstool der Giftpilz
toast der Toast
tobacco der Tabak
tobacconist's die
Tabakwarenhandlung
today heute
toddler das Kleinkind
toe die Zehe
together zusammen
toilet die Toilette

disabled toilet die Behindertentoilette
toilet brush die Toilettenbürste
toilet paper das Toilettenpapier
toiletries die Toilettenartikel
toll (motorway) die Maut
tomato die Tomate
tinned tomatoes die Dosentomaten
tomato juice der Tomatensaft
tomorrow morgen
tomorrow morning morgen früh
tomorrow afternoon morgen
Nachmittag
tomorrow evening morgen Abend
tongue die Zunge
tonic water das Tonic
tonight heute Abend
tonsillitis die Mandelentzündung
too (also) auch
too big zu groß
too small zu klein
too noisy zu laut
tools das Werkzeug
toolkit der Werkzeugkasten
tooth der Zahn
toothache die Zahnschmerzen
I have toothache ich habe
Zahnschmerzen
toothbrush die Zahnbürste
toothpaste die Zahnpasta
toothpick der Zahnstocher
top: *the top floor* das oberste
Stockwerk
top (of mountain) der Gipfel
(lid) der Deckel
(clothing) das Oberteil
on top of... oben auf...
topless oben ohne
torch (flashlight) die Taschenlampe
torn zerrissen
total (amount) die Endsumme
to touch anfassen
tough (meat) zäh
tour die Fahrt
guided tour die Führung
tour guide der Reiseführer/die
Reiseführerin
tour operator der Reiseveranstalter

tourist der Tourist/die Touristin
tourist information die Touristeninformation
tourist office das Fremdenverkehrsbüro
tourist route die Touristenroute
tourist ticket die Touristenkarte
to tow (car) abschleppen
towbar (car) die Abschleppstange
tow rope das Abschleppseil
towel das Handtuch
tower der Turm
town die Stadt
town centre das Stadtzentrum
town hall das Rathaus
town plan der Stadtplan
toxic giftig
toy das Spielzeug
toy shop der Spielzeugladen
tracksuit der Jogginganzug
traditional traditionell
traffic der Verkehr
traffic jam der Stau
traffic lights die Ampel
traffic policeman der Verkehrspolizist
trailer der Anhänger
train der Zug
by train mit dem Zug
trainers die Turnschuhe
tram die Straßenbahn
tranquilliser das Beruhigungsmittel
to translate übersetzen
to travel reisen
travel agent's das Reisebüro
travel documents die Reisepapiere
travel guide der Reiseführer
travel insurance die Reiseversicherung
travel sickness die Reisekrankheit
traveller's cheques die Reiseschecks
tray das Tablett
tree der Baum
trekking poles die Trekkingstöcke
trip der Ausflug
trolley (luggage) der Gepäckwagen
(shopping) der Einkaufswagen
trousers die Hose
truck der Laster

true wahr
trunk der Koffer
trunks die Badehose
to try versuchen
to try on anprobieren
T-shirt das T-Shirt
Tuesday der Dienstag
tumble dryer der Wäschetrockner
tuna der Thunfisch
tunnel der Tunnel
to turn (right/left) abbiegen
to turn around umdrehen
to turn off (light) ausmachen
(TV, radio, etc) ausschalten
(tap) zudrehen
to turn on (light) anmachen
(TV, radio, etc) anschalten
(tap) aufdrehen
turnip die Steckrübe
turquoise (colour) türkis
tweezers die Pinzette
24-hour 24-Stunden-
twice zweimal
twin-bedded room das Zweibettzimmer
twins die Zwillinge
to type Maschine schreiben
typical typisch
tyre der Reifen
tyre pressure der Reifendruck
Tyrol das Tirol

U

ugly hässlich
ulcer das Geschwür
umbrella der Regenschirm
(sun) der Sonnenschirm
uncle der Onkel
uncomfortable unbequem
unconscious bewusstlos
under unter
undercooked nicht gar
underground die U-Bahn
underpants die Unterhose
underpass die Unterführung
understand verstehen
I don't understand ich verstehe nicht

underwear die Unterwäsche
unemployed arbeitslos
to unfasten aufmachen
United Kingdom das Vereinigte
  Königreich
United States die Vereinigten Staaten
university die Universität
unleaded petrol das bleifreie Benzin
unlikely unwahrscheinlich
to unlock aufschließen
to unpack auspacken
unpleasant unangenehm
to unplug herausziehen
to unscrew aufschrauben
until bis
unusual ungewöhnlich
up: *to get up* aufstehen
upside down verkehrt herum
upstairs oben
urgent dringend
urine der Urin
us uns
USB flash drive der USB-Stick
USB port der USB-Port
to use benutzen
useful nützlich
username der Benutzername
usual(ly) gewöhnlich
U-turn die Wende

V
vacancy (in hotel) Zimmer frei
vacant frei
vacation der Urlaub
vaccination die Impfung
vacuum cleaner der Staubsauger
vagina die Vagina
valid gültig
valuable wertvoll
valuables die Wertsachen
value der Wert
valve das Ventil
van der Lieferwagen
vase die Vase
VAT die Mehrwertsteuer (MwSt)
vegan: *I'm vegan* ich bin Veganer
vegetables das Gemüse

vegetarian vegetarisch
I'm vegetarian ich bin Vegetarier(in)
vehicle das Fahrzeug
vein die Ader
Velcro® das Klettband
vending machine der Automat
venereal disease die
  Geschlechtskrankheit
ventilator der Ventilator
very sehr
vest das Unterhemd
vet der Tierarzt
via über
to video (from TV) auf Video
  aufnehmen
(to film) filmen
video das Video
video camera die Videokamera
video cassette/tape die
  Videokassette
video game das Videospiel
video recorder der Videorekorder
Vienna Wien
view die Aussicht
villa die Villa
village das Dorf
vinegar der Essig
vineyard der Weinberg
virus der Virus
visa das Visum
to apply for a visa ein Visum
  beantragen
visit der Besuch
to visit (person) besuchen
(place) besichtigen
visiting hours (hospital) die
  Besuchszeit
visitor der Besucher
vitamin das Vitamin
voice die Stimme
voicemail die Voicemail
volcano der Vulkan
volleyball der Volleyball
voltage die Spannung
volts die Volt
to vomit erbrechen
voucher der Gutschein

156

W

wage der Lohn
waist die Taille
waistcoat die Weste
to wait for warten auf
waiter/waitress der Kellner/
  die Kellnerin
waiting room der Warteraum
to wake up aufwachen
Wales Wales
walk der Spaziergang
to go for a walk einen Spaziergang
  machen
to walk spazieren gehen
(go on foot) zu Fuß gehen
walking boots die Wanderschuhe
walking stick der Wanderstock
Walkman® der Walkman®
wall die Mauer
wallet die Brieftasche
to want wollen
I want... ich möchte...
we want... wir möchten...
war der Krieg
ward (hospital) die Station
wardrobe der Kleiderschrank
warehouse die Lagerhalle
warm warm
it's warm es ist warm
to warm up (milk, etc) aufwärmen
warning triangle das Warndreieck
to wash waschen
(to wash oneself) sich waschen
wash and blow dry Waschen und
  Föhnen
washing machine die
  Waschmaschine
washing powder das Waschpulver
washing-up bowl die
  Abwaschschüssel
washing-up liquid das Spülmittel
wasp die Wespe
wasp sting der Wespenstich
waste bin der Abfalleimer
to watch zuschauen
watch die Armbanduhr
water das Wasser

cold water kaltes Wasser
drinking water das Trinkwasser
hot water warmes Wasser
mineral water das Mineralwasser
sparkling water das Sprudelwasser
still water stilles Wasser
water heater das Heißwassergerät
watermelon die Wassermelone
waterproof wasserdicht
water sports der Wassersport
to waterski Wasserski fahren
water wings die Schwimmflügel
waves (on sea) die Wellen
way der Weg
way in (entrance) der Eingang
way out (exit) der Ausgang
we wir
weak schwach
(tea, coffee) dünn
to wear tragen
weather das Wetter
weather forecast die
  Wettervorhersage
website die Website
website address die Internetadresse
wedding die Hochzeit
wedding anniversary der
  Hochzeitstag
wedding present das
  Hochzeitsgeschenk
Wednesday der Mittwoch
week die Woche
last week letzte Woche
next week nächste Woche
this week diese Woche
weekday der Werktag
weekend das Wochenende
weekly wöchentlich
weekly ticket das Wochenticket
to weigh wiegen
weight das Gewicht
welcome willkommen
well gut
he's not well ihm geht es nicht gut
well (for water) der Brunnen
well-done (steak) durch
wellington boots die Gummistiefel

Welsh *adj* walisisch
m/f der Waliser/die Waliserin
west der Westen
wet nass
wetsuit der Taucheranzug
what was
wheat der Weizen
wheel das Rad
wheelchair der Rollstuhl
wheel clamp die Parkkralle
when wann
where wo
which: *which man?* welcher Mann?
which woman? welche Frau?
which book? welches Buch?
while während
in a while bald
white weiß
who wer
whole vollständig
wholemeal bread das Vollkornbrot
whose wessen
why warum
wide breit
widow die Witwe
widower der Witwer
wife die Frau
wi-fi die Wi-Fi
wig die Perücke
to win gewinnen
wind der Wind
windmill die Windmühle
window das Fenster
(of shop) das Schaufenster
windscreen die Windschutzscheibe
windscreen wipers die
Scheibenwischer
to windsurf surfen
windy: *it's windy* es ist windig
wine der Wein
dry wine trockener Wein
house wine der Hauswein
red wine der Rotwein
rosé wine der Roséwein
sparkling wine der Schaumwein
sweet wine süßer Wein
white wine der Weißwein

158

wine list die Weinkarte
wing der Flügel
wing mirror der Seitenspiegel
winter der Winter
wire der Draht
wireless *adj* drahtlos
with mit
without ohne
to withdraw cash Geld abheben
witness der Zeuge/die Zeugin
woman die Frau
wonderful wunderbar
wood (material) das Holz
wooden hölzern
woods (forest) der Wald
wool die Wolle
word das Wort
work die Arbeit
work permit die Arbeitsgenehmigung
to work (person) arbeiten
(machine) funktionieren
world die Welt
worried besorgt
worse schlechter
worth: *it's worth £50* es ist fünfzig
Pfund wert
to wrap up einwickeln
wrapping paper das Geschenkpapier
wrist das Handgelenk
to write schreiben
please write it down bitte schreiben
Sie das auf
writing paper das Briefpapier
wrong falsch
what's wrong? was stimmt nicht?

X
X-ray die Röntgenaufnahme
to x-ray röntgen

Y
yacht die Jacht
year das Jahr
last year letztes Jahr
next year nächstes Jahr
this year dieses Jahr
yearly jährlich

yellow gelb
Yellow Pages die Gelben Seiten
yes ja
yesterday gestern
yet: *not yet* noch nicht
yoghurt der Joghurt
plain yoghurt Naturjoghurt
yolk das Eigelb
you (polite sing. and pl.) Sie
(familiar sing.) du; ihr (pl.)
young jung
your dein/Ihr

(with der words) dein/Ihr
(with das words) dein/Ihr
(with die words) deine/Ihre
youth hostel die Jugendherberge

Z
zebra crossing der Zebrastreifen
zero null
zip der Reißverschluss
zone die Zone
zoo der Zoo
zoom lens der Zoom

Dictionary

●●

A

Aal *m* eel
ab off; from
ab 8 Uhr from 8 o'clock
ab Mai from May onward
abbestellen to cancel
abbiegen to turn *(right/left)*
Abbildung *f* illustration
abblenden to dip *(lights)*
Abblendlicht *nt* dipped headlights
Abend *m* evening
Abendessen *nt* evening meal
abends in the evening(s)
aber but
abfahren to depart; to leave
Abfahrt *f* departures
Abfahrtszeit *f* departure time
Abfall *m* rubbish
Abfertigungsschalter *m* check-in desk
abfliegen to take off
Abflug *m* flight departures
Abflug Inland domestic departures
Abflug Ausland international departures
Abflughalle *f* departure lounge
Abflugzeit *f* departure time
Abfluss *m* drain
Abführmittel *nt* laxative
abholen to fetch; to claim *(baggage, etc)*
abholen lassen to send for
Abkürzung *f* shortcut
abladen to dump; to offload
ablaufen to expire
ablehnen to refuse
Abonnement *nt* subscription
Abreise *f* departure
absagen to cancel
Absatz *m* heel
abschalten to switch off *(machine)*
abschicken to dispatch
Abschleppdienst *m* breakdown service

abschleppen to tow *(car)*
Abschleppseil *nt* towrope
Abschleppstange *f* towbar
Abschleppwagen *m* breakdown van
Absender *m* sender
abstellen to turn off; to park car
abstürzen to crash *(computer)*
Abszess *m* abscess
Abtei *f* abbey
Abteil *nt* compartment
Abteilung *f* department
Abtreibung *f* abortion
Abtreibungspille *f* abortion pill
Abzug *m* print *(photo)*
Achse *f* axle
achten auf to pay attention to
Achtung *f* caution; danger
Ader *f* vein
Adler *m* eagle
Adressbuch *nt* address book
Adresse *f* address
adressieren to address
Affe *m* monkey
ähnlich similar
Akku *m* rechargeable battery
mein Akku ist leer I've run out of charge *(phone)*
Aktentasche *f* briefcase
Akzent *m* accent *(pronunciation)*
akzeptieren to accept
Alarmanlage *f* alarm
Alge *f* seaweed
Alkohol *m* alcohol
alkoholfrei non-alcoholic
alkoholisch alcoholic *(drink)*
alle all; everybody; everyone
alle zwei Tage every other day
Allee *f* avenue
allein alone
Allergie *f* allergy
allergisch gegen allergic to
Allerheiligen *nt* All Saints' Day
alles everything; all

allgemein general; universal
Alpen *pl* Alps
alt old
Altar *m* altar
Altbier *nt* top-fermented dark beer
Alter *nt* age *(of person)*
ältere(r/s) older; elder
Altglascontainer *m* bottle bank
Alufolie *f* aluminium foil
am at; in; on
am Bahnhof at the station
am Abend in the evening
am Freitag on Friday
Ameise *f* ant
Amerika *nt* America
Amerikaner(in) *m/f* American
amerikanisch *adj* American
Ampel *f* traffic light
Amtszeichen *nt* dialling tone
Amüsierviertel *nt* nightclub district
an at; on *(light, radio, etc)*; near
Frankfurt an 1300 arriving Frankfurt
  at 1300
an/aus on/off
Ananas *f* pineapple
anbauen to grow *(cultivate)*
anbieten to offer
andere(r/s) other
ändern to change *(to alter)*
Änderung *f* change
Anfall *m* fit *(seizure)*
Anfang *m* start *(beginning)*
anfangen to begin; to start
Anfänger(in) *m/f* beginner
Anfängerhügel *m* nursery slope
Anfrage *f* enquiry
Angaben *pl* details; directions *(to a place)*
angeben to give
Angebot *nt* offer
im Angebot on offer
Angehörige(r) *m/f* relative
angeln to fish
Angeln *nt* fishing; angling
Angeln verboten no fishing
Angelrute *f* fishing rod
Angelschein *m* fishing permit

angenehm pleasant
Angestellte(r) *m/f* employee
Angina *f* angina
angreifen to attack
Angst haben vor to be afraid of
Anhänger *m* trailer; fan *(supporter)*
Anker *m* anchor
ankommen to arrive
ankündigen to announce
Ankunft *f* arrivals
Anlage *f* park; grounds; facilities
öffentliche Anlage public park
Anlasser *m* starter *(in car)*
Anlegeplatz *m* mooring
Anlegestelle *f* landing stage; jetty
anmachen to turn on
Anmeldeformular *nt* registration
  form
Anmeldung *f* registration; reception
  (place)
Annahme *f* acceptance; reception
annehmen to assume; to accept
anprobieren to try on
Anruf *m* phone call
Anrufbeantworter *m* answerphone
anrufen to phone
anschalten to turn on
anschauen to look at
Anschlagbrett *nt* notice board
Anschluss *m* connection *(train, etc)*
Anschlussflug *m* connecting flight
anschnallen to fasten
Anschrift *f* address
anschwellen to swell
Ansicht *f* view
Ansichtskarte *f* picture postcard
Ansprechpartner(in) *m/f* contact
  person
anstatt instead of
ansteckend infectious
anstehen to queue
anstellen to switch on *(gas, water)*
Anteil *m* share *(part)*
Antenne *f* aerial; antenna
Antibiotikum *nt* antibiotic
antik ancient
Antiquitäten *pl* antiques

Antiquitätenladen m antique shop
Antiseptikum nt antiseptic
Antwort f answer; reply
antworten to answer; to reply
Anweisungen pl instructions
Anzahl f number
Anzahlung f deposit
Anzeige f advertisement; report (to police)
Anzug(-züge) m suit(s) (man's)
anzünden to light; to set fire to
Apfel (Äpfel) m apple(s)
Apfelsaft m apple juice
Apfelsine(n) f orange(s)
Apfelwein m cider
Apotheke f pharmacy
Apotheker(in) m/f pharmacist
Apparat m appliance; camera; extension
Aprikose(n) f apricot(s)
April m April
Aquarium nt fish tank
Arbeit f employment; work
arbeiten to work (person)
arbeitslos unemployed
Architekt(in) m/f architect
Architektur f architecture
arm poor
Arm m arm
Armband nt bracelet
Armbanduhr f watch
Ärmelkanal m English Channel
Art f type; sort; manner
Arthritis f arthritis
Artikel m article; item
Artischocke f artichoke
Arznei f medicine
Arzt (Ärztin) m/f doctor
Aschenbecher m ashtray
Aspirin nt aspirin
Ast m branch (of tree)
Asthma nt asthma
Atlantik m Atlantic Ocean
atmen to breathe
attraktiv attractive
Aubergine f aubergine
auch also; too; as well

auf onto; on; upon; on top of
auf Deutsch in German
auf Wiedersehen goodbye
aufdrehen to turn on (tap)
Aufenthalt m stay; visit
Aufenthaltsgenehmigung f residence permit
Aufenthaltsraum m lounge
Auffahrt f slip-road
Aufführung f performance; show
aufgeben to quit; to post; to check in (baggage)
aufhalten to delay; to hold up
sich aufhalten to stay
Aufhängung f suspension (in car)
aufladen to charge (battery)
ich muss mein Handy aufladen I need to charge my phone
auflegen to hang up
aufmachen to open (shop, bank etc); to unfasten
sich aufmachen to set off
aufregend exciting
aufschließen to unlock
aufschrauben to unscrew
aufschreiben to write down
aufstehen to get up
Aufstieg m ascent
aufwachen to wake up
aufwärmen to heat up (food, milk)
Aufzug m lift/elevator
Auge(n) nt eye(s)
Augenblick m moment; instant
Augentropfen pl eye drops
August m August
Auktion f auction
Au-pair-Mädchen nt au pair
aus off (light, radio, etc); made of...; from; out of
Ausdruck m expression; print-out; term (word)
ausdrucken to print out
Ausfahrt f exit (motorway)
Ausfall m failure (mechanical)
Ausflug(-flüge) m trip(s); excursion(s)
Ausfuhr f export(s)
ausführen to export; to carry out (job)

ausfüllen to fill in *(form)*
bitte nicht ausfüllen please leave blank *(on form)*
Ausgabe *f* issue *(of magazine)*; issuing counter
Ausgaben *pl* expenses
Ausgang *m* exit; gate *(at airport)*
ausgeben to spend *(money)*
ausgehen to go out *(for amusement)*
ausgeschaltet off *(radio)*
ausgestellt issued at *(passport)*
ausgezeichnet excellent
auskugeln to dislocate *(joint)*
Auskunft information
Ausland *nt* foreign countries; abroad; international
aus dem Ausland from overseas
Ausländer(in) *m/f* foreigner
ausländisch foreign
Auslandsgespräch *nt* international call
auslassen to leave out; to omit
auslaufen to sail *(ship)*
ausmachen to turn off *(light)*; to put out *(fire, etc)*
Ausnahme *f* exception
auspacken to unpack
Auspuffrohr *nt* exhaust pipe
Ausrüstung *f* kit; equipment
ausschalten to switch off *(light, TV, radio)*
Ausschank *m* bar; drinks
Ausschlag *m* cold sore; skin rash
ausschließlich excluding; exclusive(ly)
Außenkabine *f (on ferry)* outside cabin
Außenseite *f* outside
Außenspiegel *m* outside mirror
außer Betrieb out of order
äußerlich exterior
Aussicht *f* view; prospect
aussprechen to pronounce
Ausstattung *f* equipment *(of car)*
aussteigen to get out of *(vehicle)*
Ausstellung *f* show; exhibition
Ausstellungsdatum *nt* date of issue
Austausch *m* exchange
Australien *nt* Australia

Australier(in) *m/f* Australian
australisch *adj* Australian
Ausverkauf *m* sale
ausverkauft sold out
Auswahl *f* choice
auswählen to choose
auswärts essen to eat out
ausweichen to avoid
Ausweis *m* identity card; pass *(permit)*
auszahlen to pay
Auto(s) *nt* car(s)
Autobahn *f* motorway
Autobahngebühr *f* toll
Autofähre *f* car-ferry
Autokarte *f* road map
Automat *m* vending machine
Automat wechselt change given
Automatikauto *nt* automatic car
automatisch automatic
Automobilklub *m* automobile association
Autor(in) *m/f* author
Autoreisezug *m* motorail service
Autoschlüssel *pl* car keys
Autovermietung *f* car hire

B

Baby *nt* baby
Babyflasche *f* baby's bottle
Babymilch *f* baby milk
Babynahrung *f* baby food
Babyraum *m* mother and baby room
Babysitter(in) *m/f* baby-sitter
Babytücher *pl* baby wipes
Bach *m* stream
Bäckerei *f* baker's
Backofen *m* oven
Bad *nt* bath; spa
Badeanzug *m* swimsuit
Badehose *f* swimming trunks
Badekappe *f* bathing cap
Badelatschen *pl* flip flops
baden to bathe; to swim
Baden verboten no swimming
Badewanne *f* bath(tub)
Badezimmer *nt* bathroom
Baguette *nt* French bread

Bahn *f* railway; rink
per Bahn by rail
Bahnhof *m* station; depot
Bahnlinie *f* line *(railway)*
Bahnsteig *m* platform
Bahnübergang *m* level crossing
bald soon
Balkon *m* balcony
Ball *m* ball
Ballett *nt* ballet
Ballon *m* balloon
Banane(n) *f* banana(s)
Band (Bänder) *nt* ribbon(s); tape(s)
Band *f* band *(musical)*
Bank *f* bank; bench
Bankkonto *nt* bank account
Bar *f* nightclub; bar
Bär *m* bear *(animal)*
Bargeld *nt* cash
Bart *m* beard
Basel Basle
Batterie *f* battery
Bauarbeiten *pl* roadworks;
construction work
bauen to build
Bauer (Bäuerin) *m/f* farmer
Bauernhaus *nt* farmhouse
Bauernhof *m* farm(yard)
Bauernmarkt farmers' market
Baum *m* tree
Baumarkt *m* DIY shop
Baumwolle *f* cotton *(fabric)*
Baustelle *f* roadworks; construction
site
Bayern *nt* Bavaria
beachten to observe; to obey
beantworten to answer
Bedarfshaltestelle *f* request stop
bedeckt cloudy *(weather)*
Bedeutung *f* meaning
bedienen to serve; to operate
sich bedienen to help oneself
Bedienung *f* service charge
Bedingung *f* condition
Beefsteak *nt* steak
deutsches Beefsteak hamburger;
beefburger

beenden to end; to finish
Beerdigung *f* funeral
Beere *f* berry
beginnen to begin
begrüßen to greet; to welcome
behalten to keep *(retain)*
Behandlung *f* treatment
beheizt heated
behindert disabled *(person)*
Behinderte special needs: people with
special needs
Behindertentoilette *f* toilet for
disabled
Behinderung *f* obstruction; handicap
bei near; by *(beside)*; at; on; during
beide both
Beilage *f* side-dish; vegetables; side-
salad
Bein *nt* leg
Beisel *nt* pub *(Austria)*
Beispiel(e) *nt* example(s)
zum Beispiel for example
beißen to bite
Beitrag *m* contribution; subscription
(to club)
beitreten to join *(club)*
Bekleidungsgeschäft *nt* clothes
shop
bekommen to get *(receive, obtain)*
beladen to load *(truck, ship)*
Belastung *f* load
belegt no vacancies
Beleuchtung *f* lighting
Belgien *nt* Belgium
beliebt popular
Belohnung *f* reward
benachrichtigen to inform
Benachrichtigung *f* advice note
benötigen to require
benutzen to use
Benutzername username
Benzin *nt* petrol
bequem comfortable
Beratungsstelle *f* advice centre
berechtigt zu entitled to
Berechtigte(r) *m/f* authorized person
bereit ready

Bereitschaftsdienst *m* emergency service
Berg(e) *m* mountain(s)
bergab downhill
bergauf uphill
Bergführer(in) *m/f* mountain guide
Bergschuhe *pl* climbing boots
Bergtour *f* hillwalk; climb
Bergwacht *f* mountain rescue
Bergwanderung *f* hill-walking
Bericht(e) *m* report(s); bulletin(s)
berichten to report
Berliner *m* doughnut
Beruf *m* profession; occupation
beruflich professional
Beruhigungsmittel *nt* tranquilliser
berühmt famous
berühren to handle; to touch
beschädigen to damage
beschäftigt busy
Beschäftigung *f* employment; occupation
Bescheinigung *f* certificate
beschreiben to describe
Beschreibung *f* description
Besen *m* brush *(for sweeping floor)*
besetzt engaged; occupied
besichtigen to visit *(place)*
Besichtigungen *pl* sightseeing
Besichtigungstour *f* guided tour
Besitzer(in) *m/f* owner
besondere(r/s) particular; special
besorgt worried
Besprechung *f (business)* meeting
besser better
Besserung(en) *f* improvement(s)
gute Besserung get well soon
bestätigen to confirm
Bestätigung *f* confirmation *(flight, etc)*
beste(r/s) best
Besteck *nt* cutlery
bestellen to book; to order
Bestellung *f* order
Bestimmungen *pl* regulations
Bestimmungsort *m* destination
besuchen to visit *(person)*
Besucher(in) *m/f* visitor

Besuchszeit *f* visiting hours
beten to pray
Betrag *m* amount
Betrag erhalten payment received
betreten to enter
Betrieb *m* business
betrunken drunk
Bett(en) *nt* bed(s)
Bettbezug *m* duvet cover
Bettdecke *f* duvet; quilt
Bettlaken *nt* sheet *(on bed)*
Bettzeug *nt* bedclothes
Beule *f* lump *(swelling)*
bewacht guarded
bewegen to move
Bewohner(in) *m/f* resident
bewölkt cloudy
bewusstlos unconscious
bezahlen to pay; to settle bill
bezahlt paid
Bezahlung *f* payment
Bezirk *m* district
bezüglich concerning
BH *m* bra
Bibliothek *f* library
Biene *f* bee
Bienenstich *m* bee sting; type of cream cake
Bier *nt* beer
Bier vom Fass draught beer
Biergarten *m* beer garden
Bierkeller *m* beer cellar
Bierstube *f* pub that specializes in beer
bieten to offer
Bikini *m* bikini
Bild(er) *nt* picture(s)
Bilderrahmen *m* picture frame
Bildschirm *m* screen *(TV, computer)*
billig cheap; inexpensive
billiger cheaper
Billigtarif *m* cheap rate
Birne(n) *f* pear(s); lightbulb(s)
bis until; till
bis jetzt up till now
bis zu 6 up to 6
bis bald see you soon
bisschen: *ein bisschen* a little; a bit of

bitte please
bitte? pardon?
bitten um to ask for
bitter bitter *(taste)*
blass pale
Blase *f* blister, *(anat.)* bladder
Blasenentzündung *f* cystitis
Blatt (Blätter) *nt* sheet(s) *(of paper)*;
  leaf (leaves)
blau blue
Blaue Zone *f* limited parking zone
  (parking disk required)
Blei *nt* lead *(metal)*
bleiben to stay *(to remain)*
Bleichmittel *nt* bleach
bleifreies Benzin *nt* unleaded petrol
Bleistift *m* pencil
blind blind *(person)*
Blinddarmentzündung *f*
  appendicitis
Blinker *m* indicator *(in car)*
Blitz *m* lightning
Blitzlicht *nt* flash *(for camera)*
blockiert jammed *(camera, lock)*
Blockschrift *f* block letters
blond fair *(hair)*; blond
Blumen *pl* flowers
Blumenladen *m* florist's shop
Bluse *f* blouse
Blut *nt* blood
Blutdruck *m* blood pressure
bluten to bleed
Bluterguss *m* bruise
Blutgruppe *f* blood group
blutig rare *(steak)*
Bluttest *m* blood test
Blutvergiftung *f* blood poisoning
BMX-Rad *nt* BMX
Bockbier *nt* strong beer
Boden *m* floor *(of room)*; ground
Bodensee *m* Lake Constance
Bohnen *pl* beans
grüne Bohnen French beans
Bohrer *m* drill *(tool)*
Boiler *m* immersion heater
Bombe *f* bomb
Bonbon *nt* sweet

Boot *nt* boat *(small)*
Bootsfahrt *f* cruise
Bootsrundfahrt *f* round boat trip
Bootsverleih *m* boat hire
Bordkarte *f* boarding pass
borgen to borrow
Böschung *f* embankment
botanischer Garten *m* botanical
  gardens
Botschaft *f* embassy
Bowle *f* punch *(drink)*
Box loudspeaker
Brandwunde *f* burn *(on skin)*
Brat- fried; roast
braten to fry; to roast
Bratkartoffeln *pl* fried potatoes
Bratpfanne *f* frying pan
Bratwurst *f* sausage
Brauch *m* custom *(tradition)*
brauchen to need
Brauerei *f* brewery
braun brown
Bräune *f* suntan
Braut *f* bride
Bräutigam *m* bridegroom
Brechreiz *m* nausea
breit wide
Breitband *nt* broadband
Breitband-Verbindung *f* broadband
  connection
Bremse(n) *f* brake(s)
bremsen to brake
Bremsflüssigkeit *f* brake fluid
Bremslicht *nt* brake light
Bremsseil *nt* brake cable *(car)*
Bremszug *m* brake cable *(bicycle)*
brennen to burn
Brief *m* letter *(message)*
Briefkasten *m* letterbox; postbox
Briefmarke(n) *f* stamp(s)
Briefpapier *nt* writing paper
Brieftasche *f* wallet
Briefträger(in) *m/f* postman/woman
Briefumschlag *m* envelope
Brille *f* glasses *(spectacles)*
Brillenetui *nt* glasses case
bringen to bring

britisch British
Brombeeren *pl* blackberries
Bronchitis *f* bronchitis
Bronze *f* bronze
Brosche *f* brooch
Broschüre *f* brochure
Brot *nt* bread; loaf
Brötchen *nt* bread roll
Bruch *m* fracture
Brücke *f* bridge
Bruder(Brüder) *m* brother(s)
Brühe *f* stock *(for soup, etc)*
Brühwürfel *pl* stock cubes
Brunnen *m* well *(for water)*; fountain
Brust *f* breast; chest
Buch *nt* book
buchen to book
Buchhandlung *f* bookshop
Büchsen canned
Büchsenöffner *m* can-opener
Buchstabe *m* letter *(of alphabet)*
Bucht *f* bay *(along coast)*
Buchung *f* booking
Bügel *m* coat hanger
Bügel drücken! press down!
Bügelbrett *nt* ironing board
Bügeleisen *nt* iron *(for clothes)*
bügeln to iron
Bundes- federal
Bundesrepublik Deutschland *f* Federal Republic of Germany
Bungee-Springen *nt* bungee jumping
bunt coloured
Burg *f* castle; fortress *(medieval)*
Bürger(in) *m/f* citizen
bürgerlich middle-class
Bürgermeister(in) *m/f* mayor(-ess)
Bürgersteig *m* pavement; sidewalk
Büro *nt* agency; office
Bürogebäude *nt* office block
Bürste *f* brush
Bus(se) *m* bus(es); coach(es)
Busbahnhof *m* bus/coach station
Busfahrschein *m* bus ticket
Busfahrt *f* bus tour
Bushaltestelle *f* bus stop
Buslinie *f* bus route

Busreise *f* coach trip
Busverbindung *f* bus service
Büstenhalter *m* bra
Butangas *nt* Calor gas®
Butter *f* butter

C

Café *nt* coffee shop
campen to camp
Campingführer *m* camping guide(book)
Campingkocher *m* camping stove
Campingplatz *m* campsite
Campingtisch *m* picnic table
Cappuccino *m* cappuccino
CD-Brenner *m* CD writer
CD-ROM CD-ROM
CD-Spieler *m* CD player
Cent *m* cent *(euro)*
Champignon(s) *m* mushroom(s)
Charterflug *m* charter flight
Chatroom *m* chatroom *(internet)*
Check-in *m* check-in
Chef(in) *m/f* boss
chemische Toilette *f* chemical loo
Chili chilli
Chinarestaurant *nt* Chinese restaurant
Chips *pl* crisps; chips *(gambling)*
Chor *m* choir
Cocktailbar cocktail bar
Cola *f* Coke®
Computer *m* computer
Computerprogramm *nt* computer program
Computerspiel *nt* computer game
Cousin(e) *m/f* cousin
Creme *f* cream *(lotion)*
Creme(speise) *f* mousse

D

da there
nicht da out *(not at home)*
Dach *nt* roof
Dachboden *m* attic
Dachgepäckträger *m* roof-rack
daheim at home

Damen ladies
Damenbinde(n) *f* sanitary towel(s)
Dampfer *m* steamer *(boat)*
danach after *(afterwards)*
Dänemark *nt* Denmark
danke thank you
danken to thank
Darmgrippe *f* gastric flu
das the; that; this; which
Datei *f* file *(computer)*
Datum *nt* date *(day)*
Dauer *f* length; duration
Dauerwelle *f* perm
Daumen *m* thumb
Debitkarte debit card
Decke *f* blanket; ceiling
Deckel *m* top; lid
dein your *(singular familiar)*
denken to think
Denkmal(-mäler) *nt* monument(s)
Deo *nt* deodorant
der the; who(m); that; this; which
Desinfektionsmittel *nt* disinfectant
desinfizieren to disinfect
destilliertes Wasser *nt* distilled water
Details *pl* details
deutsch *adj* German
Deutsch *nt* German *(language)*
Deutsche(r) *m/f* German
Deutschland *nt* Germany
Devisen *pl* foreign currency
Dezember *m* December
Dia(s) *nt* slide(s)
Diabetes *m* diabetes
Diabetiker(in) *m/f* diabetic
Diamant *m* diamond
Diät *f* diet *(special)*
dick fat
die the; who(m); that; this; which
Dieb(in) *m/f* thief
Diebstahl *m* theft
Dienst *m* service
im Dienst on duty
Dienstag *m* Tuesday
dienstbereit open *(pharmacy)*; on duty *(doctor)*
Dienstreise *f* business trip

Dienstzeit *f* office hours
dies this
diese these
diese(r/s) this (one)
Diesel *m* diesel
Dieselöl *nt* diesel oil
Digitalkamera *f* digital camera
Digitalradio *nt* digital radio
Ding(e) *nt* thing(s)
Diplomat(in) *m/f* diplomat
direkt direct *(route, train)*
Direktflug *m* direct flight
Direktor(in) *m/f* managing director
Disco *f* disco
Diskette *f* computer disk *(floppy)*
Dokumente *pl* documents
Dollar *m* dollar
Dolmetscher(in) *m/f* interpreter
Dom *m* cathedral
Donner *m* thunder
Donnerstag *m* Thursday
Doppel- double
Doppelbett *nt* double bed
doppelt double
Doppelzimmer *nt* double room
Dorf(Dörfer) *nt* village(s)
Dorn *m* thorn
dort there *(over there)*; that one
Dose *f* box; tin; can
Dosenöffner *m* tin-opener
Download download
Downsyndrom Down's syndrome
er/sie hat Downsyndrom he/she has
Down's syndrome
Dozent(in) *m/f* teacher *(university)*
Drachenfliegen *nt* hang gliding
Draht *m* wire
drahtlos wireless
Drahtseilbahn *f* cable railway
draußen outdoors; outside
drehen to turn; to twist
Dreibettabteil *nt* three-berth
compartment
Dreieck *nt* triangle
Dreikönigstag *m* Epiphany
dringend urgent
drinnen indoors

Droge f drug
Drogerie f chemist's *(not for prescriptions)*
drücken push
Druckschrift f block letters
du you *(familiar form)*
dumm stupid
dunkel dark
dunkelblau dark blue
dünn thin; weak *(tea)*
dunstig misty
durch through; well-done *(steak)*
Durchfahrt verboten no through traffic
Durchfall m diarrhoea
Durchgang m way; passage
Durchgangsverkehr m through traffic
durchgehend direct *(train, bus)*; 24 hour
Durchsage f announcement
durchwählen to dial direct
Durchzug m draught *(of air)*
dürfen to be allowed
Dürre f drought
Durst haben to be thirsty
durstig thirsty
Dusche f shower
Duschhaube f shower cap
Duschvorhang m shower curtain
Dutzend nt dozen
DVD f DVD
DVD-Brenner m DVD writer
DVD-Laufwerk nt DVD drive
DVD-Spieler m DVD player

E

Ebbe f flow tide
echt real; genuine
Ecke f corner
Edelstein m jewel; gem
ehemalig ex-
ehrlich honest
Ei(er) nt egg(s)
Eiche f oak
eifersüchtig jealous
Eigelb nt egg yolk

Eigentum nt property
Eigentümer(in) m/f owner
Eil- urgent
Eilbrief m express letter
Eilzustellung f special delivery
Eimer m bucket
ein *(with 'das'/'der' words)* a; one
ein(geschaltet) on *(machine)*
Einbahnstraße f one-way street
Einbrecher(in) m/f burglar
einchecken to check in
eine *(with 'die' words)* a; one
einfach simple; single ticket; plain *(unflavoured)*
Einfuhr f import
einführen to insert; to import
Eingang m entrance
Eingangstür f front door
eingeschlossen included *(in price)*
eingeschneit snowed up
Eingeweidebruch m hernia
eingießen to pour
einige(r/s) some; a few
einkaufen to shop
Einkaufswagen m shopping trolley
Einkaufszentrum nt shopping centre
einladen to invite
Einladung f invitation
Einlass ab 18 no entry for under 18s
einlaufen to shrink
einlösen to cash *(cheque)*
einmal once
einnehmen to take *(medicine)*
einordnen to get in lane
Einrichtungen pl facilities
eins one
einschalten to switch on *(light, TV)*
einschieben to insert
einschließlich including
Einschreiben nt registered letter
per Einschreiben by recorded delivery
einsteigen to get in(to) *(bus, etc)*
einstellen to adjust; to appoint; to stop
Einstellplatz car port
Eintopfgericht nt stew
eintreten to enter
Eintritt m entry; admission *(fee)*

Eintritt frei free entry
Eintrittskarte(n) f ticket(s)
Eintrittspreis m admission charge/fee
einwerfen to post; to insert
einwickeln to wrap up (parcel)
Einwurf m slot; slit
Einwurf 2 Euro insert 2 euros
Einzahlung f deposit
Einzel- (not double)
Einzelbett nt single bed
Einzelfahrschein m single ticket
einzeln single; individual
Einzelzimmer nt single room
Eis nt ice cream; ice
Eisbahn f skating rink
Eisbecher m knickerbocker glory
Eisdiele f ice-cream parlour
Eisen nt iron (metal)
Eisenbahn f railway
Eisenwarenhandlung f hardware
  shop
Eiskaffee m iced coffee
Eistee m iced tea

Eiswürfel pl ice cubes
Eiweiß nt egg white
Elastikbinde f elastic bandage
elastisch elastic
Elektriker(in) m/f electrician
elektrisch electric(al)
elektrischer Schlag m electric shock
elektrische Zahnbürste electric
  toothbrush
Elektrizität f electricity
elektronisch electronic
elektronischer Organizer electronic
  organizer
Elektrorasierer m electric razor
Ellbogen m elbow
Eltern pl parents
E-Mail f e-mail
E-Mail-Adresse f e-mail address
Empfang m reception
empfangen to receive (guest); to greet
Empfangschef m receptionist
Empfangsdame f receptionist
Empfangsschein m receipt
empfehlen to recommend

Ende nt end; bottom (of page, etc)
Endstation f terminal
Endsumme f total (amount)
eng narrow; tight (clothes)
England nt England
Engländer(in) m/f
  Englishman/woman
Englisch nt English (language)
Enkel m grandson
Enkelin f granddaughter
entdecken to discover
Ente f duck
enteisen to de-ice
entfernt distant
2 Kilometer entfernt 2 km away
Entfernung f distance
entfrosten to defrost
Enthaarungscreme f depilatory
  cream
enthalten to hold (to contain)
entkoffeinierter Kaffee m
  decaffeinated coffee
entkommen to escape
entrahmte Milch f skimmed milk
entschädigen to reimburse
Entschuldigung f pardon; excuse me
entweder ... oder either ... or
entwickeln to develop (photos)
Entzündung f inflammation
Epileptiker(in) m/f epileptic
epileptischer Anfall m epileptic fit
er he; it
erbrechen to vomit
Erbsen pl peas
Erdbeben nt earthquake
Erdbeeren pl strawberries
Erde f earth
Erdgeschoss nt ground floor
Erdnuss(-nüsse) f peanut(s)
Erdrutsch m landslide
erfreut pleased
Erfrischungen pl refreshments
erhalten to obtain; to receive
erhältlich available
Erkältung f cold (illness)
erkennen to realize; to recognize
erklären to explain

Erklärung f explanation
erlauben to permit *(something)*; to allow
Ermäßigung f reduction
Ernte f harvest
Ersatz m substitute; replacement
Ersatzrad nt spare wheel
Ersatzteile pl car parts
erste(r/s) first
Erste Hilfe first aid
erste Klasse first class
ertrinken to drown
Erwachsene(r) m/f adult
erzählen to tell
es it
essbar edible
essen to eat
Essen nt food; meal
Essen zum Mitnehmen take-away food
Essig m vinegar
Esslöffel m tablespoon
Esszimmer nt dining room
Etage f floor; storey
Etagenbetten pl bunk beds
etwas something
Eule f owl
Euro m euro *(currency)*
Eurocent m euro cent
Europa nt Europe
europäisch European
Europäische Union (EU) f European Union (EU)
Exemplar nt copy
Experte (Expertin) m/f expert
exportieren to export

F

Fabrik f works; factory
Facharzt (Fachärztin) m/f specialist *(medical)*
Fächer m fan *(hand-held)*
Faden m thread
Fahne f flag
Fahrbahn f carriageway
Fähre f ferry
fahren to drive; to go

Fahrer(in) m/f driver *(of car)*
Fahrgast m passenger
Fahrkarte f ticket *(train, bus, etc)*
Fahrkartenschalter m ticket office
Fahrplan m timetable *(trains, etc)*
Fahrplanhinweise pl travel information
Fahrpreis(e) m fare(s)
Fahrrad(-räder) nt bicycle(s)
Fahrradflickzeug nt bicycle repair kit
Fahrradschloss nt bicycle lock
Fahrradvermietung f bike hire
Fahrschein(e) m ticket(s)
Fahrscheinentwerter m ticket stamping machine
Fahrscheinheft nt book of tickets
Fahrspur(en) f lane(s)
Fahrstuhl m lift; elevator
Fahrt f journey; drive; ride *(in vehicle)*
gute Fahrt! safe journey!
Fahrzeug nt vehicle
Fall m instance
im Falle von in case of
fallen to fall
fällig due *(owing)*
falsch false *(name, etc)*; wrong
Falten pl wrinkles
Familie f family
Familienname m surname
Familienstand m marital status
Familienzimmer nt family room
Fan m fan *(football)*
Farbe f colour; paint; suit *(cards)*
färben to dye
farbenblind colour-blind
Farbfilm m colour film
farbig coloured
Farbstoff m dye
Fasching m carnival
Fass nt barrel
vom Fass on tap; on draught
Fassbier nt draught beer
Fastnachtsdienstag m Shrove Tuesday
faul lazy
Fax nt fax
faxen to fax

Faxnummer f fax number
Februar m February
Feder f spring *(coil)*; feather
Federball m badminton
Federung f suspension *(in car)*
fehlen to be missing
Fehler m fault; mistake
Fehlgeburt f miscarriage
feiern to celebrate
Feiertag m holiday
Feige f fig
Feile f file *(nail)*
Feinkostgeschäft nt delicatessen
Feld nt field
Felsen m cliff *(in mountains)*
Fenster nt window
Fensterladen m shutter *(on window)*
Fensterplatz m window seat
Ferien pl holiday(s)
Ferienhaus nt chalet *(holiday)*
Ferienwohnung f holiday flat
Fern- long-distance
Fernbedienung f remote control
Ferngespräch nt long-distance call
Fernglas nt binoculars
Fernlicht nt full beam *(headlights)*
Fernsehen nt television
Fernseher m TV set
Fernsprecher m public phone
fertig ready; finished
Fest nt celebration; party; festival
Festnetz nt landline *(phone)*
Festplatte f hard drive
Fett nt fat; grease
fettarm low-fat
fettarme Milch f low-fat milk
fettig greasy
feucht damp
Feuchtigkeitscreme f moisturizer
Feuer nt fire
feuerfeste Form f ovenproof dish
feuergefährlich inflammable
Feuerlöscher m fire extinguisher
Feuermelder m fire/smoke alarm
Feuertreppe f fire escape
Feuerwehr f fire brigade
Feuerwehrauto nt fire engine

Feuerwerk nt fireworks
Feuerzeug nt cigarette lighter
Fieber nt fever
Fieber haben to have temperature
Filet nt sirloin; fillet *(of meat, fish)*
Filiale f branch *(of store, bank, etc)*
Film m film *(at cinema, for camera)*
filmen to film
Filter m filter
Filzstift m felt-tip pen
finden to find
Finger m finger
Fingernagel m fingernail
Firma f company *(firm)*
Fisch m fish
Fischladen m fishmonger's
FKK-Strand m nudist beach
flach flat *(level)*; shallow *(water)*
Flamme f flame
Flasche f bottle
Flaschenbier nt bottled beer
Flaschenöffner m bottle opener
Fleck m mark *(stain)*
Fleckenmittel nt stain-remover
Fleisch nt meat; flesh
Fleischerei f butcher's
Flickzeug nt puncture repair kit
Fliege f bow tie; fly
fliegen to fly
Flitterwochen pl honeymoon
Flöhe pl fleas
Flohmarkt m flea market
Floß nt raft
Flug(Flüge) m flight(s)
Fluggast m passenger
Fluggesellschaft f airline
Flughafen m airport
Flughafenbus m airport bus
Flugplan m flight schedule
Flugauskunft f flight information
Flugschein(e) m plane ticket(s)
Flugsteig m gate
Flugstrecke f route; flying distance
Flugticket(s) nt plane ticket(s)
Flugzeug nt plane, aircraft
Flur m corridor
Fluss(Flüsse) m river(s)

Flussfahrt *f* river trip
Flüssigkeit *f* liquid
Flut *f* flood; high tide
Föhn *m* hairdryer
föhnen to blow-dry
folgen to follow
Forelle *f* trout
Form *f* shape; form
Formular *nt* form *(document)*
Fortsetzung *f* sequel *(book, film)*
Foto *nt* photo
Fotoapparat *m* camera
Fotogeschäft *nt* photo shop
Fotografie *f* photography
fotografieren to take a photo
Fotohandy camera phone
Fotokopie *f* photocopy
fotokopieren to photocopy
Fracht *f* cargo; freight
Frage *f* question
fragen to ask
frankieren to stamp *(letter)*
Frankreich *nt* France
Franzose (Französin) *m/f*
  Frenchman/woman
französisch *adj* French
Frau *f* wife; Mrs; Ms; woman
Frauenarzt (Frauenärztin)
  gynaecologist
Fräulein *nt* Miss
frei free; vacant
im Freien outdoor
Freibad *nt* open-air pool
freiberuflich freelance; self-employed
Freigepäck *nt* baggage allowance
Freiland- free-range
Eier aus Freilandhaltung free-range
  eggs
freimachen to stamp
Freisprecheinrichtung hands-free
  kit *(for phone)*
Freitag *m* Friday
Freizeichen *nt* ringing tone
Freizeit *f* spare time; leisure
Freizeitzentrum *nt* leisure centre
fremd foreign; strange *(unknown)*
Fremde(r) *m/f* stranger

Fremdenführer(in) *m/f* tourist guide
Fremdenverkehrsbüro *nt* tourist
  office
Freude *f* joy
Freund *m* friend; boyfriend
Freundin *f* friend; girlfriend
freundlich friendly
Frieden *m* peace
Friedhof *m* cemetery
frisch fresh; wet *(paint)*
Frischhaltefolie *f* cling film
Frischkäse *m* cream cheese
Friseur (Friseuse) *m/f* hairdresser
Frosch *m* frog
Frost *m* frost
Frostschutzmittel *nt* antifreeze
Früchte *pl* fruit
Früchtetee *m* fruit tea
Fruchtsaft *m* fruit juice
früh early
früher earlier
Frühling *m* spring *(season)*
Frühstück *nt* breakfast
Fuchs *m* fox
fühlen to feel
führen to lead
Führer(in) *m/f* guide
Führerschein *m* driving licence
Führung(en) *f* guided tour(s)
füllen to fill
Fundbüro *nt* lost property office
Fundsachen *pl* lost property
funktionieren to work *(machine)*
für for
Benzin für 30 Euro 30 euros worth
  of petrol
für immer forever
Fuß(Füße) *m* foot(feet)
zu Fuß gehen to walk
Fußball *m* football; soccer
Fußballer(in) *m/f* football player
Fußballplatz *m* football pitch
Fußballspiel *nt* football match
Fußgänger(in) *m/f* pedestrian
Fußgängerüberweg *m* pedestrian
  crossing
Fußgängerzone *f* pedestrian precinct

Fußpfleger(in) chiropodist
Fußweg m footpath
füttern to feed

G

Gabel f fork *(for eating)*
Gabelung f fork *(in road)*
Galerie f gallery
Gang m course *(of meal)*; aisle *(theatre, plane)*
Gangschaltung f gears
Gans f goose
ganz whole; quite
ganztägig full-time
Garage f garage *(private)*
Garantie f guarantee; warrant(y)
Garderobe f cloakroom
Garten m garden
Gartenlokal nt garden café
Gärtner(in) m/f gardener
Gas nt gas
Gasflasche f gas cylinder
Gasherd m gas cooker
Gaspedal nt accelerator
Gasse f alley; lane *(in town)*
Gast m guest
nur für Gäste patrons only
Gästezimmer nt guest-room
Gasthaus nt inn
Gasthof m inn; guesthouse
Gastritis f gastritis
Gaststätte f restaurant
Gaststube f lounge; restaurant
Gate nt gate *(airport)*
Gebäck nt pastry (cake)
gebacken baked
Gebäude nt building
gebeizt cured; marinated
geben to give
Gebiet nt region; area
Gebiss nt dentures
geboren born
geborene Schnorr née Schnorr
gebraten fried
gebrauchen to use
Gebraucht- used *(car, etc)*
gebrochen broken

Gebühr f fee
gebührenpflichtig subject to fee
Geburt f birth
Geburtsdatum nt date of birth
Geburtsort m place of birth
Geburtstag m birthday
Geburtstagsgeschenk nt birthday present
Geburtstagskarte f birthday card
Geburtsurkunde f birth certificate
Gedeckkosten pl cover charge *(in restaurant)*
gedünstet steamed
Gefahr f danger
gefährlich dangerous
Gefälle nt gradient
Gefängnis nt prison
Geflügel nt poultry; fowl
gefroren frozen *(food)*
gefüllt stuffed
gegen versus; against; toward(s)
Gegend f district; region
gegenüber opposite; facing
Gegenverkehr m two-way traffic
gegrillt grilled
Geheimzahl f PIN number
gehen to go; to walk
wie geht es Ihnen? how are you?
Gehirnerschütterung f concussion
gehören to belong to
gekocht boiled; cooked
Geländewagen m 4x4
gelb yellow; amber *(traffic lights)*
Gelbe Seiten pl Yellow Pages
Gelbsucht f jaundice
Geld nt money
Geld abheben withdraw cash
Geld einwerfen insert money
Geldautomat m cash dispenser; ATM
Geldbeutel m purse
Geldrückgabe f coin return
Geldschein m banknote
Geldstrafe f fine *(to be paid)*
Geldstück nt coin
gelegentlich occasionally
Gelenk nt joint *(of body)*
Geltungsdauer f period of validity

gemischt mixed; assorted
Gemüse *nt* vegetables
Gemüseladen *m* greengrocer's
genau accurate; precise; exact
Genehmigung *f* approval; permit
genfrei GM-free
genmanipuliert genetically modified
genug enough
Genuss *m* enjoyment
geöffnet open
Gepäck *nt* luggage
Gepäckablage *f* luggage rack
Gepäckaufbewahrung *f* left-luggage office
Gepäckausgabe *f* baggage reclaim
Gepäckermittlung *f* luggage desk *(for queries)*
Gepäcknetz *nt* luggage rack *(in train)*
Gepäckschließfach *nt* left-luggage locker
Gepäckträger *m* luggage rack *(on car)*; porter
Gepäckversicherung *f* luggage insurance
Gepäckwagen *m* luggage trolley
gerade even *(number)*
geradeaus straight ahead
Gerät *nt* appliance; gadget
geräuchert smoked *(food)*
Gericht *nt* court *(law)*; dish *(food)*
gerieben grated *(cheese)*
geröstet sauté; fried; toasted
Geruch *m* smell
Gesamtsumme *f* total amount
Geschäft(e) *nt* business; shop(s)
Geschäftsadresse *f* business address
Geschäftsführer(in) *m/f* manager
Geschäftspartner(in) *m/f* partner *(business)*
Geschäftsstunden *pl* business hours
Geschäftszentrum business centre
geschehen to happen
Geschenk(e) *nt* gift(s)
Geschenkeladen *m* gift shop
Geschenkpapier *nt* wrapping paper
Geschichte *f* history
geschieden divorced

Geschirrspülmaschine *f* dishwasher
Geschirrspülmittel *nt* washing-up liquid
Geschirrtuch *nt* tea/dish towel
Geschlecht *nt* gender; sex
Geschlechtskrankheit *f* venereal disease
geschlossen closed/shut
Geschmack *m* taste; flavour
geschmort braised
geschnittenes Brot *nt* sliced bread
Geschoss *nt* storey
geschützt sheltered
Geschwindigkeit *f* speed
geschwollen swollen
Geschwür *nt* ulcer
Gesellschaft *f* company
Gesetz *nt* law
gesetzlicher Feiertag *m* public holiday
Gesicht *nt* face
Gesichtswasser *f* cleanser *(for face)*
Gesichtspflege *f* facial *(beauty treatment)*
gesperrt closed
Gespräch *nt* talk; phone call
Gesprächsguthaben *nt* credit *(on mobile phone)*
Gestank *m* smell *(unpleasant)*
gestattet permitted
gestern yesterday
gestochen stung; bitten *(by insect)*
gestreift striped
gesund healthy
Gesundheit *f* health; bless you!
Getränk(e) *nt* drink(s)
Getränkekarte *f* list of beverages
getrennt separated *(couple)*
getrennt bezahlen to pay separately
Getriebe *nt* gearbox; gears
Gewehr *nt* gun
Gewicht *nt* weight
gewinnen to win
Gewitter *nt* thunderstorm
gewöhnlich usual(ly)
Gewürz *nt* spice; seasoning
Gezeiten *pl* tide
gibt es...? is/are there...?

Gift nt poison
giftig poisonous
Gigabyte nt gigabyte
Gigahertz nt gigahertz
Gipfel m summit; mountain top
Gips m plaster (for broken limb)
Gitarre f guitar
Glas nt glass; jar
Glatteis nt black ice
Glatteisgefahr f danger – black ice
glatzköpfig bald (person)
glauben to believe; to think (be of opinion)
gleich same
Gleise pl platforms; tracks
Gletscher m glacier
Glocke f bell
Glück nt happiness; luck
glücklich happy; lucky
Glühbirne f light bulb
gluten gluten
glutenfrei gluten-free
Gold nt gold
Golf nt golf
Golfplatz m golf course
Golfschläger m golf club
gotisch Gothic
Gott m God
Gottesdienst m church service
GPS GPS (global positioning system)
Grad m degree (of heat, cold)
Gramm nt gram(me)
Grapefruit f grapefruit
Gras nt grass
Gräte f fish bone
grau grey
Graubrot nt brown bread
Grenze f frontier; border (of country)
Grenzpolizei f border police
Griff m handle; knob
Grill m barbecue; grill
grillen to grill
Grillstube f steak house; grillroom
Grillteller m mixed grill
Grippe f flu
groß tall; great; big; high (number, speed)
Großbritannien nt Great Britain

Großbuchstabe m capital letter
Größe f size (of clothes, shoes); height
Großeltern pl grandparents
Großmutter f grandmother
Großraumwagen m (in train) open plan carriage
Großvater m grandfather
großzügig generous
grün green; fresh (fish)
Grünanlage f park
Grundstücksmakler m estate agent's
grüne Versicherungskarte f green card (car insurance)
grüner Salat m green salad
Gruppe f group
Gruß m greeting
Grußkarte f greetings card
Guave guava
Gulasch nt goulash
gültig valid
Gummi m rubber; elastic
Gummiband nt rubber band
Gummihandschuhe pl rubber gloves
Gummistiefel pl wellington boots
günstig convenient; cheap
Gurke(n) f cucumber(s); gherkin(s)
Gürtel m belt
Gürtelrose f shingles
Gürteltasche f bumbag; moneybelt
gut good; well; all right (yes)
alles Gute all the best; with best wishes
guten Abend good evening
guten Appetit enjoy your meal
guten Morgen good morning
gute Nacht good night
guten Tag hello; good day/afternoon
Güter pl goods
Guthabenkarte charge card (for mobile phone)
Gutschein m voucher; coupon
Gynäkologe (Gynäkologin) gynaecologist

H
H-Milch f long-life milk
Haar nt hair
Haarbürste f hairbrush

Haare *pl* hair
Haargel *nt* hair gel
Haarklemme *f* hairgrip
Haarschnitt *m* haircut
Haarspray *nt* hair spray
haben to have
Hackfleisch *nt* mince meat
Hacksteak *nt* hamburger *(usually without the bread)*
Hafen *m* harbour; port
Hafer *m* oats
Haftung *f* liability
Hagel *m* hail
Hahn *m* tap *(for water)*; cockerel
Hähnchen *nt* chicken
halb half
zum halben Preis half-price
halb durch medium rare *(meat)*
halber Fahrpreis *m* half fare
Halbfettmilch *f* semi-skimmed milk
Halbinsel *f* peninsula
Halbpension *f* half board
Hälfte *f* half
hallo hello
Hals *m* neck; throat
Halskette *f* necklace
Halspastillen *pl* throat lozenges
Halsschmerzen *pl* sore throat
Halstuch *nt* scarf *(round neck)*
Halt *m* stop
Haltbarkeitsdatum *nt* sell-by date
Haltebucht *f* layby
halten to hold; to stop
Halten verboten no stopping
Haltestelle *f* bus stop
Hammer *m* hammer
Hämorrhoiden *pl* haemorrhoids
Hand *f* hand
Handbremse *f* handbrake
Handel *m* trade; commerce
Handgelenk *nt* wrist
handgemacht handmade
Handgepäck *nt* hand-luggage
Handschuhe *pl* gloves
Handtasche *f* handbag
Handtuch *nt* towel
Handwerker(in) *m/f* tradesman/
tradeswoman
Handy mobile *(phone)*
Handy-Ladegerät *m* mobile phone charger
Handynummer mobile number
Harke *f* rake
hart hard *(not soft)*
hart gekochtes Ei *nt* hard-boiled egg
Hase *m* hare
Haselnuss(-nüsse) *f* hazelnut(s)
hässlich ugly
häufig frequent; common
Haupt- major; main
Hauptbahnhof *m* main station
Hauptgericht *nt* main course
Hauptstadt *f* capital *(city)*
Hauptstraße *f* major road
Hauptverkehrszeit *f* peak hours; rush hour
Haus *nt* house; home
zu Hause at home
Hausarbeit *f* housework
Hausbrauerei micro-brewery
Hausfrau (Hausmann) *f/m* housewife/househusband
Haushaltswaren *pl* household goods
Hausschuhe *pl* slippers
Haustier *nt* pet
Hauswein *m* house wine
Haut *f* hide *(leather)*; skin
Hecht *m* pike
Hefe *f* yeast
Heft *nt* exercise book
Hefter *m* stapler
Heftklammern *pl* staples
Heftpflaster *nt* sticking plaster
Heidelbeeren *pl* blueberries
heilig holy
Heiligabend *m* Christmas Eve
Heim *nt* home *(institution)*; hostel
Heimweh haben to be homesick
heiraten to marry
heiß hot
heiße Schokolade *f* hot chocolate
heißen to be called
wie heißen Sie? what's your name?
Heißwassergerät *nt* water heater

Heizgerät *nt* heater
Heizkörper *m* radiator
Heizung *f* heating
helfen to help
Helikopter *m* helicopter
hell light *(pale)*; bright
hellblau light blue
helles Bier *nt* lager
helles Fleisch *nt* white meat
Helm *m* helmet
Hemd(en) *nt* shirt(s)
Hepatitis *f* hepatitis
Herbst *m* autumn
Herd *m* cooker; oven
herein in; come in
hereinkommen to come in
Hering *m* herring; tent peg
Herr *m* gentleman; Mr
Herren gents *(toilet)*
heruntergehen to go down
herunterladen to download
Herz *nt* heart
Herzanfall *m* heart attack
herzliche Glückwünsche!
  congratulations!
Herzschrittmacher *m* pacemaker
Heuschnupfen *m* hay fever
heute today
heute Abend tonight
hier here
hiesig local *(wine, speciality)*
Hilfe *f* help
Himbeeren *pl* raspberries
Himmel *m* heaven; sky
hin there
Hin- und Rückfahrt *f* round trip
hineingehen to go in
hinten behind
hinten einsteigen enter at rear
hinter behind
Hinweis *m* notice; information
Hirnhautentzündung *f* meningitis
historisch historic
hoch high
Hochsaison *f* high season
Höchstgeschwindigkeit *f* maximum
  speed

Höchsttarif *m* peak rate
Hochzeit *f* wedding
Hochzeitsgeschenk *nt* wedding
  present
Hochzeitskleid *nt* wedding dress
Hochzeitstag *m* wedding anniversary
Hochzeitstorte *f* wedding cake
Hoden *pl* testicles
Hof *m* court
hoffen to hope
höflich polite
Höhe *f* altitude; height
hoher Blutdruck *m* high blood
  pressure
höher higher
höher stellen to turn up *(heat, volume)*
Höhle *f* cave
holen to fetch
holländisch Dutch
Holz *nt* wood *(material)*
Holzkohle *f* charcoal
Homepage *f* homepage
Homöopathie *f* homeopathy
homöopathisch homeopathic
  (remedy, etc)
homosexuell homosexual
Honig *m* honey
hören to hear
Hörer *m* receiver *(phone)*
Hörgerät *nt* hearing aid
Hörnchen *nt* croissant
Hose *f* trousers
Hotel *nt* hotel
Hotel garni *nt* bed and breakfast hotel
hübsch pretty
Hubschrauber *m* helicopter
Hüfte *f* hip
Hügel *m* hill
Huhn *nt* hen
Hühnchen *nt* chicken
Hummer *m* lobster
Hund *m* dog
Hundeleine *f* dog lead
hundert hundred
Hunger haben to be hungry
Hupe *f* horn *(of car)*
husten to cough

Husten *m* cough
Hustenbonbons *pl* cough sweets
Hustensaft *m* cough mixture
Hut *m* hat
Hütte *f* mountain hut

I

ich I
Idiotenhügel *m* nursery slope
ihm him
ihnen them
ihr(e) her; their
Imbiss *m* snack
Imbissstube *f* snack bar
immer always
Immunisierung *f* immunisation
Impfung *f* vaccination
in in *(place, position)*; inside; into
in Ordnung all right *(agreed)*
Infektion *f* infection
Informationsbüro *nt* information office
Ingenieur(in) *m/f* engineer
Inhalationsapparat *m* inhaler *(medication)*
Inhalt *m* contents
inklusive inclusive
Inland *nt* domestic *(flight, etc)*
Inlandsgespräch(e) *nt* national call(s)
innen inside
Innenkabine *f (on ship/ferry)* inside cabin
Innenstadt *f* city centre
innerlich for internal use *(medicine)*
Insekt *nt* insect
Insektenschutzmittel *nt* insect repellent
Insel *f* island
Insulin *nt* insulin
intelligent intelligent
interessant interesting
Internet *nt* internet
haben Sie Internet-Anschluss? do you have internet access?
Internetcafé *nt* cybercafé
Internet-Seite *f* website
Internetadresse *f* website addres

Intrauterinpessar coil *(IUD)*
iPOD iPOD®
Ire (Irin) *m/f* Irishman/woman
irgendjemand someone
irgendwo somewhere
irisch *adj* Irish
Irland *nt* Ireland
Irrtum *m* mistake
Isomatte *f* camping mat; sleeping mat
Italien *nt* Italy
Italiener(in) *m/f* Italian
italienisch *adj* Italian

J

ja yes
Jacht *f* yacht
Jachthafen *m* marina
Jacke *f* jacket; cardigan
Jagderlaubnis *f* hunting permit
jagen to hunt
Jahr *nt* year
Jahrestag *m* anniversary
Jahreszeit *f* season
Jahrgang *m* vintage
Jahrhundert *nt* century
jährlich annual; yearly
Jahrmarkt *m (fun)* fair
Januar *m* January
jeder everyone
Jeans *pl* jeans
jede(r/s) each
jemand somebody; someone
jene those
jetzt now
Jod *nt* iodine
joggen to jog
Jogginganzug *m* tracksuit
Joghurt *m* yoghurt
Johannisbeere(n) *f* currant(s)
Journalist(in) *m/f* journalist
jucken to itch
Jude/Jüdin *m/f* Jew
Jugendherberge *f* youth hostel
Jugendliche(r) *m/f* teenager
Juli *m* July
jung young
Junge *m* boy

Junggeselle m bachelor
Juni m June
Juwelier m jeweller's

K

Kabel nt cable; lead (electrical)
Kabelfernsehen nt cable TV
Kabine f cabin; berth (train, ship)
Kaffee m coffee
Kaffeehaus nt café
Kaffeemaschine f percolator
Kai m quayside
Kakao m cocoa
Kakerlake f cockroach
Kalb nt calf (young cow)
Kalbfleisch nt veal
kalt cold
Kamera f camera
Kameratasche f camera case
Kamillentee m camomile tea
Kamin m fireplace
Kamm m comb; ridge
kämpfen to fight
Kanada nt Canada
Kanadier(in) m/f Canadian
kanadisch adj Canadian
Kanal m canal; (English) Channel
kandiert glacé
Kaninchen nt rabbit
Kanister m (petrol) can
Kanu nt canoe
Kapelle f chapel; orchestra
kaputt broken; out of order
kaputtmachen to break (object)
Kapuze f hood (of jacket)
Karaffe f decanter; carafe
Karfreitag m Good Friday
Karotten pl carrots
Karte f card; ticket; map; menu
Kartentelefon nt cardphone
Kartoffel(n) f potato(es)
Kartoffelpüree nt mashed potato
Kartoffelsalat m potato salad
Karton m box (cardboard); carton
Käse m cheese
Kasino nt casino
Kasse f cash desk

Kasserolle f casserole
Kassette f cassette; cartridge; tape
Kassierer(in) m/f cashier
Kastanie f chestnut
Katalog m catalogue
Katalysator m catalytic converter (car)
Kater m hangover; tomcat
katholisch Catholic
Katze f cat
kaufen to buy
Kaufhaus nt department store
Kaugummi m chewing gum
Kaution f deposit
Kehle f throat
Keilriemen m fan belt
kein... no...
keine(r/s) no; none
Keks(e) m biscuit(s) (sweet)
Keller m cellar
Kellner(in) m/f waiter/waitress
kennen to be acquainted with
Keramik f pottery
Kern m pip
Kerze f candle
Kette f chain
Kfz-Versicherung f car insurance
Kiefer f pine
Kiefer m jaw
Kilo(gramm) nt kilo(gram)
Kilometer m kilometre
Kind(er) nt child(ren)
Kinderbett nt cot
Kinderkrippe f crèche
Kindermädchen nt nanny
Kindersitz m child seat (car)
Kinderstuhl m high chair
Kinderteller m child's helping
Kinderwagen m pram; pushchair
Kinn nt chin
Kino nt cinema
Kiosk m kiosk
Kirche f church
Kirmes f funfair
Kirsche(n) f cherry (cherries)
Kissen nt cushion; pillow
Kiste f box (wooden)
Kiwi kiwi fruit

Klage *f* complaint
klar clear
Klarer *m* schnapps
Klärgrube *f* septic tank
Klasse *f* class; grade
Klavier *nt* piano
Klebeband *nt* adhesive tape
kleben to stick *(with glue)*
Klebstoff *m* glue
Kleid *nt* dress
Kleider *pl* clothes
Kleiderbügel *m* coat hanger
Kleiderschrank *m* wardrobe
klein little *(small)*; short
Kleingeld *nt* change *(money)*
Klempner(in) *m/f* plumber
Klettband *nt* Velcro®
klettern to climb *(mountains)*
Klimaanlage *f* air-conditioning unit
klimatisiert air-conditioned
Klingel *f* doorbell
klingeln to ring *(bell, phone)*
Klinik *f* clinic
Klippe *f* cliff *(along coast)*
klopfen to knock *(on door)*
Kloß *m* dumpling
Kloster *nt* monastery; convent
Klub *m* club
Kneipe *f* pub
Knie *nt* knee
Kniestrümpfe *pl* pop socks
Knoblauch *m* garlic
Knöchel *m* ankle
Knochen *m* bone
Knödel *m* dumpling
Knopf *m* button; knob *(radio, etc)*
Knoten *m* knot
Koch *m* chef
kochen to boil; to cook
Kocher *m* cooker; stove
Köchin *f* cook
Kochschinken *m* cooked ham
Kochtopf *m* saucepan
Kode *m* code
Köder *m* bait *(for fishing)*
koffeinfreier Kaffee *m* decaffeinated coffee

Koffer *m* suitcase; trunk
Kofferanhänger *m* luggage tag
Kofferraum *m* carboot
Kognak *m* brandy
Kohl *m* cabbage
Kohle *f* coal
Kohlrübe *f* swede
Koje *f* berth *(in ship)*; bunk
Kollege (Kollegin) *m/f* colleague
Köln Cologne
Kölnischwasser *nt* eau de cologne
Kombi *m* estate car
komisch funny *(amusing)*
kommen to come
Kommode *f* chest of drawers
Komödie *f* comedy
Kompass *m* compass
Komponist(in) *m/f* composer
Kondensmilch *f* condensed milk
Konditorei *f* cake shop; café
Kondom *nt* condom
Konfektions- ready-made *(clothes)*
Konferenz *f* conference
Konfitüre *f* jam
König *m* king
Königin *f* queen
königlich royal
können to be able to; to know how to
Konsulat *nt* consulate
Kontaktdaten *pl* contact details
Kontaktlinsen *pl* contact lenses
Kontaktlinsenreiniger *m* contact lens cleaner
Konto *nt* bank account
Kontrolle *f* check; control
kontrollieren to check *(passports, tickets)*
Konzert *nt* concert
Konzertsaal *m* concert hall
Kopf *m* head
Kopfhörer *pl* headphones
Kopfkissen *nt* pillow
Kopfsalat *m* lettuce
Kopfschmerzen *pl* headache
Kopftuch *nt* scarf *(headscarf)*
Kopie *f* copy *(duplicate)*
kopieren to copy

Kopiergerät photocopier
Korb _m_ basket
Korinthe _f_ currant
Korken _m_ cork _(of bottle)_
Korkenzieher _m_ corkscrew
Körper _m_ body
Körperpuder _m_ talc
Kortison _nt_ cortisone
Kosmetiksalon _m_ beauty salon
Kosmetiktücher _pl_ paper tissues
kosten to cost
Kosten _pl_ cost _(price)_
kostenlos free of charge
köstlich delicious
Kostüm _nt_ suit _(woman's)_
Krabbe _f_ crab
Kräcker _m_ cracker
Kraftstoff _m_ fuel
Kragen _m_ collar
Krämpfe _pl_ cramps
krank ill; sick
Krankenhaus _nt_ hospital
Krankenkasse _f_ medical insurance
Krankenwagen _m_ ambulance
Krankheit _f_ disease
Kräuter _pl_ herbs
Kräutertee _m_ herbal tea
Krawatte _f_ tie
Krebs _m_ crab _(animal)_; cancer _(illness)_
Kreditkarte _f_ credit card
Kreisverkehr _m_ roundabout
Kreuz _nt_ cross _(also crucifix)_
Kreuzfahrt _f_ cruise
Kreuzschlitzschraubenzieher _m_
   Phillips screwdriver®
Kreuzung _f_ junction; crossroads
Kreuzworträtsel _nt_ crossword
Krieg _m_ war
Kristall _nt_ crystal
Krone _f_ crown
Krücken _pl_ crutches
Krug _m_ jug
Küche _f_ kitchen; cuisine
Kuchen _m_ flan; cake
Küchenbrett _nt_ chopping board
Küchenpapier _nt_ kitchen paper
Kugel _f_ ball; scoop _(of ice cream)_

Kugelschreiber _m_ pen; biro
Kuh _f_ cow
kühl cool
Kühlbox _f_ cool-box _(for picnic)_
kühlen to chill _(wine, food)_
Kühler _m_ radiator _(of car)_
Kühlschrank _m_ fridge
Kümmel _m_ caraway seed; cumin;
   schnapps
Kunde (Kundin) _m/f_ client; customer
Kundenkarte _f_ store card
Kunst _f_ art
Kunstfaser _f_ man-made fibre
Kunstgewerbearbeiten _pl_ crafts
Kunsthalle _f_ art gallery
Kunsthandwerksmarkt _m_ craft fair
Künstler(in) _m/f_ artist
künstlich artificial; man-made
künstliche Hüfte _f_ hip replacement
Kupfer _nt_ copper
Kupplung _f_ clutch _(of car)_
Kupplungsflüssigkeit _f_ clutch fluid
Kurierdienst _m_ courier service
Kurort _m_ spa
Kurs _m_ course; exchange rate
Kurve _f_ curve; corner; bend
kurz short; brief
Kurz(zeit)parkplatz _m_ short-stay car
   park
kurzsichtig short-sighted
Kurzwarengeschäft _nt_ haberdasher's
Kuss _m_ kiss
küssen to kiss
Küste _f_ coast; seaside
Küstenwache _f_ coastguard

L

lächeln to smile
Lächeln _nt_ smile
lachen to laugh
Lachs _m_ salmon
Lack _m_ varnish
Ladegerät _nt_ charger
Laden _m_ shop; store
Lagerhalle _f_ warehouse
Lakritze _f_ liquorice
Lamm _nt_ lamb

Lampe *f* lamp
Land *nt* country (Italy, France, etc); land
landen to land
Landkarte *f* map (of country)
Landschaft *f* countryside
Landung *f* landing (of plane)
Landwein *m* table wine
lang long
Länge *f* length
Langlauf *m* cross-country skiing
langsam slow(ly)
langsamer werden to slow down
langweilig boring
Langzeitparkplatz *m* long-stay car park
Lappen *m* cloth (rag)
Laptop *m* laptop
Laptop-Tasche laptop bag
Lärm *m* noise
lassen to let (allow)
Last *f* load
Laster *m* truck
Lastwagen *m* truck; lorry
Lätzchen *nt* bib (baby's)
Lauch *m* leek
laufen to run
Laugenbrezel *f* soft pretzel
laut noisy; loud(ly); aloud
läuten to ring (doorbell)
Lautsprecher *m* loudspeaker
Lautstärke *f* volume (of sound)
Lawine *f* avalanche
Lawinengefahr *f* danger of avalanches
leben to live (exist)
Lebensgefahr *f* danger to life
Lebensmittel *pl* groceries
Lebensmittelvergiftung *f* food poisoning
Lebensversicherung *f* life insurance
Leber *f* liver
Lebkuchen *m* gingerbread
Leck *nt* leak (of gas, liquid)
Lederwaren *pl* leather goods
ledig single (not married)
leer empty; flat (battery); blank (disk/tape)

Leerlauf *m* neutral (gear)
im Leerlauf in neutral
legen to lay
Lehrer(in) *m/f* teacher (school); instructor
leicht light (not heavy); easy
Leid *nt* grief
es tut mir leid (I'm) sorry
leider unfortunately
leihen to rent (car); to lend
Leihgebühr *f* rental (fee)
Leinen *nt* linen (cloth)
leise quietly; soft; faint
leiser stellen to turn down (volume)
Leiter *f* ladder
Leitung *f* telephone line
Lenker *m* handlebars
Lenkrad *nt* steering wheel
lernen to learn
Lernschwäche *f* learning disability
lesbisch lesbian
lesen to read
letzte(r/s) last; final
Leuchtturm *m* lighthouse
Leute *pl* people
Licht *nt* light
das Licht anschalten to switch on lights
Lichtmaschine *f* alternator
Lichtschalter *m* light switch
Lichtschutzfaktor factor (sunblock)
Lichtschutzfaktor 25 factor 25
Lidschatten *m* eye shadow
liebe(r) dear (in letter)
Liebe *f* love
lieben to love
liebenswürdig kind
lieber rather
Lieblings- favourite
Lied *nt* song
Lieferwagen *m* van
Liegestuhl *m* deckchair
Liegewagen *m* couchette
Lift *m* elevator; lift
Liftpass *m* lift pass (on ski slopes)
Likör *m* liqueur
Limonade *f* lemonade

Limone f lime (fruit)
Lineal nt ruler
Linie f line (row, of railway)
Linienflug m scheduled flight
linke(r/s) left(-hand)
links to the left; on the left
Linkshänder(in) m/f left-handed person
Linse f lens
Linsen pl lentils
Lippen pl lips
Lippenpflegestift m lip salve
Lippenstift m lipstick
Liste f list
Liter m litre
Loch nt hole
lochen to punch (ticket, etc)
locker loose (screw, tooth)
Löffel m spoon
Loge f box (in theatre)
Lohn m wage
Loipe f cross-country ski run
Lokal nt pub
Lorbeerblatt nt bayleaf
los(e) loose
was ist los? what's wrong?
Los nt lot (at auction); ticket (lottery)
lösen to buy (ticket)
löslich soluble
Lounge f lounge
Löwe m lion
LSF (or **SF**) SPF (sun protection factor)
LSF (or **SF**) **30** SPF 30
Luft f air
Luftfilter m air filter
Luftfracht f air freight
Luftkissenboot nt hovercraft
Luftmatratze f air bed/mattress
Luftpost f air mail
Luftpumpe f pump (bike/air mattress)
Lüge f lie (untruth)
Lunge f lung
Lupe f magnifying glass
Lutscher m lollipop
Luxus m luxury

M

machen to make; to do
das macht nichts that doesn't matter
Mädchen nt girl
Mädchenname m maiden name
Made f maggot
Magen m stomach
Magenschmerzen pl stomachache
Magentabletten pl indigestion tablets
Magenverstimmung f indigestion
Magermilch f skimmed milk
Magnet m magnet
Magnetkarte swipecard
Mai m May
Mais m sweetcorn
Make-up nt make-up
malen to paint
Malzbier nt malt beer
man one
managen to manage (be in charge)
manchmal sometimes
Mandarine f tangerine
Mandel f almond; tonsil
Mandelentzündung f tonsillitis
Mangel m flaw
Mango m mango
Maniküre manicure
Mann m man; husband
Männer pl men
männlich masculine; male
Manschettenknöpfe pl cufflinks
Mantel m coat
Margarine f margarine
marineblau navy blue
mariniert marinated
Marke f brand (of product); token (for phone)
Markise f awning (on house)
Markt m market
Marktplatz m market place
Marmelade f jam
Marmor m marble
März m March
Maschine f machine
Maschine schreiben to type
Masern pl measles
Maßband nt tape measure

Maße pl measurements
Massage f massage
Mast m mast
Material nt material
Matratze f mattress
Mauer f wall
Maus f mouse (animal/computer)
Maut f toll (motorway)
Mayonnaise f mayonnaise
MB Mb (megabyte)
Mechaniker(in) m/f mechanic
Medikament nt drug; medicine
Medizin f medicine
Meer nt sea
Meeresfrüchte pl seafood
Megabyte nt megabyte
128 Megabyte 128 megabytes
Megahertz nt megahertz
Mehl nt flour
mehr more
Mehrwegflasche f returnable bottle (usually with a deposit)
Mehrwertsteuer (MwSt) f value-added tax (VAT)
meiden to avoid (person)
Meile f mile
mein my
meiste(n) most
Meisterwerk nt masterpiece
melden to report (tell about)
Melone f melon; bowler hat
Memorystick m memory stick (for camera, etc)
Menge f crowd
Messe f fair (commercial); mass (church)
Messegelände nt exhibition centre
messen to measure
Messer nt knife
Messing nt brass
Metall nt metal
Meter m metre
Metro f metro (underground)
Metzgerei f butcher's
mich me (direct object)
Mikrofon microphone
Mietauto nt hire car
Miete f rent

mieten to hire; to rent (house, etc)
Mietgebühr f rental charge
Mietvertrag m lease (rental)
Migräne f migraine
Mikrowelle f microwave oven
Milch f milk
Milchprodukte pl dairy produce
Milchpulver nt powdered milk
Millimeter m millimetre
Million f million
minderwertig low-quality
Mindest- minimum
Mineralwasser nt mineral water
Minidisk minidisk
Minimum nt minimum
Minister(in) m/f minister (politics)
Minute(n) f minute(s)
Minze f mint (herb)
mir me (indirect object)
mischen to mix
Missverständnis nt misunderstanding
mit with
Mitfahrgelegenheit f lift (in car)
Mitglied nt member (of club, etc)
mitnehmen to give a lift to
zum Mitnehmen take-away (food)
Mittag m midday
Mittagessen nt lunch
Mitte f middle
Mitteilung f message
Mittel nt means
ein Mittel gegen a remedy for
mittelalterlich medieval
Mittelmeer- Mediterranean
Mitternacht f midnight
Mittwoch m Wednesday
Mixer m blender; mixer
Möbel pl furniture
Möbelpolitur f furniture polish
Mobiltelefon nt mobile phone
möbliert furnished
Modem nt modem
modern fashionable; modern
mögen to enjoy (to like)
möglich possible
Mohn m poppy
Möhre(n) f carrot(s)

Mole f jetty
Monat m month
monatlich monthly
Mond m moon
Monitor m monitor
Montag m Monday
Moped nt moped
Morgen m morning
morgen tomorrow
Morgendämmerung f dawn
Morgenmantel m dressing gown
Moschee f mosque
Moskitonetz nt mosquito net
Motor m motor; engine
Motorboot nt motor boat
Motorhaube f bonnet (car)
Motorrad nt motorbike
Motte f moth (clothes)
Mountainbike nt mountain bike
Mountainbiking nt mountain biking
MP3-Spieler m MP3 player
Mücke f midge
müde tired
Müll m rubbish
Müllbeutel m bin liner
Mülleimer m bin (dustbin)
Mülltrennung f waste separation (for recycling)
Mumps m mumps
München Munich
Mund m mouth
Mundwasser nt mouthwash
Münster nt cathedral
Münze(n) f coin(s)
Münzfernsprecher m payphone
Münztelefon nt payphone (with coins)
Muscheln pl mussels
Museum nt museum
Musik f music
Muskat m nutmeg
Muskel m muscle
müssen to have to; must
mutig brave
Mutter f mother
Mütze f cap (hat)
MwSt f VAT

N
nach after; according to; to (with names of places)
Nachbar(in) m/f neighbour
Nachmittag m afternoon
nachmittags pm; in the afternoon
Nachname m surname
Nachricht f note (letter); message
Nachrichten pl news
Nachspeise f dessert; pudding
nächste(r/s) next
Nacht f night
über Nacht overnight
Nachtdienst m night duty (chemist)
Nachthemd nt nightdress
Nachtisch m dessert
Nachtklub m night club
nachzahlen to pay extra
nackt nude; naked; bare
Nadel f needle
Nagel m nail (metal)
Nagelbürste f nailbrush
Nagelfeile f nail file
Nagellack m nail polish/varnish
Nagellackentferner m nail polish remover
Nagelschere f nail scissors
Nähe f proximity
in der Nähe nearby
nähen to sew
Name m name; surname
Narkose f anaesthetic
Nase f nose
nass wet
national national
Nationalität f nationality
Natur- natural
Naturlehrpfad m nature trail
Naturschutzgebiet nt nature reserve
Nebel m mist; fog
neben by (next to); beside
Nebenstraße f minor road
Nebensaison f low season
neblig foggy
Neffe m nephew
Negativ nt negative (photo)

nehmen to catch (bus, train); to take (remove)

nein no

Nektarine f nectarine

Nelke f carnation

nennen to quote (price)

Nervenzusammenbruch m nervous breakdown

Nest nt nest

nett nice (person); kind

Netto- net (income, price)

Netz nt net; network

neu new

neueste(r/s) newest; latest

Neujahr New Year's Day

Neuseeland nt New Zealand

nicht not; non-

Nichte f niece

Nichtraucher m non-smoker

nichts nothing

nie never

Niederlande pl Netherlands

Niedersachsen nt Lower Saxony

niedrig low

Niedrigwasser nt low tide

niemand no one; nobody

Niere(n) f kidney(s)

niesen to sneeze

nirgends nowhere

noch still (up to this time); yet

noch ein(e) extra (more); another

Norden m north

Nordirland nt Northern Ireland

nördlich north; northern

Nordsee f North Sea

Normal(benzin) nt regular (petrol)

normal standard (size)

Notarzt m emergency doctor

Notaufnahme f accident & emergency

Notausgang m emergency exit

Notdienstapotheke f on-duty chemist

Notfall m emergency

nötig necessary

Notizblock m note pad

Notruf m emergency number

Notrufsäule f emergency phone (on motorway)

Notsignal nt distress signal

notwendig essential; necessary

November m November

nüchtern sober

Nudeln pl pasta; noodles

Null f nil; zero; nought

numerieren to number

Nummer f number; act

Nummernschild nt numberplate

nur only

Nürnberg Nuremberg

Nuss (Nüsse) f nut(s)

nützlich useful

O

oben upstairs; above; this side up

oben auf on top of...

Oberschenkel m thigh

obligatorisch compulsory

Obst nt fruit

Obstkuchen m fruit tart

oder or

offen open

offene Weine pl wine served by the glass

öffentlich public

öffnen to open; to undo

Öffnungszeiten pl business hours

oft often

ohne without

ohnmächtig fainted

ohnmächtig werden to faint

Ohr(en) nt ear(s)

Ohrenschmerzen pl earache

Ohrringe pl earrings

okay OK

ökologisch ecological

ökonomisch economic

Ökotourismus m eco-tourism

Oktober m October

Öl nt oil

Ölfilter m oil filter

Olive f olive

Olivenöl nt olive oil

Ölstandsanzeiger m oil gauge

Ölwechsel m oil change
Omelett nt omelette
Onkel m uncle
Oper f opera
Operation f operation (surgical)
Optiker m optician's
orange orange (colour)
Orange f orange (fruit)
Orangensaft m orange juice
Orchester nt orchestra
Ordner m file (for papers)
Oregano m oregano
organisch organic
organisieren to organize
Organspenderausweis m donor card
Ort m place
an Ort und Stelle on the spot
örtlich local
örtliche Betäubung f local
  anaesthetic
Ortschaft f village; town
Ortsgespräch nt local call
Ortszeit f local time
Osten m east
Osterei nt Easter egg
Ostermontag m Easter Monday
Ostern nt Easter
Österreich nt Austria
Österreicher(in) m/f Austrian
österreichisch adj Austrian
Ostersonntag m Easter Sunday
östlich eastern
Ozean m ocean

188

P

Paar nt pair; couple
ein paar a couple of
packen to pack (luggage)
Paket nt parcel; packet
Palast m palace
Palmtop m palmtop computer
Pampelmuse(n) f grapefruit(s)
Panne f breakdown (of car)
Papier(e) nt paper(s)
Papiertaschentücher pl tissues
Pappe f cardboard
Paprikaschote f pepper (vegetable)

Parfüm nt perfume
Parfümerie f perfumery
Park m park
parken to park
Parken verboten no parking
Parkett nt stalls (in theatre)
Parkhaus nt multi-storey car park
Parkkralle f wheel clamp
Parkplatz m car park
Parkscheibe f parking disk
Parkschein m parking ticket (to display)
Parkuhr f parking meter
Parkverbot nt no parking zone
Partei f political party
Partner(in) m/f partner (boy/girlfriend)
Party f party (celebration)
Pass m passport; pass (in mountains)
Pass geschlossen pass closed
Passagier m passenger
passen to fit
passieren to happen
Passionsfrucht f passionfruit
Passkontrolle f passport control
Passnummer f passport number
Passwort nt password
Patient(in) m/f patient (in hospital)
Pauschalreise f package tour
Pauschaltarif m flat-rate tariff
Pause f pause; interval
keine Pausen no intervals
PDA m PDA (Personal Digital Assistant)
Pelz m fur
Pelzmantel m fur coat
Pendelverkehr m shuttle (service)
Penis m penis
Penizillin nt penicillin
Pension f boarding house
pensioniert retired
Peperoni chilli
per via; by
per Express by express mail
per Post by post
perfekt perfect
Periode f period (menstruation)
Perlen pl pearls
perlend sparkling
Person f person

German – English

Personal *nt* staff
Personalausweis *m* identity card
Personalien *pl* particulars
persönlich personal(ly)
Perücke *f* wig
Pessar *nt* cap *(diaphragm)*
Petersilie *f* parsley
Pfalz *f* Palatinate
Pfand *nt* deposit
Pfandflasche *f* returnable bottle
  (with deposit)
Pfannkuchen *m* pancake
Pfarrer(in) *m/f* church minister
Pfeffer *m* pepper *(spice)*
Pfefferkuchen *m* gingerbread
Pfefferminzbonbon *nt* mint *(sweet)*
Pfefferminztee *m* mint tea
Pfeife *f* pipe *(smoker's)*
Pferd *nt* horse
Pferderennen *nt* horse-racing
Pfirsich(e) *m* peach(es)
Pflanze *f* plant *(green)*
Pflaster *nt* plaster *(for cut)*
Pflaume(n) *f* plum(s)
Pflegespülung *f* conditioner *(hair)*
Pforte *f* gate
Pfund *nt* pound
Pfund Sterling *nt* sterling *(pound)*
Picknick *nt* picnic
Picknickdecke *f* picnic rug
Pier *m* jetty; pier
pikant savoury
Pille *f* pill
Pilot(in) *m/f* pilot
Pils/Pilsner *nt* lager
Pilz(e) *m* mushroom(s)
Pilzkrankheit *f* thrush *(candida)*
Pinzette *f* tweezers
Pistazie *f* pistachio
Piste *f* runway; ski run
Pizza *f* pizza
planmäßig scheduled
Planschbecken *nt* paddling pool
Plastik- plastic *(made of)*
Plastikbeutel *m* plastic bag
Platte *f* plate; dish; record
Plattern blowout *(bicycle)*

Platz *m* seat; space; square *(in town)*;
  court
Plätzchen *nt* biscuit(s)
Platzkarte *f* seat reservation *(ticket)*
Plombe *f* filling *(in tooth)*
plötzlich suddenly
pochiert poached *(egg, fish)*
Polen *nt* Poland
Polizei *f* police
Polizeirevier *nt* police station
Polizeiwache *f* police station
Polizist(in) *m/f* policeman/woman
Pommes frites *pl* chips *(French fries)*
Pony *nt* pony
Ponyreiten *nt* pony trekking
Porree *m* leek
Portier *m* porter *(for door)*
Portion *f* portion
Portrait *nt* portrait
Portugal *nt* Portugal
Portugiese/Portugiesin *m/f*
  Portuguese
portugiesisch *adj* Portuguese
Post *f* post; post office
Post- postal
Postamt *nt* post office
Postanweisung *f* money order
Poster *nt* poster
Postkarte *f* postcard
postlagernd poste restante
Postleitzahl *f* postcode
praktisch handy; practical
Pralinen *pl* chocolates
Präservativ *nt* condom
Praxis *f* doctor's surgery
Preis *m* prize; price
Preiselbeersaft cranberry juice
Preisliste *f* price list
Priester *m* priest
Prinz *m* prince
Prinzessin *f* princess
privat private
Privatstrand *m* private beach
Privatweg *m* private road
pro per
pro Jahr per annum
pro Kopf per person

189

pro Stunde per hour
probieren to taste; to sample
Problem nt problem
Programm nt programme
Programmierer(in) m/f computer programmer
prost! cheers!
protestantisch Protestant
provisorisch temporary
Prozent nt per cent
prüfen to check (oil, water, etc)
Prüfung f exam (school, university)
Publikum nt audience
Puderzucker m icing sugar
Pullover m sweater; jumper
Pulver nt powder
pulverförmig in powder form
Pulverkaffee m instant coffee
pünktlich on schedule; punctual
Puppe f doll; puppet
Puppenspiel nt puppet show
pur straight (drink)
Pute f turkey
Pyjama m pyjamas

Q

Qualität f quality
Qualitätswein m good quality wine
Qualle f jellyfish
Quantität f quantity
Quarantäne f quarantine
Quelle f spring (of water); source
quetschen to squeeze
Quetschung f bruise
Quittung f receipt
Quiz nt quiz show

R

Rabatt m discount
Rad nt wheel; bicycle
Rad fahren to cycle
Radfahrer(in) m/f cyclist
Radiergummi m rubber (eraser)
Radieschen pl radishes
Radio nt radio
Radweg m cycle track
Rahmen m frame (picture)

Rand m verge; border; edge
Randstein m kerb
Rang m circle (in theatre); rank
Rasen m lawn
Rasierapparat m shaver; razor
Rasiercreme f shaving cream
rasieren to shave
Rasierklinge f razor blade
Rasierschaum m shaving foam
Rasierwasser nt aftershave lotion
Rasthof m service area; travel inn
Rastplatz m picnic area
Raststätte f service area
raten to advise
Rathaus nt town hall
rau rough
Rauch m smoke
rauchen to smoke
Rauchen verboten no smoking
Raucher(in) m/f smoker
Raum m space (room)
rechnen to calculate
Rechnung f bill (account); invoice
rechte(r/s) right (not left)
rechts to the right; on the right
Rechtsanwalt m lawyer; solicitor
Rechtsanwältin f lawyer; solicitor
reden to speak
reduzieren to reduce
reduziert reduced
Reformhaus nt health food shop
Regal nt shelf
Regen m rain
Regenmantel m raincoat
Regenschirm m umbrella
regnen to rain
Reibe f grater
reich rich (person)
Reich nt empire
reichhaltig rich (food)
reif ripe; mature (cheese)
Reifen m tyre
Reifendruck m tyre pressure
Reifenpanne f blowout (tyre)
Reihe f row (line); tier
rein pure
reinigen to clean

Reinigung *f* dry-cleaner's
Reis *m* rice
Reise *f* trip *(journey)*
gute Reise! have a good trip!
Reisebüro *nt* travel agency
Reiseführer *m* guidebook
Reiseführer(in) *m/f* tour guide
Reisegruppe *f* party *(of tourists)*
Reisekrankheit *f* travel sickness
reisen to travel
Reisepapiere *pl* travel documents
Reisepass *m* passport
Reisescheck *m* traveller's cheque
Reiseveranstalter *m* tour operator
Reiseziel *nt* destination
Reißverschluss *m* zip
reiten to ride *(horse)*
Reiten *nt* riding
Rennbahn *f* racecourse
rennen to run
Rennen *nt* race *(sport)*
Rentner(in) *m/f* pensioner; senior citizen
Reparatur *f* repair
Reparaturwerkstatt *f* car repairs
reparieren to repair; to mend
reservieren to book; to reserve
reserviert reserved
Reservierung *f* booking *(in hotel)*
Reservierungen *pl* reservations
Restaurant *nt* restaurant
Restgeld *nt* change *(money)*
retten to rescue; to save *(person)*
Rettungsboot *nt* lifeboat
Rettungshubschrauber *m* air ambulance *(helicopter)*
Rettungsinsel *f* life raft
Rettungsring *m* lifebelt
Rettungsschwimmer(in) *m/f* lifeguard
Rezept *nt* prescription; recipe
Rezeption *f* reception *(front desk)*
R-Gespräch *nt* reverse charge call
Rhein *m* Rhine
Rheinfahrten *pl* Rhine cruises
Rheumatismus *m* rheumatism
Richter(in) *m/f* judge

richtig correct; right; proper
Richtung *f* direction
riechen to smell
Rinderbraten *m* roast beef
Rindfleisch *nt* beef
Ring *m* ring
Ringstraße *f* ring road
Riss *m* tear *(in material)*
Rock *m* skirt
Roggenbrot *nt* rye bread
roh raw
Rohling blank *(CD or DVD)*
Rohr *nt* pipe *(drain, etc)*
Rollo *nt* blind *(for window)*
Rollschuhe *pl* roller skates
Rollstuhl *m* wheelchair
Rolltreppe *f* escalator
Roman *m* novel
Röntgenaufnahme *f* X-ray
rosa pink
Rose *f* rose *(flower)*
Rosenkohl *m* Brussels sprouts
Rosenmontag *m* carnival *(Monday before Shrove Tuesday)*
Roséwein *m* rosé wine
Rosine(n) *f* raisin(s)
Rost *m* rust; grill
Rostbraten *m* roast
rosten to rust
rostfreier Stahl *m* stainless steel
rostig rusty
Röstkartoffeln *pl* sautéed potatoes
rot red
Rote Bete *f* beetroot
Röteln *pl* German measles; rubella
Rote Johannisbeeren *pl* redcurrants
Rotwein *m* red wine
Rücken *m* back
Rückerstattung *f* refund
Rückfahrkarte *f* return ticket
Rückfahrt *f* return journey
Rückflugticket *nt* return airticket
Rückgrat *nt* spine
Rücklicht *nt* rear light
Rucksack *m* rucksack
Rückspiegel *m* rearview mirror
rückwärts backwards

rückwärtsfahren to reverse (car)
Rückwärtsgang m reverse gear
Ruder nt rudder; oar
Ruderboot nt rowing boat
rudern to row (boat)
rufen to shout
Rufnummer f telephone number
Ruhe f rest (repose); peace (calm)
Ruhe! be quiet!
ruhen to rest
ruhig calm; quiet(ly); peaceful
Rührei nt scrambled egg
Ruine f ruin (castle, etc)
rund round
Rundfahrt f tour; round trip
Rundreise f round trip
Rundwanderweg m circular trail for ramblers
Rutschbahn f slide (chute)
rutschen to slip
rutschig slippery

S

Saal m hall (room)
Sache f thing
Sachen pl stuff (things); belongings
Sachsen nt Saxony
Sackgasse f cul-de-sac
Safe m safe (for valuables)
Saft m juice
sagen to say; to tell (fact, news)
Sahne f cream (dairy)
mit Sahne with whipped cream
Saison f season
Salat m salad
Salatsoße f salad dressing
Salbe f ointment
Salz nt salt
Salzkartoffeln pl boiled potatoes
Salzwasser nt salt water
Samstag m Saturday
Sand m sand
Sandalen pl sandals
Sandstrand m sandy beach
Sanitäter (Sanitäterin) m/f paramedic (in ambulance)
Satellitenfernsehen nt satellite TV

Satnav nt satnav (satellite navigation system, for car)
satt full
Sattel m saddle
Satteltaschen pl panniers (for bike)
Satz m set (collection); sentence
sauber clean
säubern to clean
sauer sour
Sauerkraut nt sauerkraut
Sauerstoff m oxygen
Sauger m teat (on bottle)
Säule f petrol pump
Saum m hem
Sauna f sauna
Säure f acid
saure Sahne f soured cream
S-Bahn f suburban railway
Schach nt chess
Schaden m damage
schädlich harmful
Schaf nt sheep
Schaffner(in) m/f conductor (bus, train); guard
Schale f shell (egg, nut); dish
schälen to peel (fruit)
Schalter m switch
Schaltgetriebe nt manual (gear change)
Schaltknüppel m gear lever
Schaltuhr f timer
Schaltzug gear cable (bike)
scharf hot (spicy); sharp
Schatten m shade
schätzen to value; to estimate
Schauer m rain shower
Schaufel und Handfeger dustpan and brush
Schaufenster nt shop window
Schaukel f swing (for children)
Schaum m foam
Schaumbad nt bubble bath
Schaumfestiger m hair mousse
Schaumwein m sparkling wine
Schauspiel nt play
Schauspieler(in) m/f actor/actress
Scheck m cheque

Scheckbuch *nt* cheque book
Scheckkarte *f* cheque card
Scheibe *f* slice
Scheibenputzmittel *nt* screenwash
Scheibenwischer *pl* windscreen wipers
Schein(e) *m* banknote(s); certificate(s)
scheinen to shine *(sun, etc)*; to seem
Scheinwerfer *m* headlight; floodlight; spotlight
Scheinwerfer anschalten switch on headlights
Schere *f* scissors *(pair of)*
scherzen to joke
Scheuerlappen *m* floorcloth
Scheune *f* barn
Schi- *see* Ski-
schicken to send
schießen to shoot
Schiff *nt* ship
Schild *nt* sign; label
Schinken *m* ham
Schirm *m* umbrella; screen
Schlachterei *f* butcher's
schlafen to sleep
Schlafsack *m* sleeping bag
Schlaftablette *f* sleeping pill
Schlafwagen *m* sleeping car *(on train)*
Schlafzimmer *nt* bedroom
Schlag *m* shock *(electric)*
Schlaganfall *m* stroke *(medical)*
schlagen to hit
Schläger *m* racket *(tennis, etc)*
Schlagloch *nt* pothole
Schlagsahne *f* whipped cream
Schlange *f* queue; snake
Schlangenbiss *m* snake bite
Schlauch *m* hosepipe; inner tube
Schlauchboot *nt* dinghy *(rubber)*
schlecht bad; badly
Schlepplift *m* ski tow
schließen to shut; to close
Schließfach *nt* locker
schlimm serious
Schlitten *m* sleigh; sledge
Schlittschuh laufen to iceskate
Schlittschuh(e) *m* ice skate(s)

Schlittschuhbahn *f* ice rink
Schloss *nt* castle; lock *(on door, etc)*
Schluss *m* end
Schlüssel *m* key
Schlüsselbein *nt* collar bone
Schlüsselkarte *f* cardkey *(for hotel)*
Schlüsselring *m* keyring
Schlusslichter *pl* rear lights
Schlussverkauf *m* sale
schmecken to taste
schmelzen to melt
Schmerz *m* pain; ache
schmerzhaft painful
Schmerzmittel *nt* painkiller
Schmerztablette *f* painkiller
Schmuck *m* jewellery; decorations
schmutzig dirty
Schnäppchen *nt* bargain
Schnaps *m* schnapps; spirit
schnarchen to snore
Schnee *m* snow
Schneebrille *f* snow goggles
Schneeketten *pl* snow chains
Schneepflug *m* snowplough
schneiden to cut
schnell fast; quick
Schnellboot *nt* speedboat
Schnellimbiss *m* snack bar
Schnellzug *m* express train
Schnittbohnen *pl* green beans
Schnittlauch *m* chives
Schnittwunde *f* cut
Schnorchel *m* snorkel
Schnorcheln *nt* snorkelling
Schnuller *m* dummy *(for baby)*
Schnur *f* string
schnurloses Telefon cordless phone
Schnurrbart *m* moustache
Schnürschuhe *pl* boots *(ankle)*
Schnürsenkel *pl* shoelaces
Schokolade *f* chocolate
schön lovely; fine; beautiful; good *(pleasant)*
Schornstein *m* chimney
Schotte (Schottin) *m/f* Scot
schottisch Scottish
Schottland *nt* Scotland

Schrank m cupboard
Schraube f screw
Schraubenmutter f nut (for bolt)
Schraubenschlüssel m spanner
Schraubenzieher m screwdriver
schrecklich awful
schreiben to write
Schreibmaschine f typewriter
Schreibtisch m desk
Schreibwarenhandlung f stationer's
schriftlich in writing
Schritt m pace; step
Schritt fahren! dead slow
Schublade f drawer
Schuh(e) m shoe(s)
Schuhcreme f shoe polish
Schuhgeschäft nt shoe shop
Schuhputzmittel nt shoe polish
schulden to owe
Schulden pl debts
Schule f school
Schulter f shoulder
Schuppen pl scales (of fish); dandruff
Schürze f apron
Schüssel f bowl (for soup, etc)
Schuster m shoe mender's
Schutzhelm m helmet (for bike)
Schutzimpfung f vaccination
schwach weak
Schwager m brother-in-law
Schwägerin f sister-in-law
Schwamm m sponge
schwanger pregnant
schwarz black
Schwarzbrot nt rye bread
Schwarze Johannisbeeren pl
  blackcurrants
Schwarzweißfilm m black and white
  film
Schwein nt pig
Schweinefleisch nt pork
Schweiß m sweat
Schweiz f Switzerland
Schweizer(in) m/f Swiss
schweizerisch adj Swiss
Schwellung f swelling
schwer heavy

Schwester f sister; nurse; nun
Schwiegermutter f mother-in-law
Schwiegersohn m son-in-law
Schwiegertochter f daughter-in-law
Schwiegervater m father-in-law
schwierig hard (difficult)
Schwimmbad nt swimming pool
schwimmen to swim
Schwimmflossen pl flippers
Schwimmweste f life jacket
schwindelig dizzy
schwitzen to sweat
See f sea
See m lake
seekrank seasick
Segel nt sail
Segelboot nt sailing boat
segeln to sail
sehen to see
Sehenswürdigkeit f sight
Sehne f tendon
sehr very
seicht shallow (water)
Seide f silk
Seife f soap
Seil nt rope
Seilbahn f cable railway; funicular
sein(e) his
sein to be
seit since
Seite f page; side
Seitenspiegel m wing mirror
Seitenstraße f side street
Seitenstreifen m hard shoulder
Sekretär(in) m/f secretary
Sekt m sparkling wine
Sekunde f second (time)
Selbstbedienung f self-service
Sellerie m celery
selten rare (unique)
seltsam strange (odd)
Senf m mustard
September m September
servieren to serve (food)
Serviette f napkin
Servolenkung f power steering
Sessel m armchair

Sessellift *m* chairlift
setzen to place; to put
sich setzen to sit down
setzen Sie sich bitte please take a seat
Sex *m* sex *(intercourse)*
Shampoo *nt* shampoo
Shorts *pl* shorts
sicher sure; safe; definite
Sicherheit *f* safety; security
Sicherheitsgurt *m* seatbelt; safety belt
Sicherheitskontrolle security check
Sicherheitsnadel *f* safety pin
Sicherung *f* fuse
Sicherungskasten *m* fuse box
sie she; they
Sie you *(polite singular and plural)*
Sieb *nt* sieve; colander
Signal *nt* signal
ich bekomme kein signal there's no signal *(mobile phone)*
Silber *nt* silver
Silvester *m* New Year's Eve
SIM-Karte SIM card
singen to sing
Sitz *m* seat
Sitzerhöhung *f* booster seat
sitzen to sit
Ski(er) *m* ski(s)
Ski fahren to ski
Skianzug *m* ski suit
Skihose *f* ski pants
Skijacke *f* ski jacket
Skilanglauf *m* cross-country skiing
Skilaufen *nt* skiing
Skilehrer(in) *m/f* ski instructor
Skilift *m* ski lift
Skipass *m* ski pass
Skipiste *f* ski run
Skistiefel *pl* ski boots
Skistock *m* ski stick/pole
Skiverleih *m* ski hire
Slip *m* knickers; underpants
Slipeinlage *f* panty liner
SMS *f* text message
eine SMS schreiben to text
ich schreibe Ihnen/dir eine SMS I'll text you

Snack *m* snack
Snowboard *nt* snow board
Socken *pl* socks
Soda *nt* soda water
Sodbrennen *nt* heartburn
Sofa *nt* sofa
Sofabett *nt* sofa bed
sofort at once; immediately
Software *f* computer software
Sohle *f* sole *(of shoe)*
Sohn *m* son
Sojabohnen *pl* soya beans
Sojamilch *f* soya milk
Sommer *m* summer
Sommerfahrplan *m* summer timetable
Sommerferien *pl* summer holidays
Sonder- special
Sonderangebot *nt* special offer
sonn- und feiertags Sundays and public holidays
Sonnabend *m* Saturday
Sonne *f* sun
Sonnenaufgang *m* sunrise
sonnenbaden to sunbathe
Sonnenbrand *m* sunburn
Sonnenbräune *f* suntan
Sonnenbrille *f* sunglasses
Sonnencreme *f* suncream
Sonnendach *nt* sunroof
Sonnenöl *nt* suntan oil
Sonnenschirm *m* sun umbrella; sunshade
Sonnenstich *m* sunstroke
Sonnenuntergang *m* sunset
sonnig sunny
Sonntag *m* Sunday
Sonntagsdienst *m* Sunday duty *(chemist, doctor, etc)*
sorgen für to look after; to take care of
Soße *f* dressing; sauce
Souterrain *nt* basement
Souvenir *nt* souvenir
Spam spam *(e-mail)*
Spanien *nt* Spain
Spanier(in) *m/f* Spaniard
spanisch *adj* Spanish

Spannung f voltage
sparen to save *(money)*
Spargel m asparagus
Sparpreis m economy fare
Spaß m fun; joke
spät late
Spaten m spade
Spätvorstellung f late show
Spaziergang m stroll; walk
Speck m bacon
Speicherkarte f memory card
Speise f dish; food
Speiseeis nt ice cream
Speisekarte f menu
Speisesaal m dining hall
Speisewagen m dining car
Spesen pl expenses
Spezialität f speciality
Spiegel m mirror
Spiegelei nt fried egg
Spiel nt game; pack *(of cards)*
Spielbank f casino
spielen to gamble; to play
Spielkarte f card *(playing)*
Spielplatz m playground
Spielzeug nt toy
Spielzeugladen m toy shop
Spielzimmer nt playroom
Spinat m spinach
Spirale f coil *(IUD)*; spiral
Spirituosen pl spirits *(alcohol)*
Spitze f lace; point *(tip)*
Splitter m splinter
Sportartikel pl sports equipment
Sportgeschäft nt sports shop
Sporttauchen nt scuba diving
Sprache f speech; language
Sprachführer m phrase book
Spraydose f aerosol
sprechen to speak
sprechen mit to talk to
Sprechstunde f surgery *(hours of opening)*
springen to jump
Spritze f injection; hypodermic needle
sprudelnd fizzy
Sprudelwasser nt sparkling water

Sprungschanze f ski jump
Spucktüte f sick bag
Spülbecken nt sink *(kitchen)*
spülen to flush toilet; to rinse
Spülkasten m cistern *(of toilet)*
Spülmittel nt washing-up liquid
Spur f lane *(of motorway/main road)*
Squash nt squash *(drink, game)*
Staatsangehörigkeit f nationality
Stachel m sting
Stadion nt stadium
Stadt f town; city
Stadtführung f guided tour of the town
Stadtmitte f city centre
Stadtplan m map *(of town)*
Stadtzentrum nt town/city centre
Stahl m steel
Stand m stall; taxi rank
ständig permanent(ly); continuous(ly)
Standlicht nt sidelight
stark strong
Starthilfekabel nt jump leads
Station f station; stop; hospital ward
statt instead of
stattfinden to take place
Statue f statue
Stau m traffic jam
Staub m dust
Staubsauger m vacuum cleaner
Staubtuch nt duster
stechen to bite *(insect)*
Stechmücke f mosquito; gnat
Steckdose f socket *(electrical)*
Stecker m plug *(electric)*
Steckrübe f turnip
stehen to stand
stehlen to steal
steil steep
Stein m stone
Stelle f job; place; point *(in space)*
stellen to set *(alarm)*; to put
Stellplatz pitch *(for tent/caravan)*
stempeln to stamp *(visa)*
Steppdecke f quilt
sterben to die
Stereoanlage f stereo

Stern *m* star
Steuer *f* tax
Steuerung *f* controls
Steward (Stewardess) *m/f* steward/ stewardess
Stich *m* bite *(by insect)*; stitch *(sewing)*; sting
Stiefel *pl* boots *(long)*
Stiefmutter *f* stepmother
Stiefvater *m* stepfather
Stift *m* pen
still still *(motionless)*
stilles Wasser *nt* still water
Stimme *f* voice
stimmt so! keep the change!
Stirn *f* forehead
Stock *m* cane *(walking stick)*; stick; floor
Stockwerk *nt* storey
Stoff *m* cloth *(fabric)*
Stoppschild *nt* stop *(sign)*
Stöpsel *m* plug *(in sink)*
stören to disturb *(interrupt)*
bitte nicht stören do not disturb
stornieren to cancel
Stornierung *f* cancellation
Störung *f* hold-up; fault; medical disorder
Stoßdämpfer *m* shock absorber
stoßen to knock; to push
Stoßstange *f* bumper *(car)*
Stoßzeit *f* rush hour
Strafe *f* punishment; fine
Strafzettel *m* parking ticket *(fine)*
Strand *m* beach
Strandkorb *m* wicker beach chair with a hood; beach hut
Straße *f* road; street
Straße gesperrt road closed
Straßenarbeiten *pl* roadworks
Straßenbahn *f* tram
Straßenkarte *f* road map
Streichhölzer *pl* matches
Streifenkarte *f* multiple journey travelcard
Streik *m* strike *(industrial)*
streiten to quarrel
Stress *m* stress

stricken to knit
Strickjacke *f* cardigan
Stricknadel *f* knitting needle
Strohhalm *m* straw *(for drinking)*
Strom *m* current; electricity
Stromanschluss *m* electric point
Strömung *f* current *(water)*
Stromzähler *m* electricity meter
Strümpfe *pl* stockings
Strumpfhose *f* tights
Stück *nt* bit; piece; cut of meat; play *(theatre)*
Student(in) *m/f* student
Studentenermäßigung *f* student discount
Stufe *f* step *(stair)*
Stuhl *m* chair
stumpf blunt *(knife, blade)*
Stunde *f* hour; lesson
Sturm *m* storm
Sturzhelm *m* crash helmet
suchen to look for
Suchmaschine *f* search engine
Süden *m* south
südlich southern
Summe *f* sum *(total amount)*
Sumpf *m* marsh
Super(benzin) *nt* premium petrol
Supermarkt *m* supermarket
Suppe *f* soup
Surfbrett *nt* surfboard
surfen to surf
im Internet surfen to surf the Net
süß sweet
Süßigkeiten *pl* sweets
Süßstoff *m* sweetener; saccharin
Süßwaren *pl* confectionery
Süßwasser *nt* freshwater
Synagoge *f* synagogue
Szene *f* scene

T
Tabak *m* tobacco
Tabakwarenhandlung *f* tobacconist's
Tablett *nt* tray
Tablette(n) *f* tablet(s); pill(s)

Tacho(meter) *m* speedometer
Tafel *f* table; board; bar of chocolate
Tafelwein *m* table wine
Tag *m* day
jeden Tag every day
Tageskarte *f* day ticket; menu of the day
Tagespauschale *f* daily unlimited rate
Tagessuppe *f* soup of the day
täglich daily
Taille *f* waist
Tal *nt* valley
Tampons *pl* tampons
Tank *m* fuel/petrol tank
Tankanzeige *f* fuel gauge
Tankdeckel *m* petrol cap
Tanksäule *f* petrol pump
Tankstelle *f* petrol station
Tanne *f* fir
Tante *f* aunt
Tanz *m* dance
tanzen to dance
Tarif *m* rate; tariff
Tasche *f* pocket; bag
Taschenbuch *nt* paperback
Taschendieb *m* pickpocket
Taschenlampe *f* torch; flashlight
Taschenmesser *nt* penknife
Taschenrechner *m* calculator
Taschentuch *nt* handkerchief
Tasse *f* cup
Taste *f* button; key *(on keyboard)*
Taste drücken push button
taub deaf
Taube *f* pigeon
tauchen to dive
Tauchen *nt* diving
Taucheranzug *m* wetsuit
Taucherbrille *f* goggles *(swimming)*
tauschen to exchange
tausend thousand
Taxi *nt* taxi; cab
Taxifahrer(in) *m/f* taxi driver
Taxistand *m* taxi rank
Tee *m* tea
Teebeutel *m* tea bag
Teekanne *f* teapot

Teelöffel *m* teaspoon
Teig *m* pastry
Teil *nt* part
teilen to divide; to share
Teilkaskoversicherung *f* third party, fire and theft insurance
Telefon *nt* telephone
Telefonauskunft *f* directory enquiries
Telefonbuch *nt* phone directory
telefonieren to telephone
Telefonkarte *f* phonecard
Telefonnummer *f* phone number
Telefonzelle *f* phonebox
Telegramm *nt* telegram
Teller *m* plate
Tempel *m* temple
Temperatur *f* temperature
Tennis *nt* tennis
Tennisplatz *m* tennis court
Tennisschläger *m* tennis racket
Teppich *m* rug
Teppichboden *m* fitted carpet
Termin *m* date; deadline; appointment
Terminal *m* terminal *(airport)*
Terminkalender *m* diary; Filofax®
Terminplaner Filofax®
Terrasse *f* patio; terrace *(of café)*
Terrorist(in) *m/f* terrorist
Tesafilm® *m* Sellotape®
teuer dear *(expensive)*
Theater *nt* theatre
Theke *f* counter *(in shop, bar, etc)*
Thermometer *nt* thermometer
Thermosflasche *f* flask *(thermos)*
Thunfisch *m* tuna
Thüringen *nt* Thuringia
Thymian *m* thyme
tief deep; low *(in pitch)*
Tiefkühltruhe *f* deep freeze; freezer
Tier *nt* animal
Tierarzt (Tierärztin) *m/f* vet
Tinte *f* ink
Tintenfisch *m* octopus; squid
Tisch *m* table
Tischdecke *f* tablecloth
Tischler(in) *m/f* carpenter
Tischtennis *nt* table tennis

Tischwein *m* table wine
Toastbrot *nt* sliced white bread for toasting
Tochter *f* daughter
Tochtergesellschaft *f* subsidiary
Toilette *f* toilet; lavatory
Toilettenartikel *pl* toiletries
Toilettenbürste *f* toilet brush
Toilettenpapier *nt* toilet paper
Tollwut *f* rabies
Tomate *f* tomato
Tomatenpüree *nt* tomato purée
Tomatensaft *m* tomato juice
Tomatensoße *f* tomato sauce
Ton *m* sound; tone; clay
Tönung *f* hair dye
Töpferwaren *pl* pottery
Tor *nt* gate; goal *(sport)*
Törtchen *nt* cake *(small)*
Torte *f* gâteau; tart
tot dead
töten to kill
Tourist(in) *m/f* tourist
Touristeninformation *f* tourist information
Touristenkarte *f* tourist ticket
Touristenklasse *f* economy class
Touristenroute *f* tourist route
Touristenticket *nt* tourist ticket
tragbar portable
tragen to carry; to wear
Tragflügelboot *nt* hydrofoil
Trainingsschuhe *pl* trainers
trampen to hitchhike
Trauben *pl* grapes
traurig sad
Treffen *nt* meeting
treffen to meet
Trekkingstöcke *f* trekking poles
Treppe *f* stairs
Tresor *m* safe
Tretboot *nt* pedalo
trinken to drink
Trinkgeld *nt* tip *(for waiter, etc)*
Trinkwasser *nt* drinking water
trocken dry; stale *(bread)*
Trockenmilch *f* powdered milk

Trockenobst *nt* dried fruit
trocknen to dry
Truthahn *m* turkey
Tschechien *nt* Czech Republic
tschüs cheerio; bye
T-Shirt *nt* T-shirt
Tuch *nt* cloth; scarf; towel; shawl
tun to do; to put
Tunfisch *m* tuna
Tunnel *m* tunnel
Tür *f* door
türkis turquoise *(colour)*
Turm *m* tower
Turnschuhe *pl* gym shoes
typisch typical

U

u.A.w.g. RSVP
U-Bahn *f* metro
übel sick *(nauseous)*; bad
über over; above; about; via
überall everywhere
überbuchen to overbook
Überfahrt *f* crossing *(sea)*
Überfall *m* mugging
überfällig overdue
überfüllt crowded *(train, shop, etc)*
übergeben to hand over; to present *(give)*
sich **übergeben** to vomit
Übergewicht *nt* excess baggage; overweight
überhitzen to overheat
überholen to overtake
Überholverbot *nt* no overtaking
Übernachtung mit Frühstück bed and breakfast
überprüfen to check *(to examine)*
Überschwemmung *f* flash flood
übersetzen to translate
Übersetzung *f* translation
überweisen to transfer *(money)*
Überzelt *nt* fly sheet
Überzieher *m* overcoat
übrig left over; extra *(spare)*
Ufer *nt* bank *(of river)*; shore
Uhr *f* clock; watch

Uhrarmband *nt* watch strap
Uhrmacher *m* watchmaker's
um around
um 4 Uhr at 4 o'clock
umdrehen to turn around
umgeben von surrounded by
Umgehungsstraße *f* ring road; bypass *(road)*
Umkleidekabine *f* changing room *(at swimming pool, in shop)*
Umleitung *f* diversion
Umschlag *m* envelope
umsonst free *(costing nothing)*
umsteigen to change
umstoßen to knock over *(object)*
Umweg *m* detour
Umwelt *f* environment
unbefugt unauthorized
Unbefugten Zutritt verboten no entry to unauthorized persons
unbegrenzt unlimited
und and
Unfall *m* accident

Unfallstation *f* casualty department
ungefähr approximately
ungefährlich safe *(not dangerous)*
ungerade odd *(number)*
ungewöhnlich unusual
Unglück *nt* accident
ungültig invalid
ungültig werden to expire *(ticket, passport)*
Universität *f* university
unmöglich impossible; unsafe
uns us
unser(e) our
unsicher uncertain *(fact)*
unten downstairs; below
nach unten downward(s); downstairs
unter under(neath)
unter Wasser underwater
unterbrechen to interrupt
Unterbrecher *m* circuit breaker
Unterbrecherkontakte *pl* points *(in car)*
untere(r/s) lower; bottom
Unterführung *f* subway; underpass

(for pedestrians)
Unterhemd *nt* vest
Unterhose *f* underpants
Unterkunft *f* accommodation
unterrichten to teach
Unterrichtsstunde *f* lesson
unterschreiben to sign
Unterschrift *f* signature
Untersuchung *f* test; medical examination
Untertasse *f* saucer
Untertitel *pl* subtitles
Unterwäsche *f* underwear; lingerie
unwohl unwell
Urin *m* urine
Urlaub *m* leave; holiday
auf Urlaub on holiday; on leave
Urlaubsgebiet *nt* resort *(holiday)*
Ursprungsland *nt* country of origin
USA *pl* USA
USB-Port *m* USB port
USB-Stick *m* USB flash drive

V

Vagina *f* vagina
Van *m* people carrier
Vanille *f* vanilla
Vanilleeis *nt* vanilla ice cream
Vanillesoße *f* custard
Vase *f* vase
Vater *m* father
Vegetarier(in) *m/f* vegetarian
vegetarisch vegetarian
Veilchen *nt* violet *(flower)*
Ventil *nt* valve
Ventilator *m* fan *(electric)*; ventilator
Verband *m* bandage
Verbandskasten *m* first aid kit
verbinden to connect *(join)*
Verbindung *f* connection *(train, etc)*; service *(bus, etc)*; line *(phone)*
verboten forbidden
Verbrechen *nt* crime
verbrennen to burn
Verbrennung *f* burn
verbringen to spend *(time)*
verderben to go bad *(food)*; to spoil

verdienen to deserve; to earn
verdorben bad *(fruit, vegetables)*
Verein m society *(club)*
vereinbaren to agree upon; to arrange
Vereinbarung f agreement
Vereinigtes Königreich nt United Kingdom
Vereinigte Staaten (von Amerika) pl United States (of America)
Verfallsdatum nt expiry date; eat-by date
verfault rotten *(fruit, etc)*
Vergangenheit f past
Vergaser m carburettor
vergeben to forgive
vergessen to forget
vergewaltigen to rape
Vergewaltigung f rape
Vergnügen nt enjoyment; pleasure
viel Vergnügen! have a good time!
Vergnügungspark m amusement park
vergoldet gold-plated
Vergrößerung f enlargement
verhaften to arrest
verheiratet married
verhindern to prevent
Verhütungsmittel nt contraceptive
Verkauf m sale
verkaufen to sell
Verkäufer(in) m/f salesman/woman
Verkehr m traffic
Verkehrspolizist(in) m/f traffic warden
Verkehrszeichen nt road sign
verkehrt wrong
verkehrt herum upside down
verlängern to extend *(stay)*; to renew *(visa)*
Verlängerungskabel nt extension cable
Verleih m rental company; hire company
verletzen to injure
verletzt injured *(person)*
Verletzung f injury
verlieren to lose

verlobt engaged *(to be married)*
Verlobte(r) m/f fiancé(e)
verloren lost *(object)*
vermeiden to avoid
vermieten to rent; to let *(room, house)*
Vermieter(in) m/f landlord/lady
Vermietung f hire
vermisst missing *(person)*
Vermittlung f telephone exchange; operator
verpassen to miss *(plane, train, etc)*
Verrenkung f sprain
verschieben to postpone
verschieden different
verschiedene several; different
verschlucken to swallow
verschmutzt polluted
verschreiben to prescribe
verschwinden to disappear
verschwunden missing
versichern to insure
versichert sein to be insured
Versicherung f insurance
Versicherungsbescheinigung f insurance certificate
versilbert silver-plated
verspätet delayed
Verspätung f delay
versprechen to promise
Verstauchung f sprain
verstecken to hide
verstehen to understand
verstopft blocked *(pipe, road)*; constipated
versuchen to try
Vertrag m contract
Vertreter(in) m/f sales rep
Verwandte(r) m/f relative
verwenden to use
verwirrt confused
verwöhnt spoilt *(child)*
Verzeihung! sorry; excuse me
verzollen to declare goods *(customs)*
Video nt video
Videokamera f video camera
Videokassette f video cassette/tape
viel much
viele many

vielleicht perhaps
Viertel *nt* quarter
Viertelstunde *f* quarter of an hour
vierzehn Tage fortnight
Villa *f* villa
violett purple
Virus *nt* virus
Visitenkarte *f* business card
Visum *nt* visa
Vitamin *nt* vitamin
Vlies *nt* fleece
Vogel *m* bird
Voicemail *f* voicemail
Volkslied *nt* folk song
Volkstanz *m* folk dance
voll full
Volleyball *m* volleyball
Vollkornbrot *nt* dark rye bread; wholemeal bread
Vollmilchschokolade *f* milk chocolate
Vollnarkose *f* general anaesthetic
Vollpension *f* full board
vollständig whole
volltanken to fill up *(petrol)*
Volt *pl* volts
von from; of
vor before; in front of
vor 4 Jahren 4 years ago
voraus ahead
im Voraus in advance
vorbei past
vorbereiten to prepare
Vorbestellung *f* reservation
Vorder- front
Vorderradantrieb *m* front-wheel drive
Vorfahrt *f* right of way *(on road)*
Vorfahrt beachten give way
vorgekocht ready-cooked
Vorhang *m* curtain
Vorhängeschloss *nt* padlock
Vorname *m* first name
vorne einsteigen enter by front door
Vorschrift *f* regulation *(rule)*
Vorsicht *f* caution
Vorspeise *f* starter *(in meal)*; hors d'œuvre
Vorstellung *f* performance
Vor- und Zuname *m* first name and surname
Vorverkauf *m* advance booking
Vorwahl(nummer) *f* dialling code
Vorzelt *nt* awning *(caravan)*
vorziehen to prefer
Vulkan *m* volcano

W

Waage *f* scales *(weighing)*
wach awake
Wache *f* security guard
Wachsbehandlung *f* waxing
Waffe *f* gun
Wagen *m* car; carriage *(railway)*
Wagenheber *m* jack *(for car)*
Wahl *f* choice; election
wählen to dial *(number)*; to choose
Wählton *m* dialling tone
während while; during
Währung *f* currency
Wald *m* wood; forest
Waldlehrpfad *m* nature trail
Wales *nt* Wales
Waliser(in) *m/f* Welshman/woman
walisisch Welsh
Walnuss(-nüsse) *f* walnut(s)
wandern to hike
Wanderschuhe *pl* walking boots
Wanderstock *m* walking stick
Wanderung *f* hike
Wanderweg *m* trail for ramblers
Wange *f* cheek
wann? when?
Waren *pl* goods
warm warm
Wärmflasche *f* hot-water bottle
Warmwasser *nt* hot water
Warnblinkanlage *f* hazard warning lights
Warndreieck *nt* warning triangle
Warnung *f* warning
Wartehalle *f* lounge *(at airport)*
warten (auf) to wait (for)
Wartesaal *m* waiting room
warum? why?
was? what?
waschbar washable

Waschbecken *nt* washbasin
Wäsche *f* linen; washing *(clothes)*
Wäscheklammer *f* clothes peg
Wäscheleine *f* clothes line
waschen to wash
Waschen und Föhnen wash and blow dry
Wäscheraum *m* laundry room
Wäscherei *f* laundry
Wäschereiservice *m* laundry service
Wäschetrockner *m* tumble dryer
Waschmaschine *f* washing machine
Waschmittel *nt* detergent
Waschpulver *nt* washing powder
Waschsalon *m* launderette
Wasser *nt* water
wasserdicht waterproof
Wasserfall *m* waterfall
Wasserhahn *m* tap
Wassermelone *f* water melon
Wasserski fahren to waterski
Wassertreter *m* pedal boat/pedalo
Watte *f* cotton wool
Wattebausch *m* cotton bud
Website site *(website)*
Wechsel *m* change
Wechselgeld *nt* change *(small coins)*
Wechselkurs *m* exchange rate
wechseln to change *(money);* to give change
Wechselstube *f* bureau de change
Weckdienst *m* early morning call
Wecker *m* alarm clock
Weckruf *m* alarm call
weder ... noch neither ... nor
Weg *m* path; way; country lane
wegfahren to leave in vehicle
Wegfahrsperre immobilizer *(on car)*
weggehen to leave on foot
Wegweiser *m* signpost
Wegwerfwindeln *pl* disposable nappies
wehtun to ache; to hurt *(be painful)*
weiblich female; feminine
weich soft
weich gekochtes Ei *nt* soft-boiled egg
Weihnachten *nt* Christmas
Weihnachtsgeschenk *nt* Christmas present

Weihnachtskarte *f* Christmas card
weil because
Wein *m* wine
Weinberg *m* vineyard
Weinbrand *m* brandy
weinen to cry *(weep)*
Weinhandlung *f* wine shop
Weinkarte *f* wine list
Weinkeller *m* wine cellar
Weinprobe *f* wine-tasting
Weinstube *f* wine bar
Weintrauben *pl* grapes
weiß white
Weißbrot *nt* white bread
Weißwein *m* white wine
weit far; loose *(clothing)*
weiter farther; further on
weitermachen to continue
weitsichtig long sighted
Weizen *m* wheat
welche(r/s) which; what; which one
Wellen *pl* waves *(on sea)*
Welt *f* world
Wende *f* U-turn *(in car)*
wenden to turn
wenig little
weniger less
wenn if; when *(with present tense)*
wer? who?
Werbespot *m* advert *(on TV)*
werden to become
Werk *nt* plant *(factory);* work *(of art)*
Werkstatt *f* garage *(for repairs)*
Werktag *m* weekday
Werkzeug *nt* tool
Werkzeugkasten *m* toolkit
Wert *m* value
Wertbrief *m* registered letter
Wertsachen *pl* valuables
wertvoll valuable
wesentlich essential
Wespe *f* wasp
wessen? whose?
Weste *f* waistcoat
Westen *m* west
westlich western

Wetter *nt* weather
Wetterbericht *m* weather forecast
Wettervorhersage *f* weather forecast
Wettkampf *m* match *(sport)*
Whirlpool *m* jacuzzi
wichtig important
wie like; how
wie viel? how much?
wie viele? how many?
wieder again
wieder aufladen to recharge *(battery)*
wiederholen to repeat
wiegen to weigh
Wien Vienna
Wiese *f* lawn; meadow
Wi-Fi *f* wi-fi
Wild *nt* game *(hunting, meat)*
Wildleder *nt* suede
Wildschwein *nt* boar
willkommen welcome
Wimpern *pl* eyelashes
Wimperntusche *f* mascara
Wind *m* wind

Windeln *pl* nappies; diapers
windig windy
Windmühle *f* windmill
Windpocken *pl* chickenpox
Windschutz *m* windbreak *(camping)*
Windschutzscheibe *f* windscreen
windstill calm *(weather)*
Winter *m* winter
Winterreifen *pl* snow tyres
wir we
wirksam effective *(remedy, etc)*
Wirt(in) *m(f)* landlord (landlady)
Wirtschaft *f* pub; inn; economy
wissen to know *(facts)*
Witwe(r) *f(m)* widow(er)
Witz *m* joke
wo? where?
Woche *f* week
Wochenende *nt* weekend
Wochenmarkt farmers' market
Wochentag *m* weekday
wöchentlich weekly
woher? where from?
wohin? where to?

Wohnadresse *f* home address
wohnen to stay; to live *(reside)*
Wohnheim *nt* hostel
Wohnmobil *nt* dormobile
Wohnort *m* home address
Wohnung *f* flat *(apartment)*
Wohnwagen *m* caravan
Wohnzimmer *nt* living room; lounge
wolkig cloudy
Woll- woollen
Wolldecke *f* blanket
Wolle *f* wool
wollen to want *(wish for)*
Wort *nt* word
in Worten in words *(on cheques)*
Wörterbuch *nt* dictionary
Wunde *f* wound *(injury)*
Würfel *m* dice
Wurst *f* sausage
Würstchenbude *f* hot-dog stand
würzig spicy
Würzmischung *f* seasoning

Y
Yachthafen *m* marina

Z
zäh tough *(meat)*
Zahl *f* number *(figure)*
zahlen to pay
Zähler *m* meter
Zahn *m* tooth
Zahnarzt (Zahnärztin) *m/f* dentist
Zahnbürste *f* toothbrush
Zahncreme *f* toothpaste
Zähne *pl* teeth
Zahnpasta *f* toothpaste
Zahnschmerzen *pl* toothache
Zahnseide *f* dental floss
Zahnstocher *m* toothpick
Zange *f* pliers
Zäpfchen *nt* suppository
z.B. e.g.
Zebrastreifen *m* zebra crossing
Zehe *f* toe
Zeichentrickfilm *m* cartoon
Zeichnung *f* drawing

zeigen to show
Zeit f time (of day)
Zeitkarte f season ticket
Zeitschrift f magazine
Zeitung f newspaper
Zeitungskiosk m newsstand
Zelt nt tent
Zeltboden m groundsheet
zelten to camp
Zentimeter m centimetre
zentral central
Zentralheizung f central heating
Zentralverriegelung f central locking (car)
Zentrum nt centre
zerbrechlich fragile; breakable
zerrissen torn
Ziege f goat
Ziegel m brick
ziehen pull
Ziel nt destination; goal; target
ziemlich quite (rather)
Zigarette(n) f cigarette(s)
Zigarettenpapier nt cigarette papers
Zigarre(n) f cigar(s)
Zimmer nt room (in house, hotel)
Zimmer frei vacancies
Zimmermädchen nt chambermaid
Zimmernummer f room number
Zimmerservice m room service
Zirkus m circus
Zitrone f lemon
Zitronengras lemongrass
Zitronentee m lemon tea
Zoll m customs/toll
zollfrei duty-free
Zone f zone
Zoo m zoo
Zopf m plait
zornig angry
zu to; off; too; at
zu Hause at home
zu mieten for hire
zu verkaufen for sale
zu viel too much
zu viel berechnen to overcharge
zubereiten to prepare

Zucchini pl courgettes
Zucker m sugar
zuckerfrei sugar-free
Zuckerkrankheit f diabetes
zudrehen to turn off (tap)
Zug m train
Zuhause nt home
zuhören to listen
Zukunft f future
Zulassung f log book (vehicle registration document)
zum Beispiel f for example
Zuname m surname
Zündkerzen pl spark plugs
Zündschlüssel m ignition key
Zündung f ignition
Zunge f tongue
zurück back
zurückfahren to go back (by car)
zurückgeben to give back
zurückgehen to go back (on foot)
zurückkommen to come back
zurücklassen to leave behind
zusammen together
Zusammenstoß m crash (collision)
zusätzlich extra; additional
zuschauen to watch
Zuschlag m surcharge; supplement
zuschließen to lock
Zustellung f delivery (of mail)
Zutaten pl ingredients
Zutritt m entry; admission
Zutritt verboten no entry
zu viel too much
zuzüglich extra
zwanglose Kleidung f informal dress
zwei two
Zweigstelle f branch (office)
zweimal twice
zweite(r/s) second
zweite Klasse f second class
Zwiebel f bulb; onion
Zwillinge pl twins
zwischen between
Zwischenlandung f stopover (plane)
Zwischenstecker m adaptor
Zyste f cyst

German – English

Further titles in Collins' phrasebook range
Collins Gem Phrasebook

Also available as **Phrasebook CD Pack**

Other titles in the series

Afrikaans	Japanese	Russian
Arabic	Korean	Thai
Cantonese	Latin American	Turkish
Croatian	Spanish	Vietnamese
Czech	Mandarin	Xhosa
Dutch	Polish	Zulu
Italian	Portuguese	

Collins Phrasebook and Dictionary

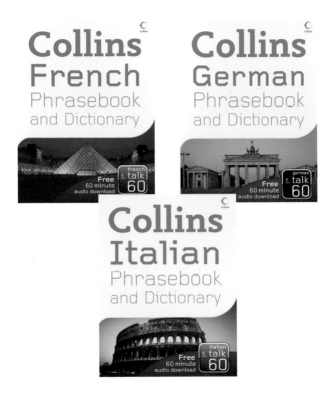

Other titles in the series
Greek Japanese Mandarin Polish Portuguese Spanish Turkish

Collins Easy: Photo Phrasebook

Also available as
**Phrasebook
CD Pack**

**Other titles
in the series**
Easy French
Easy Greek
Easy Italian

To order any of these titles, please telephone 0870 787 1732.
For further information about all Collins books, visit our website:
www.collins.co.uk